MEXICO

MEXICO
Democracy Interrupted

JO TUCKMAN

YALE UNIVERSITY PRESS
NEW HAVEN AND LONDON

For Eduardo, Natasha and Oliver

For information about this and other Yale University Press publications, please contact:

U.S. Office: sales.press@yale.edu   yalebooks.com
Europe Office: sales@yaleup.co.uk   www.yalebooks.co.uk

Set in Minion Pro by IDSUK (DataConnection Ltd)

Printed in the United States of America

Library of Congress Cataloging-in-Publication Data

Tuckman, Jo.
   Mexico : democracy interrupted / Jo Tuckman.
      p. cm.
   ISBN 978-0-300-16031-4 (cl : alk. paper)
1. Mexico—Politics and government—2000–   2. Political culture—Mexico.
3. Political corruption—Mexico.   4. Democratization—Mexico.   5. Fox Quesada,
Vicente.   6. Calderón Hinojosa, Felipe, 1962–   I. Title.
   F1236.7.T83 2012
   972—dc23

                                                                            2012006664

A catalogue record for this book is available from the British Library.

10 9 8 7 6 5 4 3 2 1

2016 2015 2014 2013 2012

Contents

List of Illustrations

Acknowledgements

My deepest thanks go to all the people across Mexico who have told me their stories and allowed me a glimpse of their lives over the years. Whether directly referred to or not, these have all shaped the text. Foreign correspondents working in Mexico are also dependent on local reporters and photographers who generosity can be extraordinary, not only with help understanding the stories that they know so much better than we do, but not infrequently with sources as well. I am particularly grateful to Martha Olivia López, Javier Valdez, Ismael Bojorquez, Fernando Brito, Pedro Pardo, Deysy Ríos, and Luis Hinojos.

While obviously all the responsibility for the analysis within this book is my own, it feeds off too many thoughtful people to mention, from the established analysts I regularly interview to ideas that emerge in casual conversations with both Mexican and foreign friends. I am especially grateful for the ever textured take of the late pollster Daniel Lund. I am also particularly indebted to Alfonso Zárate both for the seriousness of his own analysis and for his invitation to join the rich and diverse weekly workshops he chairs at his consultancy company GCI. I contributed very little but learned so much from all the participants, with special thanks to Andrés Ayala, Raúl Fraga, Primitivo Rodríguez and Max Morales. My heartfelt gratitude also to Mark Stevenson for being my constant sounding board and devil's advocate throughout the project.

Thanks also to the support of many other colleagues and friends, especially Marion Lloyd for reading and commenting on the manuscript, and to Rachel Sieder for her ever incisive intellect. I am very grateful also to George Stern for applying his eagle eye to several chapters. Photographers Shaul Schwarz and Jorge Urzón kindly contributed amazing photographs which add so much. Thanks also to Adam Wiseman. This book would never have been written were it not for my editor, Phoebe Clapham, whose clarity and velvet-gloved firmness also improved the text immeasurably over the process. I would also like to thank my family for their encouragement and interest, particularly my father John Tuckman and Eduardo Prud'homme, whose passion for his country and independent mind enrich my own vision of Mexico every day.

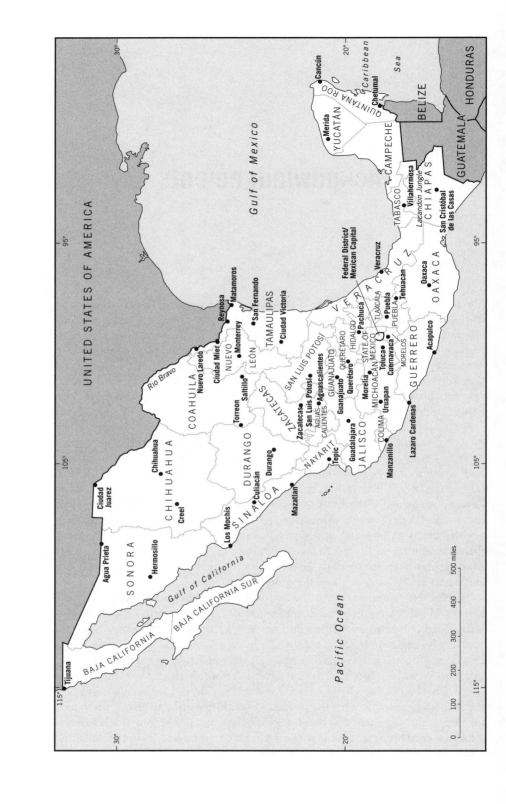

Introduction

THERE were no shots fired as Mexican democracy dawned in the year 2000, after seven decades of political hegemony exercised by the Institutional Revolutionary Party (PRI). There were no carnations in gun barrels, no failed coups, no tortuously negotiated flights into exile and no UN resolutions. Millions did not take to the streets. Instead there was one brief television message shortly before midnight on 2 July and some horn-honking in the streets.

Looking straight into the camera, President Ernesto Zedillo Ponce de León sat in front of a portrait of Benito Juárez, the nation's most revered hero, and announced that his party had lost that day's elections. Political plurality had been advancing for over a decade, but this was still the same party that had kept a hold on presidential power since 1929 with the help of soft authoritarianism and fiddled elections. Now it was preparing to leave government with almost no fuss at all. Five months later, Vicente Fox Quesada of the centre-right National Action Party (PAN) put on the green, red and white presidential sash. The new political era officially began.

Fast-forward eleven years: smooth is perhaps the last adjective that comes to mind to describe the Mexico that has emerged from that velvet transition.

As President Felipe Calderón Hinojosa, Fox's successor, who also comes from the PAN, approaches the end of his term in 2012, drug violence is battering swathes of the country. Over 50,000 people have already died, and new bodies are discovered every day. Whether it is the thirty-five corpses on a main coastal road in a big port city, the fifty-two people killed in an arson attack on a gambling centre filled with elderly women out for a day's bingo, the 250 or so bodies in a series of mass graves that the authorities began to remove with mechanical excavators, the fire fights that can last for hours, sending passers-by scrambling for cover, the child killed in his mother's arms by an army patrol, or simply the steady stream of mutilated victims dumped on the pavement, perhaps with their heads placed on a nearby car bonnet – the bloodbath continues.

President Calderón justified the military-led offensive he launched against organized crime as soon as he took office at the end of 2006 on the grounds that the local security institutions were overwhelmed; but since then the federal forces have proved unable even to contain the bloodshed on most fronts. The problem goes beyond the death and the horror. The Calderón strategy has actually seemed to fuel both the violence and the corruption that created the space for the cartels to operate in the first place. Once a cartel sets its sights on a particular area or *plaza*, all the institutions that are deemed important in safeguarding or expanding its activities in that area come under threat. Police forces, prisons, courts, local bureaucracies and political parties, newspapers and many more institutions find themselves required either to fend off infiltration or cave into it. The governability crisis already entrenched in some parts of the country is threatening to spread.

The economy, meanwhile, is still dragging itself out of one of the most acute recessions on record. Here Calderón has good reason to boast that Mexico has actually weathered the global economic storms that began in 2008 relatively well, in terms of the stability of almost all macroeconomic indicators other than growth. But neither stability, nor the laudable expansion of health services, nor indeed the increased accessibility of consumer credit is enough. Cutting into pervasive poverty and re-injecting a little optimism into the national mood requires the Mexican economy not only to grow, but to grow quickly, and there is no sign of that happening any time soon. Meanwhile the rich, in one of the world's most unequal countries, face minimal threats to their privileges.

The pervasive sense that something has gone terribly wrong extends beyond the beheadings and the employment deficit, and reflects a much broader phenomenon of weak and malleable state institutions at all levels – institutions that cannot cope with the tasks at hand. This is associated with the collapse of centralized control that came with the end of one-party hegemony, but has not been accompanied by a drive to push democratization forward. Mexican democracy – if defined narrowly to refer to the regular organization of largely free and fair elections according to rules established towards the end of the PRI regime – still seems pretty solid, despite rumbling pressures on drug-war fronts. But if it is defined in a broader, more participatory way to include systematic provisions for citizens to hold their elected representatives to account, then democracy can seem as far off now as it was before Fox took office.

Instead of providing the electorate with more control over the powers that be, political pluralism has brought a fragmentation of the state apparatus, with the different political forces seeking to monopolize different parts of it. The parties, the factions within them and the leaderships within those have concentrated on shoring up control of their bastions in the hope of winning more.

Politics as the promotion of a vision, the representation of a constituency, or the task of finding solutions to problems rarely takes centre stage. It is out there somewhere, but it is often masked by a surface layer of posturing, simulation and back-room negotiations that has brought with it a mixture of paralysis and confusion. The upshot is that whatever positive developments there have been are difficult to consolidate.

The worst traits, long associated exclusively with the regime, have been socialized across the entire political class. The PRI is probably still the worst offender, but corruption, nepotism, clientelism, ineptitude, authoritarianism, cynicism and impunity touch all parties, because all parties hold some degree of power. Now they all have vested interests in keeping further democratization at bay. In many cases they have actively resisted reforms and pressures to increase accountability or citizen participation by using a fog of mollifying rhetoric and minor concessions.

The failure to galvanize or respond to public engagement in politics, beyond the appeal for votes, contrasts with the way in which politicians and state institutions regularly protect the interests of individuals and groups that already had an established power base at the time of the transition.

Some former satellites of the old one-party system, now free to use and abuse their new autonomy, have accumulated truly extraordinary amounts of influence and wealth. A good number of state governors, once limited by presidential power, have mutated into near feudal lords. The teachers' union leader has a towering reputation for Machiavellian intrigue, at the same time as public education languishes in mediocrity.

The two commercial TV networks exploit their influence over public opinion to hold politicians hostage. Their editorial decisions are regularly defined not only by the competition for higher ratings, or even political sympathies, but by corporate interest and personal vendettas.

The economy is riddled with monopolies and oligopolies that the regulating bodies seem either unwilling or unable to rein in. While the courts regularly slap the powerless in jail for long periods of time on the merest hint of suspicion (and sometimes not even that), they ignore blatant violations of the law by well-connected people.

Some counterbalances have evolved. Genuine, if partial, advances in transparency have aided serious analysis by academics and experts, allowing them to go beyond speculation and to pick apart critical contemporary problems and suggest possible ways out. Their conclusions are often given ample coverage by the independent critical media, which have consolidated in the wake of the transition, after decades of slowly emerging from the shadow of governmental control. These are not abrupt changes, but rather an intensification of existing trends. The explosion in social media has added a genuinely new element to the mix that can pack a particularly powerful punch when it mingles with the Mexican penchant for humour underlining the absurdities of power.

The new freedom of the press is far from absolute. In some parts of the country the regional media still labour under pressure both from the local political authorities and, increasingly, from organized crime. Even so, enough outlets remain to ensure that the disturbing back stories of public life are more exposed and debated than they have ever been before.

There is also a slow but important growth of non-partisan citizen groups demanding that the institutions respond to the challenges of the times by reforming themselves. Sometimes the groups get their voices heard, and even notch up the odd significant victory that serves as a reminder that positive change is possible.

After forty-nine small children died in a fire in a state-funded crèche, their parents channelled their grief first into anger that warnings had gone unheeded, and then into activism aimed at forcing safeguards to prevent similar tragedies in the future. In another example, a couple of young lawyers transformed a typical case of miscarriage of justice into one of the most successful Mexican films ever made and thereby exerted powerful pressure aimed at shaking up the country's warped justice system. The victims of violence have begun to come together to demand that they should no longer be either criminalized or ignored, and have forced President Calderón to listen to their anger and desperation.

This does not amount to an effervescence of citizen organization. Most people face too many difficulties in their everyday lives to be able to dedicate time and effort to forcing change from below, or do not try because they are convinced that the only solutions possible are individual. In some areas with high drug-related violence it is too dangerous to even contemplate speaking out. However, those groups and individuals that do speak out represent the best hope of starting to close the enormous gulf between the governed and the governing – a gulf that underlines the partial nature of Mexico's democratic transition.

The blame for why it is all so hard rests with the entire political class, but certain leaders must shoulder a particular burden – President Fox above all. He took office with a unique opportunity to use the legitimacy he enjoyed to dismantle the old anti-democratic structures; but his reformist vigour soon dissipated when he found it was not so easy. The first president of Mexican democracy spent most of his term sitting back and watching the multi-party closed shop of the post-transition consolidate itself. His most active contribution was negative – a doomed effort to block Mexico City's leftist mayor, Andrés Manuel López Obrador of the Party of Democratic Revolution (PRD), from standing in the 2006 presidential election. This did significant damage to the credibility of even electoral democracy. It also helped ensure that López Obrador's refusal to accept defeat, when he lost by a whisker to Calderón, had more impact than it would probably otherwise have done.

We may never know whether López Obrador was cheated out of victory; but if he was, the scale of the fiddling did not compare to the crude fraud that characterized the years of political domination by the PRI. His radical challenge to the entire political system that followed not only delivered yet more body blows to the country's electoral institutions, but also damaged his own cause by making it much harder for the left to build on its unprecedented gains in the legislature and in its strongholds, and to construct a genuinely alternative platform that marked it off from the two parties that had already had a stab at the presidency. Instead the left spent years focused on self-sabotaging internal power struggles around such issues as what López Obrador's role should be in the future.

Battered by the post-electoral crisis and haunted by the legacy of Fox's lackadaisical approach to power, President Calderón paid little attention to the growing democratization deficit when he took office. Instead, the second PAN president sought to reconfigure the concept of a strong state around his offensive against organized crime – with disastrous consequences. Mounting evidence that the strategy had backfired only prompted him to intensify these efforts.

In this context, the PRI's claim to be the only party that really knows how to govern Mexico again won appeal. Its abysmal record in government in the majority of states was glossed over by a tremendously popular candidate, the governor of the State of Mexico, Enrique Peña Nieto, who, at the end of 2011, enjoyed around a twenty-point lead in the polls. Peña Nieto is young, handsome, serious, politically astute and eminently marketable; but he is also from traditional PRI stock. The party behind him has hardly transformed itself at all. The PRI has undergone some important adaptations to the new era of full pluralism and the experience of being in opposition, but it was remarkable how it prepared for a possible comeback without having first undergone a full shake-up.

Victory, of course, was not guaranteed. Ever since 2000, Mexican presidential polls have produced surprises, with first Fox and then Calderón coming from behind to win. But whatever the outcome, we still need to explain how it is that the old party of power could be the early favourite to retake the presidency less than a dozen years after it lost power – largely on account of its well-deserved reputation for dirty dealing, corruption, economic mismanagement and authoritarianism.

Exploring how Mexico has so cavalierly thrown away the chance of establishing itself as a new dynamic democracy, and has instead got itself bogged down in political decadence and a devastating saga of violence, matters not just to Mexicans. This is a giant of a country that consistently ranks within the world's top fifteen economies, in a context where middleweight nations play an increasingly important role.

Mexico claims to have more free trade agreements than any other nation on earth. Mexican products – from beer to avocados to organic chewing gum – fill the aisles of supermarkets across the world. Mexican companies – from the state-owned oil company Pemex to cement producer Cemex and industrial bakers Bimbo – are global giants. The world's richest person is a Mexican.

At least up until 2010, the security situation had not directly impacted on foreign investment. This was a particular point of pride for the Calderón administration, but many analysts wondered how long it could last if the situation continued to deteriorate. US companies are the most important investors, although European and Asian firms have increased their shares in recent years.

What happens in Mexico matters hugely to the US for many other reasons as well. Not only do the two nations have a 3,000-kilometre border, a lot of common history and a free trade agreement, but they also share a significant proportion of their populations. According to the Pew Hispanic Center there were nearly 32 million Mexican Americans living in the US in 2010, 12.4 million of them first-generation immigrants – by far the biggest immigrant population in the US. Mexicans living there without permission are also the group most directly targeted by the wave of anti-immigrant feeling that, from 2010, produced a number of state-level laws intended to squeeze 'illegals' out.

State Department documents from 2010 put the number of US citizens living in Mexico at a million, though the figure is notoriously difficult to pin down, given the high proportion of them who maintain seasonal homes. Even so, no other country provides a foreign base for so many US citizens. They make up by far the biggest immigrant population within Mexico. The bulk of the 22 million or so tourists who visit Mexico every year also come from the US.

The US also has a critical role in the drug wars: US consumption drives Mexican drug trafficking, and the cartels typically replenish their arsenals across the border. President Calderón's drug war strategy is supported by US advisers, even if Washington buzzes with concern about how effec-tively it is being applied, and there are heightened worries about the possi-bility of spill-over violence (which some claim, erroneously, is already happening). The increased direct role of US operatives within Mexico can only ensure that more attention is focused on the country in future. The possibility of a backlash in anti-American feeling is real. Mexican criminal organizations have also been linked to trafficking networks elsewhere in the world, involving Europe, Asia and even Australia, although the precise nature of these links remains sketchy.

Geography also means that Mexico is the most direct contact between the richest, most powerful nation on earth and the developing world. The way it handles this strategic position has particularly important ramifica-tions throughout Latin America, where it tends to be at odds with the prevailing political trends. Mexico's recent image problems stand in stark contrast to the rising-star status of Brazil.

Events in Mexico, meanwhile, have a direct impact on the smaller countries just across its southern border. Not so long ago, Central Americans were most worried about Mexican economic domination, but this has since been displaced by terror at the drug wars spreading south. At least one Mexican cartel also indulges in near industrial-scale kidnapping of Central American migrants travelling through the country on their way to the US. The victims have included a significant number of other Latin Americans and a smattering of Asians and Africans.

Mexico also acts as a laboratory for the exploration of issues of global relevance, of which international criminal networks are just one facet. Mass migration from Mexico has been extreme and diverse, but has now slowed, suggesting the end of a cycle; there could be lessons to learn here for many countries in the world. How to deal with entrenched poverty combined with acute inequality, at a time when deficits are condemned as the fount of most economic evils, is one of the most pressing questions for the world economy. Few countries possess such a rich natural environment, and so few can cast as much light on what works (and what doesn't) when it comes to trying to protect this environment. The way Mexican companies are able to compete abroad but at home ferociously defend their market dominance provides searing examples of the importance of effective regulation.

The international cultural significance of Mexico goes far beyond its pre-Hispanic ruins and the painter Frida Kahlo. Few Cannes film festivals in recent years have been complete without some kind of Mexican input, and contemporary artists show their work in major galleries across the US and Europe. The country also opens a globally relevant window onto a fascinating interplay between powerful religious and anti-clerical traditions, and onto the complexities of blending collective indigenous rights with individualized models of liberal democracy.

For me, however, Mexico is also my home. I moved here as a freelance journalist in early 2000, attracted by the idea that, if the PRI lost the elections that summer, I would have an enormous story to cover and plenty of work. In my naivety I imagined some kind of cross between the crumbling of the Berlin Wall and the democratic transition in Spain, with intense political change from the start and a cultural flowering.

While the elections themselves and the first year after them were pretty exciting, the energy of the story soon wilted away. President Fox really did not do very much, and nor did anybody else – or certainly not very much of interest to the international editors consumed by the Middle East (aside from the issue of migration in the US press and the plethora of presidential frivolity that made fun reading but was of little substance).

I was also initially deeply confused by Mexico. It jarred with many of my reporting experiences from when I lived and worked in Spain and Central America in the 1990s, particularly the times I spent covering the violence related to the Basque separatist organization ETA or the end of Guatemala's civil war. I did not understand how the pressures in Mexico could be there and not be there at the same time, often played out in what amounted to a kind of shadow boxing.

I arrived in February 2000, days before striking students were finally evicted from Latin America's largest university (which they had essentially shut down for a year). Radical as they obviously were, they had rarely gone beyond shouting slogans, and the authorities had largely left them to get on with it. Mexican analysts painstakingly explained to me that the history of extreme violence – and the fear of unleashing it again – helped keep a lid on both dissent and repression. But I remained confused.

Nor did Fox's election clear things up. Although his personal approval ratings throughout most of his term remained higher than those of most heads of state, they were terrible whenever the questions referred to the specifics of the job he was doing. Here the analysts drew my attention to the way that the one-party regime had instilled a basic respect for symbols of authority, but still it did not gel with the widespread distrust of the state that I encountered every day.

There seemed to be some truth in the Mexican saying *el país de no pasa nada*, the country where nothing happens. Soon, however, the irony behind that phrase became clear. I began to appreciate just how much was going on beneath the surface, and I began to focus less on the search for saleable drama and more on trying to understand a place for which, by then, I cared deeply.

The 2006 elections showed just how delicate the balance was. The campaign itself was hard and dirty, and it polarized the country with a political passion that – on the surface at least – had been lacking before. It extended into the post-electoral crisis, and then, just as it reached its climax, Andrés Manuel López Obrador suddenly disappeared and Felipe Calderón was left to step into the limelight.

'Can't say I envy you', a veteran British newshound who had 'parachuted' into Mexico to cover Calderón's chaotic inauguration remarked to me as we watched the politician field questions with dead-pan efficiency in his first press conference as head of state. 'You've got yourself one of the most boring presidents I've ever seen.' He was thinking of the colourful characters that dominated the Latin American political landscape at the time. But while Calderón lacked the theatrics of a Hugo Chávez in Venezuela, the novelty value of Evo Morales in Bolivia, or the honed charisma of Brazil's Inácio Lula da Silva, nothing could have been further from the truth: with Calderón in charge and the institutional framework that had kept things in check finally beginning to obviously wither, tensions exploded in the tragedy of the drug wars.

The stories retold in this book are primarily based on the past twelve years of reporting from Mexico, mostly for the *Guardian* newspaper in the UK, but also for a number of US publications. I also draw on the often inspirational work of other foreign correspondents, many of whom are far more experienced and intrepid than I am. The conclusions I reach are infused with analyses of established commentators and the large quantity of dedicated Mexican reporters who, not infrequently in extraordinarily adverse circumstances, still try to get to the bottom of the story.

The trouble most Mexico-watchers have in squeezing the country into easy categories and in discerning a clear trajectory today is, in many ways, a continuation of the definition problems that accompanied the PRI regime throughout its seven decades in power. In 1990, Peruvian writer Mario Vargas Llosa famously called it the 'perfect dictatorship'. This summed up the amount of control that the regime maintained over what went on in all corners of Mexico, coupled with its relative softness (compared to the military regimes in other Latin American countries). Mexican Nobel Prize winner Octavio Paz called the state a 'philanthropic ogre' to emphasize its dual role as both provider and bully. For his protégé, the historian Enrique Krauze, the PRI in power was 'a collective monarchy with the electoral forms of a republic'. The phrase underlined the regal nature of presidential power, at the same time as noting the single six-year term limit on individual occupancy of the post and the important role that elections, however perverted they might be, played in the system. Even the PRI itself enshrined an oxymoron in its own name.

The fact that the party hung onto power for so long by partially reinventing itself to go with the changing times only added to the characterization problem. By the time the PRI finally lost the presidency in 2000, it had already allowed political plurality to creep into all other levels of government, and most elections were broadly fair and the press pretty free.

Vicente Fox's undoubted talent as a candidate had been to capitalize on a moment when the electorate was ready to decide that the eternal party of power had finally had its day.

But, for all the transformations the old regime had undergone over the decades, there was an amorphous ideology and set of political styles and practices – loosely termed 'revolutionary nationalism' – that provided a degree of consistency almost right up to the end. 'There was no democracy or social justice, but there was an official epic that gave meaning and legitimacy, even to the aberrations of the regime', Héctor Aguilar Camín and Jorge Castañeda Gutman wrote in their 2009 essay 'A Future for Mexico'.

Anachronistic and exhausted though it may now be, revolutionary nationalism forms the bedrock of what the PAN presidents promised to change and did not, and so it is worth remembering some of its basic premises.

The 1910 Mexican Revolution was, in reality, a heterogeneous collection of rebellions that waxed and waned, converged and diverged, and lacked the ideological coherence of the Russian Revolution at around the same time. After the event, the victors rewrote the story into a monolithic tale of a popular uprising in the name of social justice and progress. There were heroes, villains and traitors, and there was an ultimately triumphant legacy that provided the baseline legitimacy for the PRI, slotted into a broader narrative of national liberation.

Official PRI history celebrated independence for having shaken off the yoke of Spanish rule, but deemed it incomplete, as the elites had subsequently ensured that the country fell back into a dependent relationship with foreign powers, by then primarily the USA. This was epitomized by the influence of international business interests during the dictatorship of Porfirio Díaz that ended with the Revolution.

Nation building and regime consolidation became almost interchangeable. The Partido Nacional Revolucionario, or PNR (formed in power in 1929), its successor the Partido de la Revolución Mexicana, or PRM (created in 1938) and finally the Partido Revolucionario Institucional, the PRI (proclaimed in 1946) all shared the same logo – a circle with the colours of the flag inside it and the abbreviation for the party printed on top.

The expropriation of foreign oil companies to form the state-owned Pemex in 1938 put theory into practice. With known oil reserves running low, the economic advantages of nationalization were far less clear than the symbolic ones. The slogan 'The oil is ours' rammed home the idea that Mexicans were taking control of their natural resources via their political leaders. People from all walks of life queued up to donate everything from turkeys to family heirlooms to help pay the compensation required to see the process through. Peasants and workers were brought into the system through corporatist unions with similarly surging rhetoric. Anything that made the political system stronger was, by definition, patriotic.

The Revolution was then 'institutionalized'. The 'socialism' of the 1930s and the mixed import substitution model that followed (in which tariffs on foreign imports provided local industry with a protected environment), the nationalizations that came after that, and even the opening up of the economy and the privatizations of the 1990s, were all spun to represent progressive stages of the same permanent revolutionary process, anchored in an even longer national struggle.

Foreign policy, dominated by the principle of non-intervention everywhere as the first defence of Mexican sovereignty, provided a framework that helped keep the country floating above the instability that periodically permeated the region, particularly during the Cold War. Foreigners within the country were viewed with such suspicion that a constitutional provision allowed the authorities to summarily expel them at the first hint of political activity.

Revolutionary nationalism also rested on an essentialist vision of Mexican identity, conceived of as the amalgamation of Spanish and Indian heritage destined for great things. The exaltation of the *mestizo*, however, also carried with it an emphasis on how painful the process had been. José Clemente Orozco painted a fresco of the conquistador Hernán Cortés and his Indian lover, slave and translator La Malinche over the stairway in San Ildefonso College in Mexico City in 1926. The couple sit naked and hand in hand, but while the white conquistador looks straight ahead, his free arm is stretched across his partner's chest as she looks passively down towards the lifeless Indian man at their feet. Here, in all its moral ambiguity and violent connotations, is the origin myth of the nation.

The myth of *mestizaje*, as it became known later, came with a whole range of related national stereotypes that played with the major themes and tied them into other universalizing cultural motifs emanating from Catholic tradition. Women were glorified as repositories of both comfort and virginal purity, in homage to the Virgin of Guadalupe. They were also denigrated as cunning, egocentric whores who had sold out their ethnic brothers to the conquering Spaniards, as represented by La Malinche.

Generations of intellectuals dedicated years of their lives to exploring more nuanced versions of these and other constructs that underpinned the idea of a unified identity. In his celebrated 1950 book *The Labyrinth of Solitude*, Octavio Paz concluded that Mexicans suffered from a deep loneliness of spirit, in part founded in their inability to face their conceptual roots in a rape. Other classic scholars focused on a supposed national inferiority complex that was said to be holding back the nation.

While the conclusions reached by Paz and others were often far from flattering, they did not directly challenge the idea of irreducible national traits, and so added to the narrative of uniqueness that helped the PRI claim to represent all Mexicans because, deep down, all Mexicans were the same.

The homogenizing discourse also fed into the promise of social and economic progress conceptualized as the replacement of rural indigenous communities by a new *mestizo*-dominated urban world. 'We are a *mestizo* people with a *mestizo* culture. We are proud of the two great sources of our national identity', said President Luis Echeverría Alvarez in 1970. 'Backwardness and marginalization in some indigenous groups is the product of underdevelopment. So long as we do not incorporate them into the progress of the whole community, they will be strangers in their own land.'

Anthropologist Roger Bartra was among the first to explore how the constructs of official identity and their spin-off stereotypes had helped justify exploitation and the absence of social justice under the PRI, inverting the emphasis that had dominated the works of writers such as Octavio Paz. In his 1987 book *The Cage of Melancholy*, Bartra contrasted the innocent, sad, nostalgic figure of the indigenous peasant with the quick-witted and ethically dubious urban *mestizo*, both classic Mexican archetypes of the golden years of the PRI. The peasant symbolized a past that was doomed to disappear, at the same time as he was blamed for putting a brake on development. The streetwise *mestizo* symbolized progress, even though he was also held responsible for perverting its course. Together, Bartra argued, both stereotypes formed a vision of arrested metamorphosis that provided the population with flashes of a glorious future, at the same time as it seemed to explain why they were still so far from getting there, despite decades of promises that it was just around the corner.

Revolutionary nationalism was resilient and malleable; but the gap between its promises and the reality of life on the ground began to chip away at its effectiveness in providing legitimacy for the regime.

The regime's periodic repression of dissent reached intense proportions in 1968, with the massacre of students in Mexico City; but the rot really set in with the end of the economic miracle in the 1970s. For three decades, the regime had been able to buy compliance from peasants, workers and businessmen alike with the redistribution of income and resources generated by consistently high rates of growth within a stable context. Then, from 1976 until 1994/5, every change of president every six years was accompanied by an acute economic crisis. The paternalistic narrative of the one-party system inevitably lost appeal.

The economic crises also directly challenged the old tenets of self-determination. Unable to pay its debts, the regime was forced to go cap in hand to the international finance community in 1982, and subsequently to apply austerity measures largely dictated from abroad. This sparked a debt crisis that would have an impact on the whole of Latin America, triggering the continent's so-called 'Lost Decade' and the shift to a new development model with a reduced role for the state and with priority given to financial stability and breaking down trade barriers, however painful that might be for the general population. In Mexico, US-trained economists became the dominant voices in the PRI, from where they actively pursued neoliberal reforms that aimed to fully integrate the country into the global market economy.

Party leaders continued to engage in rhetorical gymnastics that enabled them to present this dramatic change in focus as a continuation of the same narrative, but it was getting harder all the time. 'Our Revolution is different from others that have been abandoned and discredited because it is rooted in the people, in the party, and in the main political actors of the country', announced President Carlos Salinas in March 1992, with the negotiation of the North American Free Trade Agreement in full swing. 'What we are doing today is carrying out the reform of the Revolution that will guarantee its permanence and vitality.'

Glossing over the obvious contradictions was made even more difficult by the fact that the PRI had lost its monopoly on the claim to be the guardian of the legacy of both the Revolution and nationalist fervour. That evaporated towards the end of the 1980s, when Cuauhtémoc Cárdenas Solórzano led an exodus of left-leaning Priistas, who claimed that the regime had betrayed both the Revolution and nationalism, and who mounted the first real electoral challenge to one-party hegemony (although they were not allowed to win).

Soon, however, globalization began to render the debate over historical legacies rather sterile. By 1990 urban dwellers made up more than

71 per cent of the country's population, and a new generation of city-born children of the crises could not even remember the inward-looking industrialization that had underpinned the golden decades of stability and growth. They possessed new aspirations that were infused with different international references. For those who set their sights on a Sony television or Firestone tyres, there was little nostalgia for the days of Zondas and Tornels.

Mexicans from an ever greater variety of regions in the country had also joined the march across the northern border in search of better-paid work. This was particularly true in rural areas, where opening borders saw the prices of local products plummet and intensified existing economic woes. Houses built with money sent home emulated the styles on display in Californian suburbs as often as they stuck to local architectural traditions.

Foreigners were also becoming less exotic within Mexico itself. Tourism took off, with the number of international visitors (some 80 per cent of them from the US) growing from 5.7 million a year in 1970 to 17 million in 1990, as the industry became the biggest provider of jobs within Mexico. A new phenomenon of US citizens retiring to Mexico for at least part of the year provided yet another new reality that militated against the definition of 'nationhood' in oppositional terms.

The idea of a unitary national identity was under attack from the inside as well. Revolutionary nationalism had long glossed over diversity, but it had never actually got rid of it. What it meant to be Mexican remained riven with regional, ideological, age, gender, class, ethnic and countless other differences that began rising to the surface.

The Zapatista guerrilla uprising of 1994 made this dramatically clear. The rag-tag indigenous army, which demanded redress for 500 years of violence, discrimination and abandonment, directly attacked the idea that all Mexicans were integrated into a single national project. The sympathy the rebels sparked both inside and outside Mexico forced the PRI to recognize that the regime had systematically failed a section of the population that had long been made all but invisible by the assumption that only *mestizos* were really Mexican.

It also became more obvious that other identifiable groups had prospered under the regime, despite not being part of the official canon of Mexican *mestizaje*. Mexicans of Lebanese origin were particularly successful, ranging from the iconic 1950s film star María Félix to some of Mexico's most famous and influential figures of the present, such as telecoms magnate Carlos Slim Helú or the country's most famous recent export to Hollywood, Salma Hayek.

As the regime neared its end, the traditional constructs were even used to try and speed this up. The finely acted *La Ley de Herodes*, or *Herod's Law*, followed the fortunes of an initially hapless, naïve and well-meaning party man in the 1940s who, infused with the contemporary rhetoric of social justice and progress, becomes the mayor of a rural backwater. The system transforms him into a corrupt, murderous and successful national politician. *Herod's Law* was made with the help of government funding, but that did not stop belated and counterproductive attempts to keep it out of cinemas in the run-up to the 2000 elections. The perfectly timed film became a new kind of iconoclastic classic.

By the time of the 2000 elections, revolutionary nationalism had all but faded away from the political discourse. It was superseded by a contest for which a political actor made the best claim to be the standard bearer of democracy. This allowed Vicente Fox not only to win a comfortable majority in the election, but to do so despite being a repository of symbols that directly challenged the old ideology. His political party's roots, which stretched back to radical religious conservatism in the post-revolutionary period, were not a problem, and nor was the fact that his ancestors were relatively recent migrants and that he regularly boasted of his success as an executive with Coca-Cola, the ultimate representative of US economic imperialism. Fox even explicitly used his imposing physical height, regularly mocking the modest stature of his rival in an attempt to debunk the idea that the ruling party was invincible. I remember one Mexican reporter following his campaign jokily questioning the candidate on whether he risked offending the majority of Mexicans, who were similarly short. In another decade it could easily have turned into an issue of nationalist pride, but in the context of the 2000 elections it was treated as a light-hearted taunt.

The PRI's candidate, Francisco Labastida Ochoa, complained about the personal insults, but he did not claim that they were of any national import. Instead he sought to match Fox's promises of 'change' through democratization, with the value-added (he promised) of stability. His divorce from the language of revolutionary nationalism was rammed home by the often repeated pledge to ensure that English was taught in all state schools.

The stage was set for further democratization to consolidate itself as the new legitimizing narrative of power, replacing revolutionary nationalism. But in the years since, this has failed to assume a clear shape. As a result, the codes of practice and concepts that grew up under the umbrella of revolutionary nationalism retain much more relevance than they probably would have done otherwise. From the glorification of consensus to the denial of the existence of colour-based racism and the failure of the government to find an appropriate rhetoric with which to celebrate 200 years of independence in 2010, the old ideology still floats in the Mexican atmosphere and pervades many of the stories told in the chapters that follow. Instead of becoming a beacon of virtue for its 'voted transition', Mexico is now best known around the world for the brutality of its drug wars, the most acute example of how its democratic transition has got rather stuck.

CHAPTER 1

Narco Trouble

DAWN was just breaking when the first contingent of gunmen gathered at the entrance to the sleepy northern mountain town of Creel, the gateway to the spectacular Copper Canyon tourist railway. At first, the collection of figures with assault rifles slung across their backs did not do much to get noticed. They were not hiding either. They seemed to be just hanging out, watching their breath condense in the early morning air.

In the front passenger seat of a sports utility vehicle (SUV) was a round-faced man with straight eyebrows, who appeared to be in charge. At one point he waved about a piece of paper that presumably contained instructions of some kind. At another he handed around a bag filled with white powder, and then did copious amounts of snorting himself.

By the time the first rays of sunshine had crept down the sierra, the group had grown substantially and the action began. About ten of the gunmen ran across a frosted field, surrounded a two-storey white house, shot through the windows, kicked in the door, and disappeared inside.

Back at the crossroads other gunmen stopped passing cars. They roughly pulled one driver out from behind the wheel and forced him to lie on the tarmac while something was taken out of his vehicle. Back on his feet again soon after, he shook hands with one of his assailants and then drove slowly away. Eventually the commando did the same. Around thirty armed men climbed aboard thirteen vehicles that snaked out of town until they disappeared out of sight into the mountains.

I did not see any of this take place, and nor does the account come from an eye-witness. The source is more worrying. The armed organized criminal commando at work on 15 March 2010 was filmed by police cameras that were connected to a network that was supposed to mean greater coordination between different law enforcement institutions and quicker response times. There was nothing to indicate that any of those institutions responded at all that morning, during which eight people were killed in and around Creel. They included a fourteen-year-old girl shot dead in a raid on another house. The rest were abducted, killed and then dumped outside town, or else left dead inside their vehicles. Six people were also injured. It seemed the gang was free to set the death toll it wished.

By that time the Mexican drug wars, which spiralled after President Felipe Calderón launched a military-led offensive against the country's cartels in December 2006, were already producing such a litany of horror that the Creel killings warranted only a cursory mention in the national press the next day. The surrounding mountains have long been known as an area of drug cultivation, but the town was not considered particularly problematic, even within its own northern state of Chihuahua, where the daily bloodbath in the border city of Ciudad Juárez grabbed the bulk of available attention. The local Creel tourist industry was also keen to keep the news quiet, for fear of scaring off visitors.

The episode came into the spotlight only when the police video found its way onto a late-night TV news programme called *Punto de Partida*. Then it became a YouTube hit. The images themselves were far less disturbing than the pictures of dead bodies that were regularly printed in the local press, or than the filmed gun battles, torture and murder readily found on the internet. But there was something particularly shocking about the Creel film: murderers in no obvious hurry going about their business openly, while the authorities – and now the citizens, too – seemed capable of doing little more than watching and trying to stay out of the way.

The story of narcotics in Mexico goes back to the opium poppies, introduced by Chinese immigrants, that began growing in the twisted and towering Sierra Madre Occidental in the Pacific coast state of Sinaloa at the end of the nineteenth century. By the 1920s, traffickers, who dealt primarily in opium paste, had established clear routes into the US market at a time when Prohibition fomented a wider culture of cross-border contraband. Marijuana, a native crop that was cultivated more widely, initially held less interest for smugglers; but the drug-culture boom of the 1960s in the United States changed all that and provided them with their first opportunity to get really rich. A new generation of tougher players took over the trafficking scene, still largely rooted in Sinaloa.

Under pressure to get into line with President Richard Nixon's 'war on drugs', the Mexican government dispatched tens of thousands of soldiers in the mid-1970s to eradicate those plantations in the part of the sierra that was shared by the neighbouring states of Sinaloa, Durango and Chihuahua, and that is known as the Golden Triangle. Operation Condor, the closest historical precedent to the Calderón offensive of thirty years later, was billed as a great success at the time. The truth was that it did little, if anything, to slow the growing Mexican drugs industry.

Instead it instilled deep resentments in the area itself, encouraged traffickers to step up cultivation elsewhere, and prompted many drug lords, or *capos*, to move their bases out of Sinaloa. Some of the biggest went to the central city of Guadalajara. By the 1980s, many Mexican kingpins were also expanding their portfolios to include South American cocaine, making them less reliant on locally produced marijuana and opium paste anyway.

Miguel Angel Félix Gallardo, a former policeman and bodyguard of a Sinaloa governor, became the most famous trafficker of that era. Smartly dressed, urbane and famously generous, he financed a new library at the Sinaloa state university, maintained a local hospital and travelled widely to the US and Europe, as well as across Latin America. Some remember this as a kind of golden age of Mexican trafficking – a time of rapid expansion, during which violence was used only as a last resort. Félix Gallardo lived as a respectable local businessman, protected by government officials for years.

The bell tolled for this generation of Mexican *capos* after an undercover Drug Enforcement Administration (DEA) agent called Enrique Camarena was tortured and killed in 1985. The US demanded action and, after a little feet-dragging, the Mexican authorities began arresting some of the biggest traffickers and accusing them of his murder. Félix Gallardo was one of the last to fall, detained in a Guadalajara restaurant in 1989. His demise was also associated with the end of the tolerance he had enjoyed from the US authorities in return for his willingness to provide funds and weapons to the US-backed Contra counter-revolutionaries fighting the Sandinista government in Nicaragua.

The story goes that, after his arrest, the *Jefe de Jefes*, or Boss of Bosses, organized a week-long summit in a luxurious house in the Pacific resort city of Acapulco, at which second-tier figures divided up the different bases of his trafficking empire. These included key northern border crossing points such as Tijuana, Ciudad Juárez and Nuevo Laredo, as well as other trafficking hubs further south. The idea was to maintain the peace and to keep business ticking over in an era of increased pressure from law enforcement agencies.

In letters written from prison and published in Diego Enrique Osorno's 2010 book *El Cartel de Sinaloa*, Félix Gallardo denied that the fabled meeting ever took place. He claimed the turf division had been organized by the corrupt police chief who took him down. However it came about, this organization of the country into clear, geographically defined trafficking *plazas* controlled by particular groups, is sometimes referred to as the birth of the Mexican regional drug cartels. (Many academics object to the use of the word 'cartel' to describe drug-trafficking groups, because of its formal associations with price fixing. In recent years the term has become all but impossible to avoid, not least because many of the groups use it to describe themselves.)

Even if there was a peace pact, it did not last for very long, as the major *capos* of the 1990s began shoring up control of their bastions by killing rivals. Brutal as these conflicts were, compared to what was to come they now seem like playground scraps or knightly jousting. Though the point is often exaggerated, the contract killers of that era claim to have been a breed apart from today's murderers. They say they were guided by codes of mafia ethics not to hurt the families of their targets or innocent bystanders, as well as by the old axiom that it was bad for business to *calentar la plaza*, to turn up the heat on the turf.

The rapid expansion of the drug-trafficking pie that came with the demise of the major trafficking organizations based in Colombia may also have helped contain the violence. In the wake of the success of US efforts to close Caribbean smuggling routes in the 1980s, Colombian traffickers had already begun channelling ever greater quantities of cocaine to the US through Mexico. By the time the Medellín and then the Cali cartels were broken up in the 1990s, the Mexicans were ready and waiting to take more control.

The new wave of Mexican *capos* was still predominantly Sinaloa-rooted, even if their businesses were based elsewhere in the country. The most famous member of the Sinaloa diaspora, Amado Carrillo Fuentes, earned himself the nickname 'Lord of the Skies' for his audacious use of gutted commercial jets to transport tonnes of cocaine from Colombia to the northern Mexican border and then, after a change of aircraft, over into the

US. The planes then carried cargoes of cash on their way back. Carrillo Fuentes took over the cartel based in the border city of Ciudad Juárez in 1993, but died in 1997 after what appeared to be a deliberately bungled plastic surgery operation. His death came four months after the arrest of the newly appointed Mexican drug 'tsar', a general who would later be convicted of protecting the Juárez cartel.

By the time I arrived in Mexico in 2000, the glory days of the Juárez cartel were over. Vicente Carrillo Fuentes had replaced his dead brother at the top, but showed little of Amado's flair. Even so, most independent experts and government sources still identified Juárez as the biggest player on the national scene.

The cartel based in the frontier city of Tijuana and run by the numerous siblings of the Arellano Félix family was the next most notorious; however, that family's fortunes also waned in the early years of the century. Ramón Arellano Félix, the group's chief enforcer, died in a gun battle in February 2002, a month before the authorities arrested his brother Benjamín, the reputed brains of the organization. By the time Francisco Javier Arellano Félix was apprehended by the US Coast Guard off the coast of Baja California Sur in 2006, the cartel was said to be in disarray.

Analysts also mentioned the Gulf cartel, based on the other side of the country. It was run by Osiel Cárdenas Guillén from 1998 until he was arrested by the army in 2003. His broader influence was not fully recognized at the time, in part because he lacked a traditional Sinaloa pedigree.

With the Juárez cartel not what it had been, Tijuana apparently falling apart and the Gulf without its top leader, experts began predicting the end of the big drug barons. They saw a future of small cartels that deliberately kept a low profile in order to keep business ticking over, as had happened in Colombia. But rather than sending out the message that it was time to stay out of trouble, the round-up of Mexican kingpins in 2002 and 2003 helped lay the foundations for the future drug wars, as other ambitious *capos* saw opportunities to expand.

Joaquín Archivaldo Guzmán Loera became the biggest of all. Known universally as El Chapo (which, in his native Sinaloa, means 'short and stocky') the 1.68-meter (5 foot 6 inch) *capo* mutated into the symbol of Mexican drug trafficking in the new era.

Born into poverty in the drug-steeped traditions of the Golden Triangle, in a tiny village called La Tuna in the municipality of Badiraguato, El Chapo grew up under the tutelage of Félix Gallardo, but his style was very different. The older kingpin read Voltaire and García Márquez and filled one of his letters from jail with nostalgia over a trip to Geneva and his appreciation of the Swiss sense of order. Chapo, though reputedly acutely intelligent, was barely educated and is famed for using ghost-writers to finesse his love letters.

Chapo first gained public notoriety in the turf wars of the 1990s, after a shootout with the Arellano Félix brothers in the Guadalajara airport car park in 1993. They all escaped unharmed, although the battle resulted in the death of a local cardinal, Juan Jesús Posadas Ocampo, shot dead inside his car (the controversy over whether this was accidental, as police investigations concluded, lives on to this day).

Chapo was arrested within weeks in Guatemala. Taken back to Mexico, he spent the rest of the decade in a high-security prison, with ample funds at his disposal to buy special privileges that took the edge off the hardships of confinement. His escape in January 2001 was said to have been prompted by the imminent threat of extradition to the US. A recent investigation by journalist Anabel Hernández concluded that he went out the front gate in a police uniform with the complicity of high-up government officials. This contradicts the official version that he was pushed through numerous security doors in a dirty laundry cart and driven out of the prison itself in the boot of an employee's car.

Once free, Chapo spearheaded an alliance of Sinaloa-rooted kingpins that became known as The Federation. It is widely accepted that this was sketched out at an initial *capo* summit in the central city of Cuernavaca in 2001. Aside from Chapo, that meeting was reportedly attended by the top brass of Sinaloa trafficking at the time. These included Ismael 'El Mayo' Zambada García, Juan José Esparragoza Moreno or 'El Azul', Ignacio 'Nacho' Coronel Villarreal, and at least one of the four trafficking brothers with the surname Beltrán Leyva. Vicente Carrillo Fuentes of the Sinaloa-rooted Juárez cartel sent a high-level envoy.

The Sinaloa Federation, intertwined with familial as well as business ties, set out to achieve hegemony in the Mexican drug-trafficking world, but its expansion plans hit a block when it began an invasion of the Gulf cartel stronghold of Nuevo Laredo in Tamaulipas. The country's busiest inland port was an obvious jewel in any trafficker's crown. In the spring of 2005, the city erupted in a series of major shootouts in public places which broke the mould of the targeted hits that had characterized the turf wars of the past. These were not just assassinations that got out of control, but were full-on battles over physical territory.

Many date the start of the drug wars to this conflict, in which the Sinaloans badly underestimated the Gulf cartel. Despite the arrest of its top leader in 2003, the Gulf cartel both fended off the invasion and counterattacked in Sinaloa bastions elsewhere in the country, most notably Acapulco.

The Gulf's resilience stemmed from the effectiveness of its paramilitary wing, which was formed in the late 1990s from a core of around a dozen army deserters, mostly from an elite anti-drug unit. They called themselves Los Zetas, reputedly after old police radio codes, and they revolutionized the concept and practice of cartel enforcement.

The Zetas brought superior training and operational planning, a focus on weaponry, a willingness to use extreme cruelty and a disregard for who might also get killed, aside from the original target. All other major trafficking organizations in Mexico realized that they needed to form similar units if they wanted to compete. And this they did, often with the help of former police commanders. With the fighting being done by professionals on all sides, once the drug wars started, they were both particularly brutal and particularly hard to stop by the kind of *capo* peace pacts that had helped keep a lid on rivalries in the past.

Changes in business models have also given the cartels a broader range of things to fight over. As well as continuing to smuggle South American cocaine and locally produced marijuana and heroin, the Mexican traffickers started manufacturing synthetic drugs, particularly methamphetamines. Mexican production boomed after a 2005 US congressional ban on over-the-counter sales of pseudoephedrine, one of the main ingredients of the drug, made it harder for clandestine labs to operate 'stateside'.

The local user market has also grown, with the number of Mexican addicts jumping by 51 per cent between 2002 and 2008, according to government surveys. The problem is particularly acute in the big cities along the border. The proportion of Mexican drug users in the general population is still only about a tenth of the figure in the US or Europe, and is significantly lower than in much of Latin America. Nevertheless, managing distribution networks for key local markets with the potential to grow requires the cartels to maintain tighter control of their territories than is necessary when the objective is merely to move cargos through the country unseen.

Explicit territorial domination is also required by the parallel trend of diversification out of drugs and into other types of organized crime. The Zetas have been among the most aggressive in this respect, running extensive extortion rackets, systematically kidnapping Central American migrants on their way north, siphoning crude oil out of pipelines and selling it over the border, and producing their own label of pirated movies. There was even a bottle of brandy in the shape of a letter 'Z' at one point, though this said more about the symbolic power of the label than about its money-making potential. The Zetas are believed to operate as a kind of franchise, lending the terror of their name to budding criminal gangs across the country (which are not necessarily integrated into the structure), and then taking a cut of the profits.

The intensity of the drug wars also stems from the extraordinary arsenals the cartels accumulate, aided by the end of the ten-year ban on assault-weapon sales in the US in 2004. In the first four years of the Fox administration, the government seized nearly 29,000 weapons. In the first four years of the Calderón administration, the figure was 93,000. A single haul in Tamaulipas in November 2008 yielded over 500 firearms, including .50-calibre sniper rifles, rocket and grenade launchers, assault rifles and half a million rounds of ammunition.

Important as all these factors are, it was Mexico's political transition away from one-party rule by the PRI that knitted them together into such a murderous tapestry.

Social historian Luis Astorga Almanza has spent much of his career chronicling and analysing the intimate association between trafficking organizations and politics that goes back to the beginning of the business. It started off, he says, with local politicians directly controlling local drug traffickers. The relationship became more complex when traffickers got richer and governments were politically required to be at least seen to be chasing them, though it was never broken. One-party hegemony meant that the regime could still impose limits on the autonomy of both the traffickers and the corrupt security officials and individual politicians in their pay, but this began to break down as the PRI slowly lost its monopoly of political power.

The burgeoning political plurality of the end of the twentieth century freed the traffickers to play the new political game and to expand their influence, especially in the provinces. The weakening of central government meant that it was more useful than ever for the cartels to control local police forces and local politicians. Genuinely competitive elections meant that politicians with access to cartel funds had a better chance of winning – and a larger debt to repay if they did.

In cartel bastions around the country there began what Astorga calls 'a parallel transition'. One-party rule had meant that the mafia bosses were required not to make life too difficult for the local authorities, for fear of incurring the wrath of centralized power. Now the federal institutions were just one player among many, and their ability to define and enforce the rules of the game was drastically cut. 'In the old days the state held the balance defining the correlation of forces', says Astorga. 'With the referee out of the picture, the struggle for hegemony among drug-trafficking groups became something very different.'

The growth of cartel power accelerated after Vicente Fox's victory in the 2000 presidential elections. Former collaborators of the president say he was never really interested in the drug trafficking issue, beyond securing US praise for the odd high-profile arrest. In those early years of the US 'War on Terror', Washington was also less concerned about the *capos* than about the idea that Al Qaeda-linked terrorists would start flowing through Mexico on their way to strike US targets. Organized criminal groups consequently faced almost no resistance as they stepped up their colonization of the power vacuums left by the completion of the transition away from one-party hegemony.

When the first wave of the new-style turf wars exploded and intensified in Nuevo Laredo and Acapulco in 2005 and 2006, Fox deployed soldiers to patrol the cities in an operation he called Secure Mexico. It looked more like a public relations exercise than a serious effort to restore order. Even so, its minimal impact should have sounded warning bells about what was likely to happen when Fox's successor employed a similar strategy, albeit on an unprecedented scale.

President Felipe Calderón's offensive began in a piecemeal way, the pattern of deployments following explosions of violence around the country, with later surges when the initial crackdowns failed. Within a few years there were said to be around 50,000 soldiers actively involved, although some observers believed the figure was substantially higher. The navy also began to take a central role from late 2009 (though the numbers involved were harder to pin down), by which time a revamped federal police force of around 35,000 was being trained up with a focus on organized crime.

In 2007 the highest-profile conflicts were in the central state of Michoacán and the north-western border city of Tijuana. Major new fronts emerged in 2008 and 2009, most dramatically in Ciudad Juárez, just over the border from Texas, and the Pacific state of Sinaloa, following the breakdown of a *capo* pact that had helped restrain burgeoning conflicts.

Ciudad Juárez remained the most violent battlefield in 2010, at the same time as new intense fronts developed in the north-eastern states of Tamaulipas and Nuevo León, and the violence spread to northern and central states such as Durango and Morelos. During 2011, the struggle to control Ciudad Juárez calmed a little, but new conflicts blew up in the Gulf state of Veracruz and the resort city of Acapulco, at the same time as violence surged again in Sinaloa. Even Mexico City itself, still an island of relative calm, showed signs of a burgeoning war on its outskirts.

The national murder rate was still well below that in many Latin American countries (such as El Salvador and Venezuela) and was similar to Brazil's. Some areas of the country boasted a genuine aura of tranquillity. Even so, almost nowhere could claim to be completely free from drug war-related violence, and parts of the country were among the most deadly in the world. The explosion of brutality also came in the wake of fifteen years of a consistently declining national murder rate. A study of death certificates by Fernando Escalante Gonzalbo showed that, after reaching a peak of 19 per 100,000 people in 1992, the rate dropped almost every year to reach a low of 8 per 100,000 in 2007 at the start of the drug wars. This trend then reversed dramatically and the number of homicides per 100,000 Mexicans was pushing 19 again by the end of 2009.

How many deaths can be directly attributed to Mexico's drug wars is a matter of intense controversy. The government had released almost no official figures until January 2011, when it published a database of all 'deaths because of criminal rivalry' up until the end of 2010. The database put the deaths in 2007 at 2,826. The number then soared in 2008 to 6,837. It carried on rising sharply in 2009 (9,614), and leapt to 15,273 in 2010. The official database total of 34,612 also included those killed in December 2006, the first month of Calderón's administration. It was considerably higher than the unofficial tallies kept by several newspapers that had already highlighted the escalation in deaths assumed to be linked to the drug wars that began in earnest in 2008. The figures the papers gave for 2007 were slightly higher than those for 2006.

The government reneged on its promise to regularly update the figures in 2011, although regional official figures were sometimes available and the newspaper *ejecutómetros* (execution counts) indicated that the killing was continuing at about the same rate or slightly higher. At the beginning of 2012, the newspaper *Reforma* reported a 7 per cent rise in its count over the previous year.

Drug-war expert Eduardo Guerrero Gutiérrez maintains his own count: based on monitoring the press and factoring in estimated underreporting, it had reached 47,500 by the end of October 2011. Some journalists and activists argue that the criteria used to define drug-war deaths are too narrow and that the real death toll is much higher. A figure of 60,000 became popular at the end of 2011.

There is also much dispute over who is dying. For the first three years of the offensive, the government routinely claimed that 90 per cent of those killed were linked to the cartels. Most of the remainder were said to be heroic members of the security forces (with a few rotten apples who would not be missed, and the occasional particularly unlucky passer-by). Federal officials later dropped this claim in light of the large number of obviously unconnected people who were also dying. It is also, at least for now, impossible even to estimate the proportion of these so-called 'innocent victims' because only a tiny fraction of all murders are properly investigated.

It is not just the number and range of the dead that speaks of the madness of war: torture and mutilation are often extreme and the defiling of corpses routine. The first two severed heads, stuck on a railing outside a government building in Acapulco in April 2006, were widely reported abroad, as well as in Mexico. A few years later decapitations barely warranted a line in the national press, unless accompanied by additional horror (as when one victim's face was stitched onto a football). The *Reforma* newspaper noted 596 decapitations during 2011 as a figure in a table, and little more. In late 2011, the director of forensic investigation in Acapulco told me that over half the decapitated bodies he saw had lost their heads before death.

The escalation of the barbarity and the offensive's failure to contain it have inevitably provided the driving narrative of drug-war coverage so far, but understanding why things got so bad also requires delving into the complexity of what is going on – beginning with who is fighting whom.

President Calderón's offensive against organized crime is central to the story, but direct confrontations between the federal forces and the cartels have been relatively rare throughout. The impact of the offensive also depends on which agencies are involved, as the army, navy and federal police all tend to pursue different strategies, and what role the local law enforcement apparatus plays. The government offensive is consequently one (hard-to-pin-down) element in the bewildering patchwork of shifting conflicts, dominated by the rivalries between different criminal groups and complicated further by fluid and changing alliances that ensure the protagonists vary from place to place and from year to year.

The clearest identifiable trend in all of this is the fragmentation of the original groups involved in the turf wars that triggered the Calderón offensive in the first place, leading to the emergence of new players, and the multiplication of rivalries. Expert Eduardo Guerrero Gutiérrez says that, at the start of the offensive in 2006, there were six important cartels: the Sinaloa Federation, the Gulf/Zetas, the Tijuana cartel, the Juárez cartel, a newer group called La Familia and its lesser-known precursor known as Los Valencia. Five years later, he counted sixteen different groups, many of them small, locally based and particularly violent organizations without the capacity to traffic large quantities of drugs, but instead almost entirely focused on activities such as extortion, kidnapping and the local drug-user market. They might have associations with the remaining bigger groups, but these are loose and unstable.

Mexico's drug wars are just that – *wars*, plural; and each one tends to emphasize different elements of the broader dynamic.

On 8 October 2009, Rubén Ramos dropped into the carpenter's workshop a few doors down from where he lived in Ciudad Juárez to see if he could borrow a drill. Minutes later he lay stretched out on the floor, a thin trail of blood trickling from a bullet hole in his chest. His frozen expression betrayed no emotion. The carpenter himself, an older man called Arturo Chávez, was in an adjacent room. He had several bullet wounds and a large pool of blood surrounded his body. The terror on his face left no doubt that he had seen the inevitable end approaching.

I arrived at the crime scene with a military patrol – five green pickups rigged up with fixed machine guns and filled with soldiers carrying assault rifles. We got there late because we had got lost. The colonel I was sitting next to had eventually abandoned his efforts to find the way via frantic radio communication strewn with exotic code names, and instead got us back on track by leaning out of his window and asking directions from a local. It seemed to sum up what the army was doing in Ciudad Juárez, by then established as the most violent front in the drug wars – riding around with lots of fire power and not much clue about what was going on, let alone how to prevent it happening.

State-level police had already evacuated and sealed off the block of the carpenter's workshop, leaving a group of men, women and children gathered at the crime tape, waiting to return to their homes once the bodies had been removed. A pre-teen girl stood on tiptoe alongside her father to get a better look. None seemed shocked as they recounted how a hit-man had got out of a red car around 2 p.m. and rushed into the workshop. Several shots later he was back in the vehicle, speeding off in a cloud of dust to be lost in the charmless urban sprawl beyond. 'This is what Juárez is like these days', said Aurora, as she pushed her baby's pram back and forth. 'We don't understand what is happening here. You can't trust anybody anymore, you can't even really talk, anybody can be killed. The best thing to do is just shut up and watch.'

After a brief look around, the army patrol headed out again, and I renewed my doomed efforts to engage the soldiers in a conversation about their mission. 'We are here to deter the criminals', a fresh-faced private told me as we rode in the back of one of the pickups. When I asked why he thought the killers did not seem deterred, he fell silent and fiddled with his gun. Eventually we were back in the barracks, set up in a conference centre a stone's throw from Texas. The death of the carpenter and his neighbour were registered on a huge map of the city in the radio control room with a coloured drawing pin.

The local newspaper *PM* registered the double murder with a cursory mention on page eight. Its front page carried a photograph of a nameless young man, found wrapped in a blanket with his lips sewn together, and a headline about a police officer gunned down as she went to buy bread. Page three contained a picture of a man slumped in an SUV with at least twelve bullet holes in his body; page five another image of two similarly unidentified males lying dead on a pavement; and page six one of a youth with white tennis shoes killed outside a church. With eight dead, it was an average day.

The annual number of murders in Ciudad Juárez jumped from 310 in 2007 to 1,607 in 2008. It shot up again in 2009 to 2,754, and climbed even further in 2010 to 3,117. Across the Río Bravo, in El Paso, there were just five murders in 2010.

The intensification of the local bloodbath coincided with a major federal operation both in the city itself and in the nearby towns along the stretch of border-facing territory known as the Valle de Juárez. The first contingent of about 2,000 soldiers and 500 federal police arrived in spring 2008. A subsequent surge a year later took troop numbers to 7,500 and the number of *federales* to 1,500, and there was a lull in the killing for a couple of months. Then it got worse than ever. Whatever else the offensive was doing in Ciudad Juárez, it certainly was not protecting the population.

The battle in Juárez had begun after Chapo Guzmán and his branch of the Sinaloa Federation activated a latent bid to eject the local Juárez cartel, led by his former ally Vicente Carrillo Fuentes. Relations between the two *capos* had been close to breaking point for some time, but at the end of 2007 Chapo jumped at the chance to exploit internal splits in the local group to recruit the dissidents into his own invasion force. He called it Gente Nueva, or New People.

The rapid escalation of the violence that followed stemmed from the wholesale recruitment of pre-existing local youth gangs into the conflict. There were hundreds of these gangs, though only a few gained national notoriety. The oldest and largest – Los Aztecas – was associated with La Linea, the enforcement arm of the Juárez cartel. The Sinaloan interlopers had ties to the Artistas Asesinos and the Mexicles.

'This started off with cartel members fighting each other, but then they realized that they were all going to end up dead, so they started to recruit from the gangs and form kind of paramilitary structures', local human rights worker and analyst Gustavo de la Rosa Hinkerman told me.

The gangs were originally associated less with the city's long trafficking tradition than with its position as a hub for *maquilas* – workshops that assemble duty-free components for export. Established in the 1960s, the sector boomed after the North American Free Trade Agreement came into effect in 1994. Job-hungry migrants flooded to the city, setting up their homes in dusty shanty towns that spread ever further into the broiling desert. Lacking the most basic services, these were soon overflowing with bored and alienated latchkey kids with minimal schooling. Joining a gang provided a sense of shared identity and offered something to do. When the turf war started, the gangs provided the cartels with a fount of disenfranchised youth, willing to be used as cannon fodder. Some reputedly accepted as little as $100 to carry out a contract killing, and even less to serve as lookouts and dealers.

The cartel war in Ciudad Juárez turned into a street-by-street battle for control of each *barrio* and a cell-by-cell battle for control of the jails, where there were several massacres of inmates. Commandos also targeted drug rehabilitation centres, said to be replete not just with recovering addicts, but also with gang members lying low. Two separate attacks on two centres in September 2009 left twenty-eight dead.

The violence spread out of gang territories, on the back of rampant extortion and kidnapping rackets. The *maquila* sector remained largely immune, but under the new sinister shadow private doctors, who had once competed for attention by advertising their services on giant bill-boards, retired behind metal doors and refused to offer appointments to patients who could not provide a recommendation from a trustworthy source. Respectable lower middle-class and poor families without ties to the gangs, and without sufficient resources to make them obvious financial targets, also got drawn into the horror.

Prior to the drug wars, the main reason for a reporting trip to Ciudad Juárez had been to cover the serial-type murders of young women that had begun in the mid-1990s. But hard, dusty and ugly as the city was, even at that time it was also a repository of hope that some form of advancement was possible. It provided employment to anybody willing to work hard, and small business people with initiative had more chance to grow there than in most Mexican cities. Many a cardboard shack was gradually transformed into a breeze-block home with flowers – and perhaps even a battered old car – outside the front door. The drug violence ensured that, although life continued in the city in a remarkably normal way, the pockets of optimism it had once prized shrivelled up.

For many in Ciudad Juárez there was a sense that the violence in their city had gone beyond the relatively simple logic of an inter-cartel turf war to evolve into a form of senseless criminal anarchy. Things were further complicated by the difficulty in establishing where the boundaries between the criminals and the authorities lay – a problem fuelled by evidence of corruption and a suspicion of dirty-war tactics and social cleansing. A number of prominent social activists who opposed the government strategy in the city were killed, raising questions about whether they had been targeted by angry officials, the cartels, or both.

The massacre of fifteen people at a teenager's birthday party in a working-class *barrio* called Villas de Salvarcar on 30 January 2010 marked a breaking point of sorts. President Calderón's initial description of the bloodbath as a gangland feud caused a national furore. An arrested leader of La Linea later confessed that he had ordered the raid, because he believed some of the partygoers belonged to a rival gang. But that was not really the point. What mattered was that so many ordinary, young, totally uninvolved people had died in a way that suggested there was no safe space left.

Calderón went to Juárez to personally apologize to the families of the victims. After sitting through hours of recriminations at a public meeting, he admitted that the strategy had not paid enough attention to what he called 'the social dimension'. His government went on to announce plans to build new schools, new hospitals and new sports grounds, and to set up a youth orchestra – all in the name of giving wayward young people reason not to become killers, and law-abiding citizens reason to trust in the good faith of the authorities. He was also keen to show the rest of the country that the government was responding to demands that it should pay more attention to the victims of the violence. The government also accelerated a plan to scale down the army presence and scale up the number of federal police, primarily in response to charges of human rights violations by soldiers.

Although the killing kept getting worse in 2010 and the daily average during the year was 8.5 murders a day, the numbers did start to fall in 2011, with the daily average for the year dropping to 5.5 murders. This was still far higher than it had been before the offensive began in the city, but it was at least a significant improvement

In the middle of 2011, Gustavo de la Rosa, the veteran activist, credited this improvement to a mixture of more efficient targeting of mid-level cartel operatives by the federal police and the creation of a citizens' watchdog (of which he was a member) that monitored progress and exerted pressure to limit abuse. However, he said, little had yet been done to address the real need for a concerted effort to design programmes to help the high-risk youth population that was either still caught up in the swirl of violence or else was vulnerable to being sucked into it – and, complained de la Rosa, there was no sign of any such effort.

Even if this happened and the murder rate continued to fall, Ciudad Juárez remained emblematic of how ineffective the offensive was in the early years, and how much of a struggle it had been to even begin to get things under control. No other front had received so much attention – first, in terms of federal firepower and then in terms of social programmes – and no other front had produced such an often seemingly incomprehensible catalogue of horror. The city and the towns around it screamed out the price paid of not thinking things through better from the start.

The development of the violence in Ciudad Juárez also underlined the fact that positive changes only came about when civil society demanded them in a way that the authorities could not ignore. This was something that was particularly hard to imagine on some other drug-war fronts, most particularly in Tamaulipas, where civil society had been beaten down over the years by the tight territorial control of the Gulf/Zetas cartel – a factor that appeared to be of little concern to the government until the group divided into two factions, which began fighting each other in 2010.

In October 2009, a group of high-ranking Mexican and US officials sat down to dinner to discuss the progress of the Mexican offensive against the cartels. According to an account of the conversation contained in a classified US embassy cable, the Mexican diners said they believed that efforts should be narrowed down to the two or three cities where the violence was most acute. Jorge Tello Peón, then national security coordinator and a former intelligence chief, argued that there was 'certainly no time to work in a few relatively safe cities such as Nuevo Laredo'. Four months later, Nuevo Laredo and the rest of the north-eastern state of Tamaulipas were transformed into the most warlike of all the drug-war battle fronts.

The Gulf/Zetas had dominated the state together, ever since they had repelled the original Sinaloa incursion in 2005, but the relationship had been under strain for some time. The Gulf's old-guard leadership were uncomfortable with the increasing autonomy of their erstwhile enforcers, while the Zetas felt little loyalty to their nominal bosses. When they finally split in early 2010, their rivalry triggered a full-scale, open confrontation for control of the state's cities and towns which involved battles between heavily armed – and at times uniformed – commandos that lasted for hours.

Locals began jokingly referring to their state as Ta . . . ta . . . ta . . . ta . . . maulipas, their fear of being caught in the crossfire augmented by the difficulty of finding out what was actually going on. The cartels terrorized the already cowed local press into what amounted to a virtual news blackout. The army and navy were also often loath to give out information about the operations they were involved in, while the local authorities revealed almost nothing.

Twitter, Facebook, blogs and YouTube became the main source of information about even the most basic dynamics of the violence, though the web was also inundated with rumour-mongers and cartel propagandists.

A climate of fear, distrust, isolation and impotence pervaded the lives of those who, in theory, should have had nothing to fear. Locals said the cartels recruited taxi drivers and street vendors en masse to report on everything – from troop movements to strangers coming to town. It was impossible to tell when cartel eyes and ears might be tuned in around office water coolers or behind the scissors in hairdressers' shops.

In rural areas that were deemed to be of strategic importance, farmers stopped tending their fields, shopkeepers closed their doors, gas-field workers ceased to turn up for work, and almost everybody avoided going out at night. People began disappearing and often nobody dared look for them.

Accepted wisdom in intelligence circles, one high-level US law enforcement official told me in 2011, expected the Gulf to 'steamroller' the Zetas. The Gulf, he said, had control of the main drug-trafficking and money-laundering networks, and most people assumed they would build up a new army that could pound their former enforcers, who would run out of resources. It didn't work out that way, he believed, because the Zetas stepped up other criminal activities, such as kidnapping, to keep the cash flowing and the battle going.

Located about half way between the frontier cities of Reynosa and Nuevo Laredo, near a junction with another road that leads to the country's business capital of Monterrey, the pretty colonial town of Ciudad Mier was always going to be in dispute. The battles that began in February 2010 were so fierce that families pushed their furniture against their doors and windows and retreated into their bathrooms. When they heard the convoys of gunmen leave, the residents emerged from their bunkers to see gaping holes in many of their houses and a carpet of bullet casings on the roads. Burnt-out or crashed vehicles abandoned by the gunmen littered the town. Some were dubbed *monstruos* – trucks encased in 3cm steel plating, complete with small holes along their sides from which guns could fire.

The cartels tended to take their dead with them, and those civilians abducted simply disappeared, which meant that the terrified residents of Ciudad Mier rarely encountered bodies. One summer night, however, a man was left hanging from a palm tree in the town square with his hands and legs cut off. The townsfolk listened to his screams until he finally died.

It all got too much for most of Mier's 8,000 odd residents after a particularly ferocious series of shootouts in November. Over the course of a couple of days they packed up their few valuables and fled. Interviewed in a temporary shelter set up for them in the nearby larger town of Ciudad Alemán, the refugees complained to reporters that they had been all but abandoned by the federal offensive. The federal police outpost in town had been burnt down months before, they said, while the military and navy only drove through the town during the day. At night there was nothing to stop the cartels. The minority who remained in town rarely ventured out of their homes. 'It is terrible and sad', one of them told me by phone. 'People don't even dare to go to Mass anymore.'

Drug-war refugees were not a new phenomenon; however, the flight from Ciudad Mier was more concentrated than anything widely reported before. It shocked the country, rather as the massacre at the Ciudad Juárez birthday party had done earlier in the year, and drove home just how deep the impact of the violence was on ordinary people. Coming just a few days after the federal offensive claimed a major victory by bringing down one of the Gulf cartel's most important leaders, it also underlined the fact that success against high-value targets was one thing, but citizen security was quite another matter.

Ezequiel Cárdenas Guillén, the brother of the group's former leader Osiel Cárdenas Guillén, was killed in an operation mounted by the Mexican army and navy in the Gulf border stronghold of Matamoros on 5 November 2010. He died after a day of shootouts that ended with the *capo* making a last, doomed stand, accompanied by his inner circle of hit-men known as Los Escorpiones, holed up in a warehouse that soldiers and marines pounded with grenades. Nicknamed Tony Tormenta, he played second fiddle to his brother's former right-hand man, Eduardo 'El Cos' Costilla, who was left to continue his battle with the Zetas.

By then, the most famous Zeta was Heriberto Lazcano Lazcano (alias El Lazca), who was one of the original members of the group formed from army deserters. He was said to lead the cartel alongside Miguel Angel Treviño Morales. By then almost all the other founders had been either killed or arrested, but new recruits had replenished these losses. The Zetas are particularly famous for hiring former members of the notorious Guatemalan army special forces unit, the Kaibiles, though the extent of this phenomenon is not yet clear.

New deployments of federal forces to Tamaulipas beginning in late 2010 reduced the number of show-stopping gun battles, but an atmosphere of terror still reigned, and the government's claims to have 'restored normality' were obviously exaggerated.

A year after the exodus from Ciudad Mier, the mayor claimed that two-thirds of the original residents were back living in the town. Many lined the main street to applaud a military parade on the day a mobile barracks on the edge of town was inaugurated, the first of several planned in the state. With roughly one soldier for every ten residents, they told reporters they felt safer; but they knew the situation was unsustainable.

More than anywhere else in the country, the federal offensive in Tamaulipas had got bogged down in a kind of holding operation. This stemmed, at least in part, from having ignored the control the Gulf and Zetas had exercised in the state before they began fighting each other in early 2010. Prior to that, Tamaulipas had been treated as unproblematic because the murder rate appeared contained, but the absence of bodies on street corners did not mean that peace and tranquillity reigned. The truth was that extortion rackets, kidnapping and a growing fear were already eating into the ability of civil society to speak out – particularly as the authorities did not seem interested in listening. The explosion in outright violence that followed silenced most of the remaining citizen voices and left the population with little choice but to keep a low profile, leave, hide, or (in places like Mier) welcome de facto martial law, with all the inherent risks of abuse.

Meanwhile, the Gulf–Zeta conflict had spread to other states, most notably Nuevo León and its capital Monterrey, the nation's business capital, which, back in 2005, had been considered the safest big city in Latin America.

Monterrey had long thought of itself as a case apart from pretty much anywhere in Mexico. Its compact elite, which mingled with the CEOs of big international companies, liked to ascribe the city's success to an abundance of entrepreneurial spirit and a furious work ethic. Many in Mexico City viewed it as unusually rich, efficient, dynamic, modern and crime free, if just a touch smug.

Drug trafficking there has a long and established presence, but nobody bothered about it too much. The city is strategically placed, just 160 kilometres from the border, and ample communications networks enabled the traffickers to go virtually anywhere else they chose. There was a growing domestic market for drugs in the poorer *barrios*, and a good few kingpins set up family homes in the mansions that abounded in wealthy districts.

Signs of burgeoning tensions aside, neither the city nor the state featured on anybody's map of major drug-war trouble spots until 2010, when local government figures saw the number of murders more than triple to 828, as the Gulf cartels and the Zetas brought their rivalry south from neighbouring Tamaulipas. That record figure had already been surpassed by the middle of 2011.

The cartels in Nuevo León also began assassinating mayors. This had happened in other trouble spots, but the targets here included politicians from well-to-do towns that had previously thought themselves immune. The August 2010 abduction and subsequent murder of Edelmiro Cavazos grabbed most attention. The young US-educated mayor of Santiago, a picturesque town filled with the weekend holiday homes of the Monterrey wealthy, had a staunchly upright reputation. The authorities later arrested six of the mayor's own police officers who were allegedly in the pay of the Zetas.

The same day as Cavazos was kidnapped, an early-afternoon gun battle outside the gates of the American School Foundation sent the children of the Monterrey elite scurrying for cover. It turned out that a Zeta commando had clashed with a group of bodyguards from the nation's biggest bottling company, Femsa, and had killed two before leaving the scene with four more. The following morning they were found alive inside a company car.

The authorities and the company said the commando had mistaken the guards for rival gunmen, but rumours were rife that it had actually been a failed effort to kidnap children from the school. Kidnapping was ballooning at the time: 'My dentist's son was kidnapped two weeks ago, the brother of a friend was kidnapped two months ago, the best friend of the entrepreneur where my fund was invested was kidnapped in December, and never returned, and this past Wednesday, a close acquaintance was kidnapped', a Mexican investment banker with children at the American school told the *Wall Street Journal*. 'The big topic is whether to move to the U.S. altogether. I don't know the actual numbers, but there's a feeling of "diaspora" from families moving to San Antonio, or Austin or Houston.'

Soon after the incident at the American school the US State Department ruled the Monterrey consulate out of bounds for the dependent minors of its employees. This is the kind of measure usually reserved for conventional war zones.

The battle for Nuevo León in general, and for Monterrey in particular, dealt an especially damaging blow to the federal offensive. It underlined the sense that violence had spun so far out of control that it was beginning to have a direct impact on the business elite. It also provided a potential model of what could happen if a strong economic elite decided to take an active role in the search for a solution. Local business leaders began helping to finance social programmes in the *barrios*, and some even got involved in organizing police recruitment drives.

The size of the challenge to turn things around was underlined in August 2011, when armed arsonists set fire to the Casino Royale gambling centre in the city, killing fifty-two people. The impact of the tragedy was measured by more than just the number of victims (most of whom were found dead in the toilets, where they had fled from the guns, only to find themselves caught by the fire and smoke in a building without adequate emergency exits); it was also associated with their primarily middle-class status – many of them elderly women out for an afternoon's bingo. This section of the population had been targeted individually in extortion rackets, but it was not generally considered vulnerable to a massacre.

Subsequent journalistic investigations also uncovered a morass of corruption that not only underpinned a recent explosion in the number of gaming houses in Monterrey, but also suggested links between these and organized crime. The fire at the Casino Royale, and the reluctance of the authorities to pursue the evidence of widespread corruption that it high-lighted, undermined the efforts of both the federal and the Nuevo León state government to frame the drug wars as a straightforward battle between the good guys and the bad guys. Nowhere, however, were the lines between the dirty and the clean more blurred, and more complex, than in Sinaloa, the so-called cradle of Mexican drug trafficking.

Martín Ferrer builds tombs for a living – and he makes a reasonably good living out of it, too. His are no ordinary tombs, but are the kind of two-storey marble extravaganzas that make the Jardines de Humaya cemetery on the outskirts of Culiacán, the capital of Sinaloa, look like a wealthy suburb for the dead – the narco dead. 'They pay well and on time, and they are good clients as long as you deliver what you promise', Ferrer told me one afternoon, as he took a break from his current project. 'If you don't, they are not so happy.' With his hand, he mimed putting a gun to his head and pulling the trigger. This was, he said, exactly what had happened to a friend a few months ago when he went over budget.

Such mortuary luxury does not come cheap. The builder pointed to one mausoleum with five-metre high Doric columns and a sweeping curved staircase up to a second floor. It had cost 1.2 million pesos to build (around $120,000 at the time), he said, though he did not specify whether that had included the solar panels on the roof (to power the air condi-tioning and in-tomb entertainment) or the bullet-proof glass in the picture window. 'It's so the family can get together and relax. They have to be careful these days.'

The view from where we were chatting suggested that domes were almost obligatory, balconies common, and that the most popular architectural inspiration could be loosely described as neo-classical. Gaudy baroque was also a favourite, and there was a smattering of modernist minimalism that Ferrer said was becoming all the rage.

Drug trafficking has a longstanding tradition in many parts of the country, but nowhere is it as organically integrated into the political, economic, social and cultural bedrock as in Sinaloa. The state has many facets: it has industrialized agriculture and is one of the last redoubts of traditional pre-Conquest ball games; but the drug business lurks in the background almost everywhere you look.

As well as being the bastion of the Sinaloa cartel, the country's most powerful trafficking organization of the contemporary period, and of Joaquín 'El Chapo' Guzmán, its most famous *capo*, the state is also the sentimental homeland of a good many other leaders of rival organizations. Though their strongholds may be elsewhere, they not infrequently end up being brought home for burial in the Humaya cemetery when their time is up. The ageing mother of the Carrillo Fuentes brothers of the Juárez cartel continued to live in the state, at least up until 2011. She occasionally allowed journalists into her home, where she kept an altar dedicated to her various dead sons.

Sinaloa was relatively peaceful at the start of the Calderón offensive, until a split at the heart of the Sinaloa Federation turned it into a major front in early 2008, at just about the same time as the Ciudad Juárez conflict got going. The spark came with the January arrest of Alfredo Beltrán Leyva, one of the four brothers whose organization had grown into one of the most powerful in the country within the Federation.

The rumour quickly spread that Alfredo, picked up by the military in a Culiacán safe house, had been 'given up' to the authorities by Chapo. Others said that Chapo had not done enough to support an escape plan in the immediate aftermath of Alfredo's detention. The simmering tension exploded into open warfare when one of Chapo's sons was gunned down outside a mall in Culiacán that May, reputedly on orders from the Beltrán Leyva brothers still at large. In the conflict that followed, Ismael 'El Mayo' Zambada and the other major Sinaloa leaders sided with Chapo. The Beltrán Leyva consolidated a budding alliance with the Zetas that may have been the root cause of the original split.

The battle raged in all the states where the groups coincided, but was most intense in Sinaloa itself. Chapo and the Beltrán Leyva family were born in the same part of the sierra, were vaguely related, and had grown up together in the business, privy to each other's secrets. They knew the location of each other's safe houses and which policemen and politicians were on whose payroll. They knew which companies laundered whose money; what restaurants their erstwhile allies liked to frequent; and which schools their children attended. The drug wars had come home.

A relatively small city of about 600,000 people, Culiacán is far more pleasant than most of Mexico's big drug-trafficking hubs on the border, with their anonymous strip-mall culture. The centre is shabby, but the tree-filled plazas are comfortable and the river promenade is populated and fun. At least they were until the priority became to avoid getting shot.

During a trip to Culiacán in January 2009, I talked to a taxi driver who had stumbled across seven separate gun battles in the space of two months. A young mother recalled watching armed men abduct another parent as they picked up their respective children from nursery school. A toddler cowered behind her mother as the woman told the story of her little girl's recent birthday party that ended when carloads of gunmen began shooting at each other not far away, leaving two small guests with shrapnel in their legs. A businessman confessed to a concern that he would become a target because he had friends whom he knew to be narcos. A family described how they had moved their bedroom so as not to have to sleep next to the wall they shared with neighbours they had seen carrying guns. The manager of a tyre-repair workshop told how he had instructed his employees to work at the double whenever obvious traffickers stopped to get new tyres – for fear that they would attract rivals. A woman said she would never recover from the death of her teenage son, killed when gunmen attacked the mechanic's workshop where he happened to be. A doctor in a private clinic recounted the time he had been forced to put a corpse on an IV drip by distraught assault rifle-wielding relatives, who refused to believe that their loved one was dead, despite seeing the brains spilling from his skull.

The stories were not only remarkable because they were so easy to find and so intimate; they also revealed a profound ambivalence among the general population about their city's status as a centre of organized crime.

The taxi driver said that, once things had calmed down, he would consider doing a little trafficking on the side to boost his income. The young mother expressed understanding for her friends who sought out the luxuries that narco boyfriends could provide (though personally she would prefer a politician – less risky). The mother of the little girl whose party had been ruined by a gun battle just wished the hit-men would take more care to fight each other in less destructive locations. The tyre-repair workshop manager recognized that his business would fold, were it not for the traffickers' insatiable appetite for new rubber on their vehicles. The mother of the dead teenager was angry with the cartels, but directed the bulk of her ire at the authorities for not tracking down his murderers. Only the doctor seemed to blame the violence entirely on the narcos, believed the solution was to run them out of town, and welcomed the 2,000 soldiers then patrolling the city as a first positive step towards this.

While hardly a scientific sample, it did suggest that even those directly affected by the violence find it hard to imagine Culiacán without drug traffickers in a significant role. The city is also replete with ordinary people who go beyond ambivalence to openly express affinity with the outlaws.

A housewife who lived next to a house pock-marked with bullet holes sat in a rocking chair with her infant daughter on her chest and complained that the economy was suffering acutely, since the offensive had made the traffickers lie low, when they were not killing each other. A waiter at my hotel told me, with evident pride, that his brother cooked for a *capo*. A little group of seven-year-olds, who had just participated enthusiastically in a violence-avoidance workshop organized by the state authorities at their school, boasted that they knew how to shoot Kalashnikov rifles. A twelve-year-old hawking newspapers to passing motorists said he wanted to be a narco. We had just watched a shiny new pickup drive by, prompting him to muse that one day he would have one just like that.

The city also moves to the sound of *narcocorridos* wafting out of car stereos – ballads recounting the exploits of outlaws, between frenetic accordion riffs, oom-pah-pah rhythms and gentle melodies that belie the bite of their lyrics. The couple of lines of a song by the band known simply as Cartel strike a near existential tone: 'A killer arrived in hell to inspect a job that he'd done. He didn't know his victims were already expecting him.'

The best-known *narcocorridos* embellish the biographies of well-known figures of the narco world, fulfilling a role similar to the songs of minstrels about medieval knights. Ambitious young traffickers pay thousands of dollars for a *corrido* about them, but the established *capos* are more likely to be asked for permission than for a fee.

Though they have been around for decades, the popularity of *narcocorridos* boomed from about 2000, and nowhere more so than in Sinaloa, where some of the biggest bands are based. '*Narcocorridos* are like action movies; they allow people to feel part of something exciting, even if they are not and don't really want to be', record producer Conrado Lugo told me. 'They grow a lot of tomatoes and chillies in Sinaloa as well as opium poppies, but I can't imagine a song about tomatoes and chillies becoming a hit.'

One night Lugo took me on a tour of some of Culiacán's sights. He showed me the house where Alfredo Beltrán Leyva was arrested. It had been scrawled with the words 'We Love You, Mochomo', referring to his nickname, which is a kind of red ant. We drove slowly by a well-tended metal cross surrounded by fresh flowers and helium balloons that stood in the place where Chapo Guzmán's son was killed. We passed in front of the modelling agency where Miss Sinaloa used to work before she was arrested with a trafficker and detained for forty days. As we went, the generous and jovial Lugo chatted about his plans to teach his three daughters to shoot, so that they wouldn't be intimidated by the violence. He was worried he might have left it too late for his eldest. She was twelve years old.

Whatever else it had done, the crackdown in Sinaloa had made little obvious progress in unravelling the ties of criminal groups to communities where roots ran deep. Some argued it had actually forced the penetration deeper.

'Narco here is not a military problem. It isn't even a police problem. It is a way of life', said Javier Valdez Cárdenas, a reporter at the investigative local weekly *Río Doce*. Valdez has also written three extraordinary books delving into the real stories that back his assertion: *Malayerba* (*Bad Grass*), *Miss Narco* and *Los Morros del Narco* (*Narco Youth*). 'We have allowed it into our homes, our kitchens, our dining rooms, our bathrooms, our bedrooms and under the sheets. I am pessimistic about whether we can get it out again.'

Relative calm returned to Sinaloa in 2009 as the government went after the Beltrán Leyva cartel and its main leader Arturo Beltrán Leyva. This culminated with him and six of his gunmen holed up in a second-floor flat in a high-end apartment complex in the central city of Cuernavaca, going down fighting as navy special forces closed in. After the operation, a photograph found its way into the public domain: it showed the lifeless kingpin lying on the floor, his trousers pulled down around his knees, his shirt up to his armpits, and his flesh covered in blood-stained dollar and peso bills. One of the most powerful drug traffickers in Mexico was dead and humiliated, but he had a powerful legacy that would continue to create havoc years later as the group he had led split into two and the killing continued.

Arturo's brother Hector headed one faction, which he renamed the Southern Pacific cartel. His former head of security, a US-born trafficker called Edgar Valdez Villarreal and nicknamed La Barbie, headed the other. Their struggle ended with La Barbie's arrest in August 2010; but that opened new conflicts, as the structures he had once controlled fell apart, most dramatically in Acapulco, where three main groups emerged from its remnants. They were the Independent Cartel of Acapulco, the Barredora (which means mechanical street-sweeper in Spanish) and the Devil's Commando. Chapo, Juárez and La Familia were also said to be hovering on the sidelines of the conflict.

By 2011 the bloodbath began spreading out of the resort's poverty-stricken outskirts into the main tourist areas, threatening to sink the local economy. A new surge in the federal presence in October was followed by a partial lull in the killing, but few of the people I talked to in the *barrios* two months later were hopeful that there would be lasting improvements for them.

'This whole thing is a pantomime to keep the tourists happy, but for people like us it will get worse again soon', a fifty-eight-year-old grandmother who did not want to give her real name told me as she rocked her coughing grandchild in a hammock at the back of the tiny shop where she sold homemade *piñatas*.

A few months before, she had got caught in the middle of a shootout inside the jail, when she was visiting her son, who was serving a sentence for robbery. 'If they can't even control the prison, how do you think they can control what happens outside.'

By then, Sinaloa was also suffering a renewed surge in violence, with Héctor Beltrán Leyva back fighting El Chapo in alliance with the Zetas. There were also said to be signs that Chapo was facing a potential rebellion within his own ranks from a new generation that was building its own power bases within his organization. 'We hear that there is a lot of stress even trying to hold it together', the same US law enforcement official who had been so surprised at the resilience of the Zetas told me. If Chapo was brought down, he predicted, the organization would fracture and there would be a lot more violence. It sounded like a scratched record.

The cartels did not just fragment in the context of the drug wars: they innovated and transformed in a way that presented yet more challenges to the authorities – none more so than La Familia, a cartel based in the central Pacific state of Michoacán, which melded drug trafficking with preaching, extortion with parallel justice, and flirted with becoming a criminal insurgency.

La Familia announced its claim to be a significant new player on the Mexican drug-trafficking scene in September 2006, when a commando burst into the Sol y Sombra disco in the small city of Uruapan and dropped five severed heads onto the dance floor. The heads were accompanied by a written message: 'La Familia does not kill for cash. It does not kill women or innocents and only those who deserve it die. Everyone should know that this is divine justice.' Beheadings were still rare at the time, and soon the group, which had been virtually unknown outside the state, became a national household name.

Michoacán is dotted with pockets of intense conservative Catholicism, but it is also famous as the cradle of the left-wing political dynasty begun by General Lázaro Cárdenas del Río in the 1930s. It has global economic relevance as a producer of avocados and mangos, and tourists from around Mexico and the world have long been drawn to its well-preserved colonial cities, vibrant indigenous culture and the exuberant beauty of its nature reserves and beaches. The state also has a long tradition of growing marijuana and opium poppies in the remote Tierra Caliente region, the Hot Land, which extends over the border with the state of Guerrero. More recently this rugged area has provided convenient cover for methamphetamine labs, which use precursor chemicals imported from Asia into the country's biggest Pacific port, Lázaro Cárdenas, which also lies within the state. Michoacán's long and largely isolated coastline likewise provides a convenient way station for South American cocaine heading north.

At the turn of the century, Michoacán was the bastion of an organization known as the Milenio, which was run by the Valencia family. Although it grew fast, it received little attention. I remember not paying sufficient attention myself around 2001 when the then drug tsar, José Luis Santiago Vasconcelos, took me over a map of the country and pointed out Michoacán as the place to watch. At the time, most independent drug-trafficking experts still largely confined their analysis to the Juárez, Tijuana and Gulf cartels.

The arrest of the new cartel's top leader, Armando Valencia Cornelio, in 2003 allowed La Familia to jump into the space this left and emerge as the new force in the Tierra Caliente. At first La Familia did this in an alliance with the Gulf/Zetas and then in direct conflict with them.

The battle between La Familia and the Zetas in Michoacán turned the state into one of the early hot spots of the drug wars. It was also the place that President Calderón, himself a native of the state, chose for the first test of his offensive and his determination to bring the cartels to heel in December 2006. The heavy federal presence led to an initial lull in the violence. But, though the violence waxed and waned over the following years, the place never settled into a comfortable peace.

La Familia, having apparently pushed the Zetas out, developed a solid social base of support. In the time-honoured traditions of veteran drug barons from Sinaloa, it cultivated an image as a local benefactor in communities long left to fester in their poverty by the state. It paid for new sports grounds, funded roads and would give wayward children a talking to on behalf of their worried mothers – all of which engendered local loyalty that acted as a buffer to efforts to arrest leaders.

La Familia also developed directly clientelistic organizations that were reminiscent of the corporatist structures that had served the PRI regimes so well for so long. 'I'm only here because they told me to come', said Francisco, as we chatted in Mexico City during a demonstration in the spring of 2009, called to protest against the recent detention of the local mayor on suspicion of links to the cartel. 'I think they are sick in the head sometimes, but they are the only people in my town who can help you out if you have a problem.'

Francisco's personal list of troubles ranged from noisy neighbours to his inability to support his large family with what he earned by selling shoes in a street market. Once he had proved his reliability by turning up to demonstrations when asked, he hoped 'they' might get him a job as a municipal police officer. 'They run everything', he smiled sheepishly. 'What can you do?' La Familia also spread far out of its heartland in the Tierra Caliente and established a network of criminal activity throughout the state. This included not only drug trafficking, but the whole range of other options – from levying taxes on illegal loggers to traditional kidnapping.

Local representatives of the cartel set themselves up in some towns as de facto judges of everything from land disputes to municipal contracts. When La Familia announced its arrival with a piece of theatrical violence, it was a foolhardy local who tried to resist, and a particularly naïve one who went to the police for help. In many places the cartel became the only authority that really mattered.

La Familia also took its struggle with the Zetas to other states. It established at least a temporary alliance with Chapo Guzmán and the Gulf cartel, and attempted incursions into the areas controlled by the troubled remnants of the Beltrán Leyva cartel, particularly Acapulco.

After the initial focus on Michoacán at the start of the offensive, La Familia's role in the drug wars generally was largely overshadowed by the parts played by the bigger cartels; but it was always there, with its decidedly odd, cult-like internal dynamic and threat to mutate into a kind of narco guerrilla group.

Training for La Familia operatives reputedly involved prayer meetings alongside target practice, and at least some recruits came from a network of religious-based drug rehabilitation centres. It also had a spiritual leader called Nazario Moreno González. Nicknamed El Chayo and El Más Loco, The Craziest One, he preached his organization's divine right to eliminate its enemies and distributed a book of his own sayings called *Pensamientos* (*Thoughts*).

The Craziest One is believed to have been killed in a battle with the federal police in Michoacán in December 2010. As La Familia's forces scrambled for safe havens, setting up burning barricades across major roads in the state as they went, another key leader called Sevando Gómez Martínez (nicknamed La Tuta) broadcast a pep talk for cartel members, urging them to stand firm: 'It had to happen one day, so don't despair, this is not over', he said in the radio recording. 'Don't worry, God is with us and we will continue until we achieve victory. *Hasta la victoria, hermanos* [to victory, brothers]', he screamed at one point, seeming to emulate the iconic Che Guevara chant *Hasta La Victoria Siempre*. 'We are fighting for our people and for our cause. This is a just cause, a social cause born of the way we have been treated.' He ended the address by promising that La Familia would not allow 'them' to enter Michoacán and occupy 'our turf'. 'They', he said, were the Zetas working under cover of the federal offensive. At one point in the recording, a young female voice is heard thanking La Tuta for his 'beautiful words that give a lot of hope to the people'. She then screams into the microphone: '*Arriba la Familia Michoacana!*' – 'Hurrah for the Michoacan Familia!'

La Familia soon split. One faction – led by Jesús Méndez Vargas, alias El Chango or The Monkey – sought an alliance with the Zetas before El Chango was arrested in June 2011. La Tuta relaunched the remaining faction under a new name, Los Caballeros Templarios, or The Knights Templar. The allusion to the Middle Ages seemed particularly appropriate.

The government claimed that the organization which had once been La Familia was all but dismantled and that it was only a matter of time before the leaders of the Caballeros Templarios were also detained or dead. Six months later this had not happened, and instead the cartel was being blamed for seriously disrupting the governorship elections in the state in October 2011.

❄ ❄ ❄

While most of the drug wars were played out in a very public way, as the years went on it became clear that there were also many hidden horrors, the full extent of which was very hard to gauge. The revelation that Central American migrants on their way through Mexico to the US were being kidnapped on a near industrial scale provided an early clue as to how serious some of these problems were.

Convinced that he could never make a go of life in his rural Honduran village, a gentle-eyed nineteen-year-old (I shall call him Juan) had set off hoping to join his brother, who had already made it to the US some years earlier. He headed north through Guatemala and into Mexico, where he managed to cross the entire country on buses unnoticed. As he was approaching the north-eastern border city of Reynosa, in Tamaulipas, a policeman took him off the bus. Juan prepared himself mentally for the disappointment of deportation, but instead the officer took him to a Zeta safe house and left him there.

For the first week of his two-month ordeal, Juan felt like a sideshow for the gunmen (who beat him regularly and gave him electric shocks to intensify his screams when they put him on the phone to his poverty-stricken family and demanded $5,000 for his life). His captors were more concerned with torturing four members of the Gulf cartel in the same room by cutting off different parts of the bodies each day, until they had revealed all the information they knew and were finally killed.

Somehow Juan's father in Honduras and his brother in Atlanta raised the required ransom and wired it to Mexico. The Zetas demanded as much again, and his family stopped answering the phone. By then, Juan had been moved to a different safe house, filled with other migrants like him. He was shifted to several more after that. In one there were eighty others; in another 120.

Every day his armed captors took the migrants out one by one, or in small groups, and beat them with baseball bats, planks and pistol butts. For the rest of the time the captives sat silently on the floor. There was no space to lie down, and moving or talking brought additional torture. Crying out in pain or weeping with anguish prompted more. The heat was suffocating, but they were rarely given water and had one small portion of rice a day. Juan estimated that every week about five migrants whose families had paid nothing were taken away: he assumed they had gone to their death. 'Sometimes I couldn't think of anything because of the pain in my body', he said when I asked him what had gone through his mind. 'I prayed a lot and at other times I would just sit there wondering how people could be that bad.'

Juan said his captors offered to spare his life if he joined them. They said this would involve twelve weeks' training in a jungle camp for a monthly salary of $5,000. If he got through the training, they said, he would become a full cartel member and have money to burn. At one point he asked if he would be allowed to see his family again if he accepted. They told him he would not, and added that the only way out of a Zeta commando was death or jail.

Juan did not know (or at least was not telling me) why they eventually spared his life and dumped him in Reynosa, unable to walk, his face so swollen that he could hardly talk. Somebody took him to a shelter for migrants run by some extraordinarily dedicated nuns, who slowly nursed him back to health.

When I met him five months later, he no longer vomited blood and his bruises had faded; but he lived in limbo – reluctant to go back to Honduras, too scared to make a final push over the border into the US, wary of venturing onto the streets of Reynosa for fear that the cartels or the authorities would get him, and nervous about spies in the shelter itself. And yet Juan felt like 'one of the lucky ones, because I got out alive'.

On 24 August 2010, a few weeks before we talked, seventy-two migrants were found shot dead in an abandoned farmhouse down the road, in the municipality of San Fernando. The navy was led there by a survivor who had played dead and got away with it. Subsequent investigations suggested that they had been killed as a message to people-smugglers trying to take the migrants through the group's territory without permission. Other versions held that the killers may have thought the fifty-eight men and fourteen women were on their way to be recruited by the Gulf cartel.

The authorities had long ignored human rights activists who tried to draw attention to the terror that, since about 2007, had faced migrants passing through Mexico; but the massacre in San Fernando made it impossible to continue to do so. A new migration law approved by the legislature in April 2011 theoretically guaranteed foreign migrants basic rights, and was greeted by activists as a step in the right direction, albeit an inadequate one. It still left migrants subject to arbitrary detention and deportation by the security forces and migration agents – the very people who, in many cases, had handed them over to the kidnappers in the first place.

Meanwhile, it was emerging that Mexican migrants were facing similar terror, if on a smaller scale. Travelling towards the border in their own country, they were pulled off buses, held in safe houses until ransoms were paid, tortured and sometimes killed. There was also evidence from human rights activists in border cities that deportees from the US were being particularly singled out as targets for forced recruitment.

Every so often there came word of telecoms technicians disappearing (perhaps forced to work fixing communications systems) or of builders rumoured to have been press-ganged into constructing elaborate tunnels under the border to shift drugs. And all over the country there were ever more stories of people simply going missing on their way to work, on their way to school, or sometimes from their own homes.

By 2011, the phenomenon of people disappearing had emerged as one of the great, largely hidden horrors of the drug wars. There were few estimates of how many had vanished, but the semi-autonomous Mexican National Human Rights Commission said in April of that year that 5,000 people had reportedly disappeared since 2006.

Previously, the focus had always been on the bodies displayed in public places or left behind after shootouts. Now it was clear that there were perhaps thousands more buried in clandestine graves around the country.

Close to two hundred bodies were discovered in mass graves in Tamaulipas in April 2011. Of the victims, several dozen at least were believed to have been kidnapped by armed gangs off buses passing through the area. Most of the victims had died from having their heads smashed in. Rumours abounded that the kidnappers had staged some kind of gladiatorial contest between their captives. Later arrests suggested that the killings had been an attempt to stop rivals bringing in reinforcements.

Another set of death pits containing around 250 bodies came to light in the northern state of Durango around the same time. One of the biggest pits was found in the back garden of a middle-class *barrio* in the state capital, which made it hard to believe that nobody had known anything about them. The authorities began removing the bodies with mechanical excavators, and even once investigative protocols were established identification was painfully slow and incomplete. Even with the corpses dug up and kept in storage they remained, on one level, almost as invisible as the

300 victims that one cartel operative arrested in Tijuana in January 2009 had admitted to dissolving in tubs of caustic soda.

The government liked to point out that, drug wars or no drug wars, daily life went on pretty much as normal in most of the country. This was even true on some of the most acute drug-war fronts, where people still went to work and kids still went to school (albeit with additional classes on how to stay safe in the event of a shootout). In Ciudad Juárez the *maquila* export sector had hardly been affected. Sinaloa still produced large quantities of tomatoes and chillies. Aside from Acapulco, the big tourist resorts were almost unaffected, and the murder rate in Mexico City itself was well below that in some US cities.

Still it was also clear that something had gone terribly and tragically wrong with President Calderón's efforts to bring organized crime under control. In order to understand what, we need to take a much closer look at the strategy he favoured and how it developed over time. I will do that in a later chapter, since it will be easier after a more general exploration of the fragmentation of authority and institutional weakness that accompanied the political transition, as well as the failure of the political elite to seize the golden opportunity presented by the demise of one-party hegemony to push forward democratization in a much more aggressive way.

CHAPTER 2

Political Wastelands

THE fire started in a government warehouse and spread quickly to the next-door day-care centre, converted from a factory. The flames were initially trapped between the corrugated iron roof and a false ceiling, but soon dark smoke started billowing into the areas where the toddlers and babies were settling down for their siesta. The flaming toxic material itself began falling down soon after that.

The centre's workers desperately ferried children out, but they did not have time to rescue them all. The choking atmosphere, decreased visibility, an emergency exit that would not open and a narrow front door did not help. A man who lived nearby rammed his truck into the solid concrete façade to create a bigger hole, but it was too late for many. Forty-nine small children died and dozens more were left permanently injured and deeply traumatized by the fire at the ABC crèche in the northern city of Hermosillo on 5 June 2009.

The families took their pain and anger onto the streets to call for justice, and their cause was taken up by the mainstream media, which began to dig about behind the event. It emerged that the crèche had repeatedly passed safety inspections, despite being an obvious hazard. Written orders to improve things had been repeatedly ignored. One of the workers had called one of the owners with her concerns about the false ceiling just a few months before the fire. She was told not to watch so many Hollywood movies.

It also turned out that some of the owners had family ties to high officials among the state authorities, and that one of them was a relative of President Felipe Calderón's wife. A little more scratching revealed a general pattern. A federal programme, started in the late 1990s, to increase the availability of childcare facilities for working parents affiliated to the Social Security Institute by financing private ventures had turned into a cash cow for people associated with the political elite all over the country.

At first the federal, state and municipal authorities sought to downplay the implications of the fire. When that proved impossible, they started blaming each other. There were efforts to buy off the protestors with promises of compensation in exchange for commitments not to pursue the matter in the courts. A core group remained determined to continue their battle, as they themselves evolved from grieving parents to activists.

Roberto Zavala, the father of Santiago de Jesús, who died in the fire, was at one of the early rallies when his wife handed him the microphone. At first he did not really know what to say, but, as he spoke, Zavala – a worker in a factory that supplied Ford – got to grips with the essence of what he felt: 'There is one person who is responsible who accepts that blame, and who carries it on their shoulders – and that is me.' The crowd shouted out that this was not true and that the guilt lay with corrupt officials, but Zavala continued: 'I am to blame for trusting; I am to blame for paying my taxes; I am to blame for voting. I am responsible for the death of my child.'

Zavala's exasperation at the uselessness of the political process and his distrust of the state in general stemmed from his personal desperation; but it also reflected a broader feeling across the country that democracy had turned out to be a bit of a con. The ABC fire became a symbol of the persistence into the new political era of the kind of lack of accountability associated with the PRI regime, suggesting that Mexico's famously smooth 'voted transition' in 2000 had not really changed very much for the electorate.

The PRI had held off the inevitable march towards full political pluralism for decades with the help of extensive and sophisticated clientelistic networks and the legitimizing narrative and political culture of revolutionary nationalism. It had also introduced reforms that partially opened up the system to other political parties in a way that put off more fundamental change until a later date. By the turn of the century, there was little wiggle room left. The Federal Electoral Institute (IFE) (the body overseeing federal elections that was set up in 1990 and made fully independent in 1996) made it all but impossible to fiddle the poll as a last resort to stay in power, as had happened in the past. The then president,

Ernesto Zedillo, was, in any case, disinclined to blot his historical legacy by trying.

Vicente Fox was the perfect candidate to deal the final blow in the 2000 presidential elections and to capitalize on the frustration with the regime that had accumulated thanks to a series of acute economic crises and the increasingly obvious gulf between a corrupt governing class and the electorate.

Fox was a latecomer to politics, which gave him a certain freshness in a country tired of familiar faces. In fact, he was never even particularly politically engaged until he joined the PAN in the 1980s, when in his forties, and became a federal deputy in 1988. Before that, he had spent his youth focused on a successful career with Coca-Cola, which he then left to run the family farm, frozen food business and boot factory in the central state of Guanajuato. Fox ran for governor of the state in 1991, in an election that he and his party energetically claimed was riddled with fraud. He tried again in 1995, won by a margin of nearly 2:1 and, shortly after taking office, announced his intention to run for president. Fox began obviously campaigning from that moment on, until he had built up such momentum that it was impossible for his party not to give him the candidacy.

No other opposition figure could match Fox's charisma. Following him on the campaign trail in 2000, I watched him strike up an immediate rapport with an extraordinary range of audiences that went far beyond the PAN's traditional right-wing, middle-class constituency. As a former businessman, he could talk to the private sector in its language; but the tall, light-skinned son of a Basque mother and the grandson of a US-born rancher of German origin could also get rallies full of short, dark and poor peasants giggling at his risqué jokes debunking the solemnity of the *ancien régime*. His voice was deep and melodic, and his swagger and grace seemed totally natural. He was able to transmit genuine enthusiasm while delivering the same speech that he had already given several times that day, and exuded hope that things would be better once the Mexican electorate had 'kicked the PRI out of Los Pinos', in reference to the presidential residence in the capital.

In this election – the first Mexican presidential campaign in which the small screen was genuinely opened up to all candidates – Fox was a TV natural with a talent for one-liners that drove home his promise of 'Change'. He was also extremely stubborn – a quality that sometimes verged on the boorish, but when handled adroitly by his team seemed appropriate for the task in hand. An initially embarrassing incident in which he was filmed banging his fist on a table at a cross-party negotiation and demanding what he wanted '*Hoy, hoy, hoy*' ('Today, today, today') was turned into an effective campaign slogan.

A small group of progressive intellectuals had also worked their way into Fox's inner circle and added a liberal veneer to his discourse that helped make it acceptable for many on the left to vote for him in the name of getting rid of the PRI. They included a respected maverick politician called Adolfo Aguilar Zínser, whose comparison of Fox to Indiana Jones will always stick in my mind. 'A road exists that theoretically leads to the change of power in Mexico, but as you proceed it gets narrower, the bridges collapse, the weather gets very bad and there are seductive temptations on the way', he told me with the campaign in full swing in 2000. 'There has never been anyone in Mexican politics before Fox able to cope with all of that.'

On 2 July Fox won the presidential election with 43 per cent of the vote, a full 6 percentage points clear of the PRI's Francisco Labastida Ochoa and 26 percentage points more than Cuauhtémoc Cárdenas, the seemingly eternal candidate of the leftist PRD. The streets of the capital filled with cars honking their horns and with people waving to Fox's entourage as it headed for a celebration rally at the Angel of Independence monument. The jubilant crowd gathered there passed a cardboard coffin above their heads on which was written 'P.R.I.'

That same night, the atmosphere in the PRI's headquarters was indeed funereal. The party had known it was possible that it might lose the election, but had not taken this fully on board. Reality struck hard. Mark Stevenson, of the Associated Press, remembers watching party operatives wandering aimlessly around the building, mumbling their anger at the upstarts who had taken power, their faces etched with disbelief rather than mere defeat. 'It was the death of PRI entitlement', he recalls.

The PRI had no experience of how to manage its vast structure, or the competing ambitions that flowed through it, without the president to keep things together. A good few observers predicted that the loss of the presidency meant its days were numbered.

The root of much of the disappointment to come is traceable to Fox's early decision to ignore the advice of his leftist advisers, who urged him to use his 'democratic bonus' to go after the PRI while it was down. They hoped to accentuate the divisions within the party and push it to collapse by, for instance, launching a truth commission to pursue paradigmatic cases of corruption. Showing mercy, they warned, would block the new administration's ability to democratize the old institutions, because the PRI was still the only political party with truly national spread, was the second largest party in the legislature (by a whisker), and was still in government in the majority of the country's thirty-two states.

Fox chose a more conciliatory approach, inspired by the pact-based democratic transition of post-Franco Spain, and pushed by Santiago Creel Miranda, a PAN politician close to Fox who had a reputation as a good mediator. This recognized the old ruling party as a legitimate political force with a role to play in the new Mexico. Creel insisted that this would both reduce the danger of political and social conflict, and would aid the passage of the new government's reform agenda through the legislature. He was given the job of putting the scheme into practice as interior minister.

The strategy did help to ensure that the transition was completed peacefully. After seven decades in power, the PRI handed over the keys to Los Pinos without much fuss at all. In time, however, the non-confrontational approach proved naïve, just as Fox's doom-saying leftist advisers had warned.

The PRI might be weakened and confused, but it was still replete with wily political animals who had no intention of throwing away their political careers, or the political culture they had grown up in, by strengthening the Fox presidency. They used the respite provided by the new government's softly-softly approach to get through their initial disarray in (just about) one piece. Then they discovered that they could maintain unity by redefining the party in opposition to Fox's government. They set about opposing pretty much everything the president proposed.

It was not just in handling the PRI that Fox faced problems; he also had trouble securing the support of his own party. Founded in 1939 in response to the anti-clericalism and early socialist tendencies of the post-revolutionary regime, the PAN had gone on to establish a solid support base among provincial business owners and religious conservatives. For the first four decades of its existence, it never really contemplated moving beyond the status of what Soledad Loaeza, an authority on the party, calls 'a loyal opposition'. Instead it swung between being a party of principled protest and a more pragmatic-minded conservative lobby seeking some influence over PRI policy, but stopping short of genuinely seeking power for its own members.

This changed when a new generation of business leaders joined the PAN after the PRI nationalized the banks in 1982, and relations between the regime and the private sector soured dramatically. The so-called *neopanistas* were not only ambitious, but they were militant too. They did not just try to win regional elections, particularly in the more industrialized north: they blocked border crossings and went on hunger strike when they believed they had been cheated of victory.

When they did make deals with the regime, they made sure they got significant returns. In 1988 the PAN helped shore up Carlos Salinas de Gortari's hold on power after he was declared the winner in an election that many believed was actually won by the left-wing candidate, Cuauhtémoc Cárdenas, on the first of his three presidential campaigns. The PAN was rewarded with several governorships and mayoralties, some of which were negotiated and some of which it was allowed to win through the ballot box. This constituted a major step towards genuine multi-party politics, and was followed by more political reforms that edged the country closer to the possibility of genuinely free national elections.

Vicente Fox was swept into the PAN on the *neopanista* wave, and this inevitably created the potential for tension between his government and the traditionalists, who still held important positions within the party. Rooted in provincial citizen politics and Vatican-directed family values, many of them were uncomfortable with Fox's unconventional style, colloquial language and overriding pragmatism. When he took office, they were also angered by the scant inclusion of old-style *Panistas* in his markedly plural cabinet, which included more former leftists and former *Priistas* than members of his own party.

The presidential reform agenda floundered quickly in this context of belligerent obstruction by the PRI and always qualified support by the PAN. The one big legislative success of Fox's administration – a freedom of information act, energetically promoted by civil society organizations – passed easily through the legislature with hardly any debate in 2002. But the structural, economic, political and institutional reforms that were supposed to be the priority of the new government, as it sought to put Mexico on a genuinely new path, fell by the wayside one by one. Some were blocked inside the legislature, and some never even got that far because the government knew it could not garner the votes.

The legislative paralysis of the Fox years is directly associated with the structural weakening of presidential control that accompanied the PRI's slow relaxation of its grip on power in the previous decades. Genuinely competitive elections – right up to the highest office – accelerated the process. The new situation did not strip the presidency of any formal constitutional attributes, but it did mean that the legislature completed its transition to becoming a real power in its own right. This was also true in the other parts of the once corporatist state that were now no longer beholden to the man in Los Pinos. The presidency had also been quietly stripped of most of the so-called 'meta-constitutional powers' that had helped Fox's predecessors get their way in the past and that included large secret budgets and a range of intimidatory options.

Fox himself has always blamed this waning of centralized power for his inability to advance his reformist agenda, and has sought to spin it as proof of his respect for the separation of powers and of how democratic Mexico became under his guidance. He does have a point, in the sense that consolidating the promised changes was never going to be easy in the new era. But it is also true that Fox's historic election victory carried with it a golden opportunity to push through new rules of the game that moved democratization forward. Genuinely encouraging citizens to become more engaged with politics could have provided an alternative motor for other changes. It could also have made the whole political process less reliant on a strongman president to keep things ticking over. In the event, however, Fox did not seem particularly bothered about even trying to live up to the challenge.

In his 2007 autobiography, *Revolution of Hope*, Fox draws on his experience in Coca-Cola to describe his move into politics as 'turning to selling the label of democracy like a cool soda on a hot day of summer'. There is no doubt that he was a supremely gifted salesman, and as a candidate he used this to great effect to push a product that resonated with the times. Once in government, he was not so talented at (or even particularly interested in) the nitty-gritty of politics.

It started with his decision not to use the momentum that swept him into power to go after the anti-democratic legacy of the PRI, and his clumsy handling of his relationship with his own party. It continued throughout his presidency, and underpinned his reputation for vacuity.

When I interviewed the former president in 2009, Fox said that he had perceived his role as primarily 'to motivate and fill with enthusiasm', which was why, he said, he had spent so much time travelling around the country as if on permanent campaign. Certainly he had never lost his ability to connect with ordinary people; but trying to galvanize them behind the idea of 'Change', with the elections shimmering on the horizon, was rather easier than generating excitement around dramatically named, but essentially empty, government projects. In 2001, Fox announced a 'crusade for forests and water'. Reporting the story at the time, I found it hard to divine if there was actually a genuine programme behind the slogan.

Lack of presidential weight also lay behind the way a good many of Fox's cabinet ministers focused on their personal ambitions and on fighting among themselves. The press dubbed the result 'The Montessori Cabinet'. The individualism and lack of coordination on display was partly a function of the political pluralism and the size of the egos involved, but it also revealed Fox's reluctance to direct the show.

This was clear in the demise of a plan to build a six-runway $2.3 billion new airport for the capital, announced in the early months of the new administration. Mexico City's only international airport was already close to capacity and was all but surrounded by urban sprawl, which made significant expansion impossible. The experts told Fox that a new airport was urgent, and that the best option was on the eastern outskirts of the capital, in a semi-rural area known as Texcoco. The government duly announced the expropriation of the land, held by local smallholders. Most meekly accepted the pitiful compensation offered, but a group living in the small town of San Salvador Atenco resisted from the start.

Soon after the project was announced, one of the Atenco protestors took me on a tour of the disputed land. I forget his name, but I will never forget his heroic efforts to add value to the windswept lake bed, where nothing seemed particularly keen to grow. At one point he earnestly claimed that a rather undistinguished looking rock we came across was actually a throne, from which the pre-Conquest poet king Nezahualcoyotl contemplated his kingdom. Talking to him and others in the group, I got the distinct impression that they were rather less emotionally attached to the land than they professed, but were genuinely terrified of being forced to give it up and join the ranks of the urban poor in the slums down the road. A compensation package that gave them another option might well have softened resistance to the project, but in those early stages the government refused to even contemplate offering significantly more.

The residents of Atenco began holding regular protest marches. Over time these became ever more militant, as well as theatrical. The protestors carried machetes wherever they went, painted murals of the revolutionary Emiliano Zapata in the town square, symbolically defended their head-quarters with toy cannons, and became a magnet for radical groups from around the country and abroad.

The conflict reached a head in July 2002 with a particularly violent clash with riot police. The farmers took officials hostage and retreated into

Atenco behind burning barricades. Four days of negotiations led to the exchange of the hostages for detained protesters, and talks began on compensation. The government raised its original offer seven-fold, but this was still rejected. It was too late. The government scrapped the new airport plans a few weeks later.

The idea that by far the biggest infrastructure project of a government could be brought down by a few irate farmers would have been unthinkable under the PRI. The old regime typically dealt with dissent by moving early to co-opt those leaders willing to be bought and to repress the others if they continued making a nuisance of themselves. President Fox's reluctance to do this suggested more democratic instincts; but his failure to do much else allowed the conflict to fester and grow, until he felt he had no choice but to back down altogether in the name of social peace.

One aspect of the mishandling of the Atenco conflict was the fact that it was never quite clear which of several ministers involved was handling the project. In their detailed account of the Fox years, collated in a book called *La Diferencia*, Fox's first foreign minister, Jorge Castañeda Gutman, and his spokesman during his last few years in office, Rubén Aguilar Valenzuela, blame the president: 'The lack of passion and scant priority given to the project [by Fox] was the origin of a considerable part of the rest of the errors and difficulties that ended leaving the airport chopped to pieces by machetes.'

In the end, the government built a second terminal at the existing airport, which will extend its life for a few years more. The tension in Atenco, meanwhile, rumbled on, with the most radical elements of the movement forming a kind of revolutionary vanguard that roamed the country, supporting the struggles of others. That was until they were viciously repressed by the PRI-controlled government of the State of Mexico following a road block that got out of hand in May 2006. The crackdown, ordered by local governor Enrique Peña Nieto, put the future presidential candidate's traditional party pedigree on early display. The leaders of the movement were subsequently sentenced to up to 112 years in high-security prisons. They were released in 2010 amid international pressure from former Nobel Peace Prize winners, but showed few signs over at least the next two years that they had any intention of returning to their former activism. Rather than becoming a symbol of the new democratic era, Atenco came to epitomize both the weakness of the PAN governments and the ever-latent temptation, within the PRI in particular, to reach for the repressive techniques of old. In this particular case, they had proved rather effective.

Some policy initiatives did move forward under Fox, such as the advance of a new federal health insurance, which targeted poor people with no access to subsidized care. This, however, was a naturally well-defined task that had no opponents worth speaking of, and was championed by an energetic health minister who did not require Fox to be decisive for him.

Encouraged by the ferociously assertive Castañeda, foreign policy proved the biggest exception to the rule of presidential nonchalance in the first few years, although by the end it, too, had drifted that way.

PRI foreign policy traditionally revolved around protecting Mexico from foreign intervention in domestic affairs. This required considerable skill, given that the country was caught between the looming presence of its superpower neighbour to the north and a vast continent to the south that was prone to intense periods of ideologically driven conflict. The PRI set Mexico up as a kind of buffer between the two – as a bulwark of stability in a volatile region for the US, and as a block to US imperialism for the rest. There was additional kudos to be gained by playing the peace-maker in Central American conflicts, or by accepting exiles from military dictatorships around the region.

The emphasis changed under President Salinas, who took office in 1988. With the Cold War out of the way, he turned his sights firmly north-ward and negotiated the North American Free Trade Agreement (NAFTA) with the US and Canada, which came into force in 1994.

Fox's bold vision consisted of a drive to develop and deepen NAFTA into something more akin to the European Union, beginning with a concerted effort to secure a much more liberal attitude to mass Mexican economic migration. President George W. Bush's initial receptiveness was encouraging, but everything changed when Mexico dropped off Washington's agenda in the wake of 9/11. Fox dropped his more audacious integrationist vision but kept the search for some kind of migration accord at the centre of his foreign policy. He achieved little. His strident pro-migrant rhetoric may even have contributed to something of a backlash against migrants in the United States. At the same time, his efforts to curry favour with Bush opened him up to accusations – both within Mexico and in the rest of the region – of fawning to the superpower.

There was, for instance, a highly embarrassing diplomatic row with Cuba in 2002. The PRI had always handled relations with Fidel Castro with particular care. It had consistently resisted US pressure to harangue the communist island during the Cold War, and Castro repaid the favour by not giving Mexican guerrilla movements the kind of support that other rebels received further south. Castro also maintained personal friendships with several Mexican leaders, ranging from Salinas to Cárdenas, with whom he liked to while away entire nights in conversation and ideological debate.

Relations soured as soon as Fox took office and Castañeda, long distrusted by the Cuban authorities for his academic work debunking the iconic status of its revolution, began insisting that a natural corollary of Mexico's decision to throw open its doors to international human rights observers was to urge other countries with dubious reputations to do the same. This included a reversal of the PRI tradition of abstaining in the vote on a resolution, tabled every spring at the UN Human Rights Council meeting in Geneva, demanding that Cuba improve its record and accept monitors.

The rising tension saw Castro storming out of an international development summit held in Mexico in March 2002, falling over in the process, and announcing that he was being forced to go because of US pressure. When Mexico went ahead and voted in favour of the human rights resolution a few weeks later anyway, Castro released a tape of a conversation he had had with Fox just prior to the summit. In it, Fox is heard asking him to promise to leave Mexico discreetly before Bush arrives (which he seems to do). A full-scale diplomatic row followed, with both countries withdrawing their ambassadors. Fox ended up looking rather silly: in the taped conversation, which became known as 'comes y te vas' or 'eat up and go', Castro, the wily old political survivor, seems to toy with his Mexican counterpart like a cat playing with a mouse.

The crisis with Cuba was followed by a general deterioration in relations with many Latin American leaders, as the continent swung to the left. Castañeda resigned in January 2003 and was replaced by a former World Bank bureaucrat, Luis Ernesto Derbéz Bautista, who was less audacious, but no more tactful.

The Summit of the Americas in Argentina in November 2005 underlined how unpopular Mexico had become. Fox voluntarily turned himself into the standard bearer for a bid to relaunch Bush's already flagging initiative to form the Free Trade Area of the Americas. It seemed like a pointless sacrifice. The presidents of Argentina, Brazil, Uruguay and Paraguay were explicitly annoyed. Hugo Chávez of Venezuela seized the opportunity to fire characteristically histrionic volleys of insults Fox's way, including the charge that he was 'a lapdog of imperialism'. Again the row escalated out of control, until both nations recalled their ambassadors. By the time Fox left office, Mexico's only ally of any weight in the region was Colombia's right-wing president Alvaro Uribe.

The weakening of the presidency dovetailed with the consolidation of an independent media – the other most important change directly associated with the political transition. The days when a president could rely on most of the newspapers and radio stations, and all of the television, to transmit his message the way he wanted were long over. Now the media used its influence over public opinion to push its own interests, ranging from the purely journalistic, to political and corporate. Fox found himself exposed in a way no president had ever been before – and exposed in a particularly personal way, given the absence of very much else to talk about and the way in which the informal style that had served him so well in the campaign backfired once he was in office. The first post-PRI government did not need to be boring, but it did need to be taken seriously, and Fox made himself an easy target for ridicule.

When the president wore patent-leather cowboy boots to a state dinner with the king of Spain in Madrid, the press derided his lack of gravitas. When he enthused about his government's achievements with nothing obvious to back it up, the media coined the phrase 'Foxilandia'. If he looked dejected, he was diagnosed with clinical depression, and when he seemed happier it was assumed he was taking Prozac. Columnists regularly described him in print as not particularly bright, mentally unstable and sexually impotent.

Particular venom was directed at the way in which Fox encouraged the excesses of his wife, Marta Sahagún de Fox. Originally his campaign manager, she had become the government's first spokesman. The couple married in an early morning civil ceremony in Los Pinos on 2 July 2001 – the first anniversary of Fox's election victory and his fifty-ninth birthday.

As first lady, Sahagún threw herself into self-promotion through a private charity she founded, called Vamos México (Let's Go, Mexico). She seemed to be on prime-time news almost every night: she hugged orphans, cried with terminal cancer patients, urged ageing lepers to look on the bright side, and tearfully proclaimed her commitment to improving the lot of the underprivileged.

Sahagún delighted in front-cover features of society magazines, showing off the way she had decorated the private quarters in Los Pinos, and was rarely seen out of designer clothing. In interviews she underlined her admiration for Mother Teresa, and encouraged comparisons with Eva Perón and Hillary Clinton. She insisted that Mexico was ready for a female president, though she coyly avoided questions about her own ambitions.

A significant sector of the Mexico City-based media laced much of its coverage of Sahagún with mockery of her unsophisticated provincial style and smug sentimentality. Some commentators went further, portraying her as a kind of Lady Macbeth figure, scheming behind the scenes as she prepared her own bid for the top job. Fox made matters worse by jumping to her defence in a way that suggested he was not quite sure where his duties as a husband ended and his role as the nation's leader began. 'All those who think they can bring down the presidential couple, all those who are waiting for us to trip up, will get a taste of their own medicine', he said in February 2003.

Sahagún's presidential ambitions were buried by opposition from within the PAN, as well as by awkward questions about the finances of Vamos México, meticulously documented in the *Financial Times*. She nevertheless remained a hate-figure for many, and was regularly accused of corruption and of using her influence to promote the business interests of her sons from her first marriage, who became obviously rich during this period. During the 2000 campaign, Fox had promised to put *peces gordos* or 'big fish' in prison, in an unprecedented anti-corruption drive. Instead he began to look complicit in the maintenance of a culture that routinely exploited the privileges of power for personal benefit.

It all fed into the widespread dismissal of Fox as the president who never really wanted power (or at least who gave up trying to do anything significant with it almost as soon as he took office). Fox told me in 2009 that he did not care: 'They said Fox was weak, etc., etc., but that's OK. I'm not bothered by that description. I prefer it to people saying that President Fox was authoritarian, that he violated human rights.'

Even so, as his term drew to a close, the Indiana Jones of Mexican politics seemed to have no priceless treasure in his sights. His hat and whip already gathering dust, Fox began to succumb to outbursts of un-statesmanlike pique. When he was refused permission by the Senate to go on an international trip that included an unexplained stopover in Australia (Mexico's thirty-second-ranked trading partner), where one of his children was studying, he used the presidential privilege of a broadcast to the nation to accuse the legislature of 'kidnapping'. At other times, he seemed to be counting the days. Caught on an open microphone just before sitting down to a television interview in the US shortly before he left office, Fox mumbled, 'I'm free, I can say any stupid thing now. It doesn't matter. I'm out of here.'

President Fox's efforts to prevent the PRD's Andrés Manuel López Obrador from winning the 2006 elections were among the few exceptions to the political detachment that characterized his last years in office. It was never really clear why Fox, who had had little trouble working with leftists before, abhorred the then Mexico City mayor to the degree he obviously did. Perhaps it had something to do with the way López Obrador constantly took personal pot-shots at the president as part of his strategy of getting momentum behind his own bid. Marta Sahagún was also said to hate the mayor. Whatever the reason, Fox set out to stop López Obrador even becoming a candidate.

The saga began when the attorney general's office received a judicial order in 2004 to prosecute López Obrador over his failure to obey an earlier ruling to stop building a slip road to a private hospital on a piece of expropriated land. With López Obrador refusing to cooperate, a strict legal reading of the order required the government to start impeachment proceedings to strip him of his immunity, so that he could be taken to court. If this happened, the left-winger would have been automatically barred from seeking electoral office until the case was resolved, which would almost certainly be after the campaign had begun.

While Fox operated behind the scenes to ensure that he could count on the necessary congressional majority in the impeachment vote in April 2005, one of the few instances in which he secured the help of the PRI, the mayor adroitly played the martyr card and mobilized his supporters. Shortly after the vote, he organized one of the biggest marches in Mexican history. Even the federal government admitted it was attended by several hundred thousand people, while López Obrador's supporters claimed over a million.

Shocked by the size and passion of the protest, and desperate to avoid any photograph of the impeached martyr to democracy behind bars (he had refused to pay the small amount of bail set), Fox cut his losses. He sacked his attorney general and found a legally acceptable way of dropping the case. López Obrador returned to his pre-election campaigning more popular than ever.

Fox admitted later that he had been forced to retreat, but had then set out to get his own back in the 2006 election. He seemed more concerned with keeping the left-winger out of Los Pinos than with aiding his own party's candidate, Felipe Calderón, with whom he had never got on particularly well. When the election campaign began, he used his considerable campaigning talents, residual popularity born of the widespread impression that he was generally quite a nice guy, and all the state resources he could muster without blatantly breaking the law requiring incumbent presidents to stay out of elections. Calderón would eventually be declared the winner with a mere 0.56 per cent edge over López Obrador.

Fox might have got away with being remembered as merely benignly ineffectual, had his determination to torpedo López Obrador's ambitions not revealed a streak of anti-democratic malevolence. The first politician to prove that elections in Mexico could lead to a change of party in government went down in history as a president who had tried to use the system in underhand ways to eliminate a rival.

More importantly, it left the country's electoral institutions vulnerable to accusations that they had let themselves be used. This helped López Obrador to sustain his resistance to accepting defeat, which played out in a protracted post-electoral crisis, in which he tried and failed to get the elections annulled. It ensured that Calderón finally took office with the legitimacy of his election in question.

President Felipe Calderón's inauguration ceremony in the national Congress, on 1 December 2006, was both the antithesis of the impeccable protocol that reigned in the days of the imperial PRI presidency, and an uncomfortably long way from the festive new-era ambience of Fox's first day in power. Instead it amounted to a study of how weak the presidency had become.

Three-metre high solid metal barriers, guarded by large numbers of riot police, surrounded the congressional building, which made it very unlikely that the planned march headed by López Obrador could disrupt the event. Even so, deputies from the PRD and affiliated smaller parties were still gearing up to sabotage the ceremony from the inside.

A physical battle for territorial control of the Chamber of Deputies itself began two days before, with pro-Calderón and pro-López Obrador deputies staking out strongholds and setting up camp. Periodic brawls were interspersed with negotiated truces that allowed for a few hours' sleep, much munching of take-out tacos, and the occasional sectarian sing-along.

Just after midnight on the big day itself, Calderón received the presidential sash in an austere and improvised handover of power inside Los Pinos that was intended as a fall-back. Even so, the president-elect was always going to ignore the advice of some in his inner circle and attempt to face down the rebels in the chamber, where dawn brought a particularly intense round of fisticuffs and jacket-pulling. At one point, a male deputy was dragged to the floor, where he was kicked repeatedly by his peers, while a female legislator let loose with a hail of soft-drink cans from above.

When the PAN ended up with control of the podium, the *Lopez-obradoristas* turned to blocking the entrances with piles of the great green-leather congressional chairs. These barricades proved unable to prevent the PRI deputies from entering the chamber and providing a quorum for the session. The *Priistas* filed in holding little Mexican flags and looking distinctly uncomfortable at their role as extras in somebody else's show.

The president-elect himself appeared soon after, followed closely by Fox, who was holding the presidential sash and wearing a rather gormless grin. They had slipped in through a back entrance hidden by the two enormous flags that are draped in a huge bow on the back wall of the chamber.

The rebels greeted the two *Panistas* with bellowed insults and piercing whistles. Their supporters cheered and chanted 'Yes, We Could'. Drowned out by the general pandemonium, the country's new president stood stony-faced and incongruously still. He put on the sash, stuck out his arm, shouted out his oath of office and then, after a short blast of the national anthem, he was gone again.

Felipe Calderón's political career is littered with other examples of stubbornness and high-stakes gambles that have often paid off. The son of one of the founders of the PAN, he had grown up in the political opposition, reputedly announcing his presidential ambitions at the age of five. By twelve, he was an enthusiastic accomplice to several of his father's doomed attempts to get elected to Congress.

After graduating in law, Calderón dedicated himself to rising quickly through the PAN ranks. He became party president in 1996 at the age of just thirty-three. After a brief break to study for a Master's degree in public administration at Harvard, Calderón returned to lead the PAN in Congress. From there he was appointed to head the state-owned development bank, before becoming energy minister in September 2003, a move designed to placate PAN traditionalists angry at the paltry number of *Panistas* in Fox's cabinet.

Fox pushed Calderón out of the job just eight months later, after the minister publicly revealed his presidential ambitions. Few gave his bid much of a chance, given the widespread assumption that Fox favoured the interior minister, Santiago Creel. Calderón eventually won the candidacy at the end of 2005, with a strategy focused on key party members that contrasted with Creel's much more showy public-relations offensive based on TV ads. But he was still around 10 percentage points behind López Obrador in opinion polls and laboured under a grey and unexciting image. He closed the gap with the help of a campaign that demonized his more charismatic rival as 'a danger to Mexico', while presenting himself as a safe pair of hands. Not even those who cried fraud ever questioned that the election had been very close.

Even after the vote, however, Calderón remained in the shadow of López Obrador and his refusal to accept defeat. Once in office he was determined to claim the limelight as his own. Calderón's genuine desire for power contrasted acutely with his predecessor's apathy, but this brought with it a different form of ineffectiveness, related to his reluctance to delegate or let others shine. It also made him no more inclined to push the cause of democratization forward.

Despite his youth – he was forty-four when he took office – Calderón was much closer to the traditional wing of the party, and saw little need to integrate other political voices into his government in the name of plurality, as Fox had done. He relied almost entirely on low-profile unknowns, loyalists and personal friends, who carried out his orders without question. The new president's dominance was further reinforced by a directive that discouraged almost all government officials from talking to the press without prior authorization from Los Pinos.

Where presidential directives were clear, ministers could go about their business energetically enough. This ensured that stability in public finances was going to remain the priority it had been since the times of Zedillo. The expansion of health coverage, targeted anti-poverty programmes and incentives to home-building that had already taken root under Fox were also continued. Elsewhere presidential micromanagement proved as stultifying as Fox's political detachment.

One long-time PAN member in a top-level bureaucratic post told me that, while he was happy to see the end of the disarray of the Fox years, there were several ministers who were too nervous to develop their own initiatives for fear of eliciting one of the president's famous withering stares. The problem only got worse, he said, as Calderón became immersed in the drug wars, which left limited room for anything else. Outside the frenetic activity on security issues, and a personal attempt to push a climate-change agenda, there was little about the Calderón administration in terms of the content or achievements of domestic policy that marked a major departure from what was already happening.

In foreign policy, Calderón spent the early years of his administration actively mending the bridges with the region's leftist leaders that Fox had broken. He had considerable success: at a summit of Latin American leaders in Mexico in 2010, he seemed to revel in smiling embraces with Raúl Castro, Hugo Chávez and Evo Morales, as well as in a new chumminess with Brazil's ascendant world luminary Luiz Inácio Lula da Silva. But the strategy seemed to stop there. Calderón might say that Mexico's regional influence should be on a par with Brazil's, but he did not seem all that concerned to make this a reality. His low-profile foreign minister, Patricia Espinosa Cantellano, had a reputation as the cabinet goody-goody, whose main concern was always to please the president. With relations with the rest of Latin America no longer problematic, Calderón's overriding concern was always the bilateral relationship with the US, seen almost exclusively through the prism of the drug wars.

Some PAN members also complained in private about the lack of presidential attention to developing the kind of administrative experience within the party that could establish a clear, new and more democratic public-service ethos. This, they said, often left those who were in a position of power in the federal bureaucracy unable to resist the temptation of slipping into the bad habits of old. By this they meant less the lure of corruption (which remained pervasive) than the way in which decisions often devoted greater effort to balancing competing vested interests than to issues of efficiency and accountability. The difference was that the PAN no longer had the resources to limit the influence of those interest groups that one-party hegemony had provided in the past.

Mexican federal bureaucrats I knew, who were fairly high up the ladder in technical jobs and had no affiliation to the governing party, were grateful to the PAN for removing the pressure they had once felt to support the government politically. Even under Zedillo, bosses were in the habit of hinting heavily to their underlings that it would be a good idea if they voted for the PRI. The tendency to simply ignore legal restrictions defining what could and could not be done in government also faded, although it did not disappear. There was a rather half-hearted attempt to create a career civil service. Taken together it all fell far short of creating a new model for exercising power. It also meant that the PAN still seemed rather uncomfortable in government, after nearly two terms in power.

Calderón was also accused of stunting the party's development outside government. Local activists in some states did not appreciate his imposition of loyalists to lead the party in a way that they felt contravened the PAN's anti-corporatist citizen roots and principles. They rarely said so too loudly, but the discontent rumbled beneath the surface and began to bubble up in the race to choose the party's presidential candidate for 2012. The president's obvious favourite, the former finance minister, Ernesto Cordero Arroyo, trailed behind other hopefuls in the polls of the party faithful.

Josefina Vázquez Mota, a former education minister and leader of the PAN in the Chamber of Deputies, became an early frontrunner in the race for the candidacy, thanks to her relative freshness. She had once been close to Calderón, but the rest of his inner circle had never fully accepted her, and this appealed to many PAN sympathizers – as did her conciliatory (but firm) tone and image. Opinion polls that focused on the presidential election showed her around 20 percentage points behind the PRI's Enrique Peña Nieto at the start of the electoral year. She was slightly ahead of Andrés Manuel López Obrador in his second coming as the left's candidate. Having secured the PAN candidacy in February, her first task became to consolidate that second place. If she managed that, she could hope to attract voters who might be deeply critical of both Fox and Calderón but were willing to tolerate another PAN government if it meant blocking the seemingly imminent return of the PRI.

President Calderón was marginally more successful than Fox in pushing his legislative agenda, at least in the first half of his administration. This, however, appeared to owe less to his government's skilled political operations than to the fact that the PRI was in a rather more cooperative mood, following its dismal showing in the 2006 presidential elections.

After surviving the initial shock of losing the presidency in 2000 and then rebounding in the 2003 mid-term elections in a way that proved its electoral machinery was still intact, the PRI had fallen into a new crisis associated with the mechanism for choosing its next presidential candidate. During the PRI regime the incumbent president had reserved the right to designate his successor, who would then go through the legitimizing ritual of elections that everybody knew he would win. This process was known as the *dedazo*, or the 'finger'. President Ernesto Zedillo, who headed what was essentially a transition government, changed the system by organizing primary elections, although these were inevitably won by his known favourite.

With no president to referee the process for 2006, the competition for the candidacy sparked a vicious internal power struggle, eventually won by party president Roberto Madrazo Pintado.

Madrazo came in a poor third in the presidential election itself, 14 percentage points behind Felipe Calderón and Andrés Manuel López Obrador. This owed much to his unpalatable reputation as a wheeler-dealer, rather humorously confirmed a year later in the Berlin Marathon. A marathon veteran, the former presidential candidate charged over the finishing line to claim the fastest time in his age category, only to be later disqualified for taking a short cut.

The size of Madrazo's defeat in 2006 also reflected his clumsy use of the party apparatus to impose his candidacy without paying due court to the new hubs of internal power that had accrued more influence now that the president no longer ran the show. Many governors had only half-heartedly activated their regional electoral machinery in Madrazo's favour on polling day, which meant that, while he got just 22 per cent of the presidential poll, in the congressional elections held at the same time the PRI as a party attracted 28 per cent of the vote.

The beating persuaded PRI leaders both to prioritize the need to keep internal conflicts out of public view and to develop a more construc-tive image than the knee-jerk opposition of the Fox years. Presenting itself as the picture of democratic responsibility in the period of intense polarization between the PAN and the PRD, the PRI helped the new president ride out the initial challenge to his legitimacy. It also cooperated with Calderón to get several early initiatives through the legislature, including pension reform and mild-mannered energy and tax reforms.

The strategy helped propel the PRI to become the big winner in the 2009 mid-term legislative elections, which it fought under the slogan 'Proven Experience, New Attitude'. The PRI's resurgence was aided by the descent of the PRD into infighting and a severe recession. It also benefited from the PAN's hard-nosed electoral campaign, which focused on promoting the still vaguely popular anti-cartel offensive and was mixed with underhand accusations against the PRI of complicity with the traf-fickers. The strategy, designed to deflect attention from an acute recession triggered by the global financial crisis of 2008, did not work.

The PAN and the PRD were left nursing their mid-term wounds, while the PRI nearly doubled its representation in the lower house, to the point where it could form an absolute majority with small-party allies. Its new position, and the PAN's aggressive campaign, gave it little incentive to continue cooperating with the government.

Calderón responded to the increased weakness of his party and to the deterioration in its relationship with the PRI by taking the counterintuitive step of announcing a much more ambitious reform agenda than he had pursued in the first half of his term. He promised new legislative efforts to combat poverty, improve education, encourage competition in the economy, eliminate corruption, boost efficiency and further democratize politics. Asked by an interviewer on Radio Formula to explain why he had got so ambitious at such an unpropitious time, Calderón responded: 'I don't want to be remembered as just one more president.' He might have added: 'I don't want to be remembered like Fox.' Most of the promised package never saw the light of day, and most of the proposals that did get to the legislature were bogged down in the usual way until they were eclipsed by the run-up to the 2012 presidential election.

Felipe Calderón's determination to exorcise the aura of frivolity and inaction that shrouded the Fox presidency also guided his relationship with the media, which he kept at a distance during the first few years of his term. Naturally a far less showy and rather more conventional public personality than Fox, this came easily. Fox had brought up his four adopted children on his own, after his first wife left him and before he threw caution to the wind with his controversial remarriage to Sahagún (a union that provoked the public disgust of one of his daughters). Calderón was the unquestioned head of a seemingly stable family, with three apparently well-behaved young children. His wife, Margarita Zavala Gómez del Campo, a former PAN deputy with her own independent political career and pedigree, seemed happy to take on a purely supportive role, which she fulfilled rather successfully.

While the decision to be dour at first helped Calderón restore seriousness to the presidency, as time went on it fuelled charges that he was living in a bubble. He began to appear insensitive to the conflictive and complex nature of the real world and to the impact of his decisions, particularly those related to the drug wars. Stories of cabinet temper tantrums began to make their way into the press, as rumours swirled of a drink problem.

From the end of 2009, Calderón sought to address this through a more open media strategy that included more interviews – and even the odd joke. By the following year he had enthusiastically embraced Twitter and had taken up the challenge of defending his drug-wars strategy in open debate with critics and victims of the violence. This was something completely unimaginable under the old PRI.

The new approach tempered Calderón's previous aloofness, and the president could be very impressive in the debates; but he never seemed able to shake off the image of stubbornness and inflexibility. 'I am fully aware that an enormous gulf has opened between the authorities and the citizens, and I hope we all try to close it by, among other things, this kind of dialogue. An effort to talk to each other, listen to each other and try to understand each other', Calderón told one meeting with his critics in October 2011. He then proceeded to make it clear that whatever anybody thought, he would continue along the same road he had already planned. The president seemed incapable of admitting the possibility that mistakes might have been made, and portrayed disappointments as the result of a lack of commitment on the part of other actors or of forces beyond his control.

Fox had left office under the shadow of his lack of political determination, which served to exacerbate the weakening and fragmentation of the state. Calderón approached the end of his *sexenio* with an image of a frustrated strongman. A leader who seemed to prize loyalty above all else, he had been unable to impose it beyond his own hand-picked inner circle. Democratization in Mexico was not served well by either. Creating a system that worked substantially better than the soft authoritarianism of the old imperial presidency, protected by a docile media, required fundamental reforms that marked a clear break with the past and traced out new ways of organizing politics that put the electorate at the centre of it all, even after the elections were over. It also required a strong narrative to keep it moving forward with a sense of purpose; but this had faded quickly as well.

By the time President Vicente Fox was preparing to leave office, his use of the word 'democracy' was beginning to sound as hollow as the PRI's use of 'The Revolution' in the final decades of its regime. 'Democracy is both the verb and the noun of national life', he said in his last state-of-the-nation address in September 2006. The speech was transmitted on television only because opposition deputies had prevented him from making it in the congressional chamber by occupying the podium. That congressional insurrection served as a rehearsal for the scenes of bedlam that accompanied Calderón's inauguration three months later. Democracy certainly did not look like it was providing the grammar of political life, as deputies punched and kicked each other on people's television screens.

Once in power, President Calderón had a neutral, negative and positive mode for referring to democracy. The first consisted of offhand references that implied it was so solid as hardly to warrant a mention. At times, the president seemed to want to avoid it altogether. He let the tenth anniversary of the election that ended one-party hegemony go without so much as a speech.

Calderón also periodically warned that democracy was in grave danger, particularly from organized crime. Paradoxically, he argued that this required all other parties – and indeed all Mexicans who valued democracy – to give his strategy in the drug wars their unqualified support.

Calderón's more optimistic vision centred on the claim that Mexicans had finally overcome the national inferiority complex associated with the years of restricted freedoms and had embraced a new, competitive spirit that befitted the new democratic era. The president frequently sought to illustrate what he termed *El Mexico Ganador* ('The Mexico that wins'), with reference to the national football team.

Football serves as a charged repository of national narratives in many countries in Latin America. But while the Brazilian, Argentinian and even Uruguayan teams have regularly provided their fans with reasons to celebrate, Mexicans traditionally end up licking their wounds and agonizing over why Mexican legs so often seem to go to jelly at the penalty spot.

A footballer called José 'El Jamaicon' Villegas gave his name to Mexican self-image of underperformance on the world stage – and not just in football: it was called El Síndrome del Jamaicon. Recognized as a world-class defender within Mexico, he fell to pieces in 1958 during a friendly game against England at Wembley that ended in an 8-0 defeat. He explained away his abysmal play by saying that he missed his mother and the food back home.

Expectations began to change when striker Hugo Sánchez did spectacularly well in the Spanish league in the 1980s, although his distinctly un-Mexican habit of blowing his own trumpet at every opportunity made him an obvious exception. By 2000, a steady trickle of Mexican players were signing for European clubs, and talk began of a new generation that had shaken off the insecurity of their forebears. This seemed to be confirmed when the under-seventeen team won its category's World Cup in 2006 – a reference that Calderón often used in his early presidential speeches.

The new golden generation was supposed to be reaching its peak around the time of the 2010 World Cup in South Africa. President Calderón did his best to associate himself with the team. He developed a personal relationship with the trainer, Javier Aguire, visited training sessions and found a limp diplomatic excuse that allowed him to be present at Mexico's first game in the competition.

Expectations got out of hand, whipped up by the feral commercial gusto of the television networks. Something even possessed the national football federation to emblazon the team bus with the slogan 'It's time for a new champion'. Such wild fantasies were balanced out by choruses of self-flagellating assertions that Mexico was fated never to get anywhere. The emotional rollercoaster intermingled with the general pessimism in the country, which was suffering from both the drug wars and an acute economic recession. When Aguire told a Spanish interviewer that the country was 'screwed' he was treated as both a traitor and a valiant plain speaker by the Mexican media. His subsequent promotional TV spots, in which he pronounced 'I love Mexico' contrasted fabulously with his earlier pronouncement.

In the end, Mexico was not even able to fulfil the down-to-earth ambition of reaching the quarter finals (something the team had only done in 1986, when the competition was on home ground). National soccer seemed once more destined for mediocrity – until young Mexican striker Javier Hernández, nicknamed 'Chicharrito' (little green pea) became one of Manchester United's new stars and helped the Mexican team win the Gold Cup in 2011. That same year, the new under-seventeen team was once again top of the world, and President Calderón once again began talking about *Mexico Ganador*.

Mexican football in the twenty-first century was actually a rather good metaphor for Mexican democracy; but not in the way Calderón intended. In politics, as in football, clear advances mixed with frustration over a failure to consolidate them. But while Mexican fans could draw genuine hope from a generation of players who were undeniably breaking new ground, politics remained dominated by old faces and anachronistic attitudes. The possibility that Mexicans would soon begin to feel significantly more in control of their elected representatives than they had done under the PRI seemed consequently rather more remote than the chances of Mexico being on the verge of becoming a world footballing power.

While both PAN presidents inevitably shoulder much of the blame for not pushing democratization further, Mexican politics cries out for a change in attitude across the entire political elite, which has manifestly failed to rise to the challenge posed by the dispersal of centralized power that came with the transition. Rather than prompt leaders to promote substantive public debate on the challenges facing the country, full pluralism has seen all the parties settle into a modus vivendi of alliances of convenience and mutual sabotage. Often they work things out in back-room negotiations, with no reference to the public at all, taking political traits seen the world over to an extreme.

There have been occasional exceptions, as with the discussions around political reform, particularly after President Calderón sent a formal proposal to the legislature in December 2009. The publicly aired debates over whether it did or did not make democratic sense to allow the re-election of deputies, senators and municipal mayors, or to open the way for citizen candidates unattached to any party, provided a brief peek at what should have been happening for years. After that, the reform was put on ice until a hotchpotch of minor measures was approved in 2011 after substantial horse-trading behind the scenes.

Legislative paralysis in the new political era was also associated with the glorification of consensus, itself a hangover from the old political culture forged within revolutionary nationalism. In the glory days of the PRI, open expression of disagreement was frequently condemned as both unproductive and potentially dangerous, as it risked turning the heat up under a supposed national tendency towards conflict – the so-called *El Mexico bronco*. National responsibility required the search for formulas to which everybody could sign up, because fissures should not exist in a unified country.

This was relatively easy to achieve under the PRI imperial presidency. Directives from the top trickled down through the system and, with a few negotiations and modifications along the way, ended up with a formula that all relevant political leaders and forces could live with. Discipline and loyalty among the party faithful were prized qualities. Bitter pills to be swallowed were sugar coated with the promise of candy at a later date. Where conflict was unavoidable, the ideal required efforts to reach back-room deals to smooth things over, followed by a public show of unity at the end. Some historians suggest that conflicts were sometimes even delib-erately staged, so that they could be solved with aplomb.

Political pluralism made it impossible to manufacture across-the-board agreements in this way, particularly in the legislature, which no party controlled from 1997. But rather than develop a new language that revolves around the need to construct majorities, the leaders of all parties have continued to publicly exalt the ideal of consensus in the name of the higher interests of the nation.

Laws that include a pick-and-mix of different positions hammered out in arduous (and usually hidden) negotiations are promoted by the political class as preferable to the victory of one set of ideas over the rest in an open debate. This ideal is not only very hard to secure, but the laws that result are often both weak and near impossible to implement, given their lack of internal coherence.

'The country is fed up of bad agreements and needs some good fights', wrote the political commentator Jesús Silva-Herzog in 2009. 'All relevant transformations in Mexico today necessarily require taking on powerful interests, and that requires confrontation and friction. The first fight we need is precisely one in favour of conflict.'

Mexico State governor Enrique Peña Nieto, the initial favourite to win the 2012 presidential election for the PRI, was a master of glossing over behind-the-scenes political hardball with the language of conflict avoidance. In the spring of 2010, Peña Nieto's own aides revealed a secret pact, in which he had promised PRI legislative support for a value-added tax rise in return for assurances from the PAN not to form an alliance with the PRD in the upcoming governorship elections in Mexico State. This showed the then governor to be a deft political operator, as well as a major voice in Congress – where, theoretically, he had no say. At the same time, however, he indulged in what famed cultural commentator Carlos Monsiváis termed 'patriotic mutism' in order to avoid giving more information about the deal. 'This is not the moment to debate', the governor said in response to a question about the furore created by the revelations. 'On the contrary, I believe that differences and everything that marks a division should be overcome in order to obtain common objectives and proposals in favour of all Mexicans.'

The only time I remember the Mexican political class in the new political era genuinely coming together over a particular issue was during a bizarre diplomatic row with the US over a commemorative stamp collection.

The stamps celebrated sixty years of a cartoon character called Memín Pinguín – a little black boy, drawn with huge lips, enormous ears, gigantic feet and wide-eyed wonder. Issued in September 2005, they caused uproar in the US, with the White House requesting they be recalled. The government jumped to the stamps' defence, supported by politicians from across the political spectrum, as well as by the bulk of the media and a good many ordinary citizens as well.

Political enemies banded together to insist that the US had no moral authority when it came to racism, while Mexico had such authority in abundance. Serious analysts argued that Mexicans could not possibly be racist because they were all brown themselves and knew what it was like to suffer prejudice in the US. Queues formed at the central post office, and the collection sold out in record time. Radio phone-in programmes buzzed with outraged citizens insisting that the hapless little Memín Pinguín, who was always getting himself into trouble alongside his more sensible and realistically drawn non-black friends, was actually a positive image of black people, because he was lovable.

Much of the backlash stemmed from a temporary recharging of traditional anti-imperialism, rooted in an understandable resistance to being lectured by the US on moral issues. More interestingly, however, it also revealed that the old myth of nationalist uniformity, promoted by revolutionary nationalism, still held currency in the new political era.

The defence of Memín Pinguín mostly ignored the fact that Mexico has an important black history all of its own. Colonial records show that around 200,000 slaves were imported into 'New Spain' in the sixteenth and seventeenth centuries to work in the silver mines, on the sugar plantations and cattle ranches. At that time, there were more black people than white in the colony.

In the colonial classification of the different 'castes' of the New World, those born in Spain were at the top and black people at the very bottom. At one time, there were more than forty classifications, including the infamous '*Salto pa tras*' (which means 'jump backwards' and was a mixture of Indian and black). But for all the classifications and theoretical rules about what each caste could and could not do, the reality was much more fluid. This, together with the demise of Mexican slavery earlier than elsewhere on the continent, helped the descendants of some slaves rise to prominence in Mexico, including two of the main leaders of the independence struggle.

The subsequent growth of nationalism around the idea that 'Mexicanness' was rooted in the mixture of indigenous and Spanish races and cultures put the black population on the road to invisibility. By the time of the furore over the Memín Pinguín stamp collection, most Mexicans with identifiably black roots were concentrated in the Gulf state of Veracruz and in a collection of small communities in a Pacific coastal region known as the Costa Chica. These latter communities had been among the most isolated in Mexico until a coastal road built in the 1960s had cut the journey time to Acapulco, the nearest city, from a week on a donkey to three hours on a bus. Electricity and television soon followed, along with black American anthropologists with their very different racial consciousness.

I visited the area shortly before the stamp episode to do a story about the small movement encouraging the local communities to begin thinking of themselves as Mexicans of African descent that was slowly taking hold, but never really took off. A fifty-year-old fisherman called Eladio García recalled the stories his grandparents used to tell him about how his ancestors arrived in the area on a ship that sank off the coast. 'They did not say where the ship came from, but now I know it was filled with slaves from Africa', he said as he threw his nets into a mangrove-ringed lagoon. 'Imagine that. All the way from Africa.'

García also had more recent stories to tell of people from the community being arrested in other parts of Mexico by immigration officials who would not believe they were Mexican. He and others like him might have found the stamp offensive; or they might have been among Memín Pinguín's fans. It would have been interesting to know, but I saw no domestic reports that asked them.

Modern Mexican politicians regularly use rhetoric that celebrates diversity in Mexico, but policies to this effect are rare. Notable exceptions include the legalization of gay marriage in the capital and some recognition of indigenous rights. Even so, the persistence of a background discourse that assumes a single national identity exists – made explicit in the Memín Pinguín episode – helps provide politicians with a latent excuse for not doing more about some of the country's most serious social problems, such as pervasive class and race-based abuse.

The tendency of the political class to fall back on the old canons of a political culture forged within one-party domination also encourages a sense that full plurality has done little to change the status of politics as an exclusive club that guarantees its members privileges for life. This is underlined by the meandering careers of a good few politicians who have fallen out with their party bosses (typically over issues of personal ambition), only to turn up on the electoral lists of their old party's rivals.

There is also a notable absence of new faces in the so-called *partidocracia* of the new political era.

The PRI is still replete with the infamous dinosaurs that roamed the corridors of power for decades and since 2000 have been kicking around influential positions in the opposition, and in state and municipal governments. After overcoming the challenges of staying together without a party member in the presidency, and after undergoing a makeover that added a veneer of slickness to old practices, the PRI remains the biggest party in the country. It is consequently well placed to take advantage of the combination of dissatisfaction with the current situation and a yearning for the re-establishment of at least some form of effective government. The fact that this even seemed possible in the run-up to the 2012 election is a measure of the partial nature of the country's democratic transition.

The PRD is hardly fresher. The coterie of dissident *Priistas*, communists and grassroots leaders who formed the party in 1989 still dominate the apparatus, the party blocs in the federal legislature and its regional power bases. New additions tend to be later defectors from the PRI. Even López Obrador, who put anti-systemic rectitude at the centre of his image, is steeped in the traditions of corporatist-style politics, learned in his early career as a PRI party organizer.

The PAN under Calderón brought in more newcomers. Most of these, however, were protégés of the president whose first priority was loyalty to him, rather than to the electorate.

There is also a smattering of established neoliberal economists who forged their political careers in the latter years of the PRI regime and now circulate among all the parties, somewhat above the political fray, but always on call when a key economic position comes up. Then there are the crude opportunists without any ideological identification, who are particularly obvious in the smaller parties. Their primary aim appears to be to secure some of the considerable amount of public money handed over to the political parties from the 1990s, originally in the name of encouraging pluralism.

The Mexican Green Party epitomizes this mercenary image, regularly securing a small but solid minority vote, by means of which it obtains favourable deals in alliances with the bigger parties. In 2000 it allied with the PAN; in 2006 and 2012 with the PRI. The Greens' electoral marketing tends to adroitly pick out a particular niche with well-designed simple messages that bear little relation to any serious political programme, have scant chance of success and usually nothing at all to do with the environment. The party won twenty-one deputies in the 2009 mid-term elections, after a campaign that focused on promising the death penalty for kidnappers.

It was all simpler back in the run-up to the 2000 election, when Fox turned the election into a referendum on whether the PRI could be trusted to fulfil its promises to lead reform from within, or whether the only way to shake things up was to change the party in power. Since then, the insider/outsider dichotomy has got all mixed up. All parties now share some degree of responsibility for the scant achievements of the democratic transition, because all but the tiniest parties hold some significant degree of power.

If anything, the political elite, seen as a class, has suffered rather more from media scrutiny than either Fox or Calderón, who could at least take some solace from residual public respect for the institution of the president, as the representative of the nation. Long-time pollster Dan Lund insisted, before he died in 2010, that this is why the personal approval ratings of both presidents rarely fell below 50 per cent. This was true even at times when positive evaluations of their governments' specific actions bumped along at 20–30 per cent. Governors fare reasonably well at a local level for similar reasons. Named political parties can also rely on baseline loyalties at least, but when electors are asked to evaluate nameless collective groups of politicians there are no such buffers.

A Demotecnia poll showed that, in early 2011, only 19 per cent of Mexicans thought that Calderón's ministers were doing a 'good' job, down from 49 per cent four years before, in the early days of the government. This dramatic fall took them close to the pitiful 14 per cent approval level for federal deputies, down from the hardly dizzying heights of 28 per cent in the same period.

Deputies and senators are particularly favoured targets of the national media, being frequently portrayed as lazy, self-serving, cynical, good-for-nothing burdens around the public's neck, and regularly pictured dozing in their seats and fiddling with their BlackBerries, when they are not trading insults and accusations of everything from alcoholism to murder from the podium. Publically funded advertising campaigns that seek to address this image problem are often laughably clumsy. One of the most widely broadcast in early 2012 began with a child proposing 'no more kidnapping' and being greeted by a chorus of voices responding 'in favour'. It ended with the slogan 'In the Senate we approve laws that benefit all Mexicans'.

Periodically, the media turns a particular issue into a full-blown campaign that requires a more specific response. This happened during the 2009 recession, when legislators approved tax hikes at the same time as they continued to enjoy publicly funded luxurious international trips, subsidized haircuts, private health insurance and many other obviously unnecessary benefits to top up salaries that are higher than those of their counterparts in many developed countries. Several politicians sought public sympathy by announcing that they would renounce some of these privileges in solidarity with the general population. When reporters followed up a few months later, they found that several had done nothing to make good on their promise.

It is perhaps unfair to dwell too much on the post-2000 sins of Mexican politicians, given that the sins of the past were never exposed in anything like the same way. But the fact that such offensive behaviour remains so prevalent, even in the new context of media scrutiny, reveals a depth of cynicism that is perhaps cause for even greater concern. Politicians caught in a scandal often appear confident that they can ride it out until a new one, involving someone else, comes along and grabs public attention. Accountability has become a buzzword, but it only stands a chance of taking on real meaning if a particular interest group with clout takes up a cause after a major scandal.

This happened in the wake of the furore unleashed when eight female deputies from various parties resigned during the first session of the newly elected lower chamber in September 2009, in order to make way for male substitutes. They had been included in electoral lists in order to meet gender quotas, but once the polls closed they were of no further use. Two years later, the lobby of female politicians seemed on the verge of pushing through legislative changes requiring all female candidates to have a female substitute.

Honourable exceptions apart, neither competitive elections nor a more confident and independent media has produced a political elite inclined to pay more than lip service to the idea that public office carries with it responsibilities as well as privileges. Mexico's political system seems stuck in a kind of dysfunctional limbo. It has left behind one-party hegemony, but has failed to make the transition to a democracy in which citizens have effective ways of demanding more than superficial attention outside of elections, and punishing the careers of those who have let them down.

The determined parents of the children killed in the ABC day-care fire in July 2009 constitute one of the glimmers of hope that widespread frustration with the limitations of the transition might eventually coalesce into enough pressure to force democratization out of its impasse.

They soon realized that the authorities – at whatever level, in whatever capacity and whichever political party they were associated with – would do nothing unless pushed. And so they kept pushing.

A year after the fire, they persuaded the Supreme Court to use its privilege to open an investigation into what had happened. Such investigations produce non-binding recommendations, designed to guide the actions of other state organs. One of the magistrates drew up a proposal for his colleagues to debate in which he argued that individual high officials from the federal, state and municipal authorities should be named as responsible for serious violations of citizen rights. The court as a whole shied away from voting in favour of this potentially system-jolting precedent, but it has at least put the issue on the agenda.

Though the campaign by the core group of relatives has subsequently lost some of its momentum, it has not disappeared. Their continued activism has kept judicial cases stemming from the fire inching forward. It has also resulted in legislative changes designed to monitor state-subsidized day-care facilities in a better way. Perhaps most importantly, the ABC parents have proved that when citizens do take up the challenge and are prepared to persist, progress is possible; but that if more do not join them, such progress is going to be excruciatingly slow.

The task is made even harder because narrowing the gulf between politicians and the run-of-the-mill electorate also requires that something is done to reduce the influence of vested interests that have colonized some of the spaces left by the receding centralized authority – the so-called 'de facto powers'.

CHAPTER 3

The Misrule of Law

Iɴ his 1997 book, *The Imperial Presidency*, historian Enrique Krauze describes the PRI regime at its height as a kind of political solar system. The president – the sun – provided the guiding force for almost everybody, from the governors to the intellectuals, the unions to the Church, and the media to the opposition political parties. They moved around the system with differing degrees of subordination to the centre, he writes, but their movements were always controlled to some degree.

Krauze's original analogy can be usefully extended into the era of political plurality. The waning of the sun's gravitational pull released the planets to roam more freely, but the absence of more concerted efforts to deepen democratization meant that they did so with their own orbits largely intact. Some floated off towards irrelevance and began to lose their satellites, but others began drawing in more floating bodies, gaining greater weight and importance in the definition of how the whole system works.

Many observers use the term 'de facto powers' to describe these former players that once upon a time were organized within the regime, and that have now not only survived it, but have occupied some of the areas left by the receding centralized state. The expansion of organized crime epitomizes how dangerous this can be; but there are plenty of other above-board organizations and individuals that have also found ways of using their new autonomy in the new fragmented reality to accumulate influence, fortune and, in some cases, infamy.

The limit to what the de facto powers can do is set by their ability to get the rules changed to fit with their interests, or to ensure that their transgressions are tolerated by the authorities. They risk little – unless the protection they enjoy fades. This could happen if they overplay their hand, lose out to their peers, or are impacted by social or economic changes beyond their control. Even so, the chances of actually being brought to book remain slim, because of a judicial system that routinely ignores the guilty (particularly the influential guilty), while it fills the jails with the poor, the vulnerable – and the innocent.

On the afternoon of 16 December 2005, a human rights activist and investigative journalist called Lydia Cacho Ribeiro was forced into a vehicle outside the high-security shelter she ran for women abused by powerful men in the Caribbean resort city of Cancún. Within a few hours it became clear that Cacho had not been kidnapped by an underworld commando, as was first feared. Instead, she had been abducted by police from the central state of Puebla, hundreds of kilometres away, to face libel charges filed by a successful textile businessman there called Kamel Nacif Borge.

Cacho had mentioned Nacif in a book she had recently published called *Los Demonios del Eden* (*The Demons of Eden*). Victims of a Cancún-based child-sex ring described him as a friend and protector of a local businessman called Jean Succar Kuri, who allegedly ran the criminal network. Succar Kuri was in the US at the time, fighting extradition to Mexico to face charges.

Cacho later stated that she had been subjected to degrading treatment and psychological torture throughout the twenty-hour road trip. This ranged from having a gun pressed into the back of her neck to malicious mockery and death threats. Once behind bars in Puebla, sympathetic prison guards kept her safe in the prison infirmary until pressure from the media and activists ensured her release on bail the following day. Two months later, a tape of a private phone conversation between Nacif and Puebla Governor Mario Marín Torres, recorded at the time of her abduction, found its way onto the broadcast media. It transformed the minor scandal into a major controversy.

'Hiya Kamel', the governor begins. 'My gorgeous guv', replies the businessman. 'My fucking hero', responds Marín. 'No, papa,' insists Nacif, 'you are the real hero of this movie.' Niceties over, the pair go on to discuss Cacho's arrest, making it clear that the governor himself was directly involved. 'Yesterday I gave that bitch a damn good slap', says the governor.

I showed her that in Puebla the law is respected and there is no impunity and anybody who breaks the law is called a criminal. And she'd better not play the victim, or try and take advantage of it to get publicity. I sent her the message and now we'll see what she says.

The call carries on in similar vein, ending with Nacif taking an enormous amount of care to pin down the exact location to which he should send 'an extra beautiful bottle of cognac' as a token of his gratitude. This raised suspicions that the liquor was code for something far less innocent. In another tape, Nacif is heard chuckling with someone else over plans to have Cacho beaten and raped in jail.

The illegally obtained recordings had no weight in a criminal court, but the extreme abuse of power they revealed could not be ignored. Here was an elected leader using his influence over the theoretically independent state judicial authorities to pursue a journalist investigating serious child sexual abuse – and all, apparently, at the behest of a local businessman with criminal intentions. There were marches in Puebla calling for Marín's resignation and vitriol in the national press. The main candidates in the 2006 presidential election campaign, in full swing at the time, expressed their outrage.

For a while it seemed hard to imagine that Marín, now widely referred to as 'El Gober Precioso' – 'The Gorgeous Guv' – could withstand the pressure. He knew better. After an initial attempt to deny the authenticity of the tape, he kept his head down. The state-level congress could theoreti-cally impeach him and force him to stand trial; but he controlled the majority of the deputies. The national Senate could declare the state ungovernable and remove him; but that required his party, the PRI, to throw him to the wolves.

In early 2007, the newly inaugurated President Felipe Calderón Hinojosa went to Puebla and extended his hand to the disgraced governor in a shameful photo opportunity. He had conveniently forgotten the campaign rally in the state a few months before, when he had held up a red card and demanded that Marín must go. In November 2007, in a non-binding resolution, the Supreme Court exonerated Marín of conspiring to violate Cacho's rights. The court refused to include the taped phone conversations in its deliberations.

A few days later, the Gober Precioso's apparent triumph was sealed when he led the PRI to an increased majority in Puebla's mid-term congressional and municipal elections. A few days after that, I interviewed

PRI voters in the state, who enumerated classic reasons for supporting the party that had held power there for an uninterrupted seventy-eight years. They talked of the sacks of cement they had received, the promises of drainage systems in their *barrios* they had believed, and their reliance on handouts of basic foodstuffs controlled by the party. Most were unwilling even to broach the subject of Marín's morality and democratic credentials. 'You can't expect politicians to be clean', a sixty-year-old farmer told me as he pulled up weeds from his field under the looming presence of the Popocatepetl volcano. 'It's in their nature to be corrupt.'

Mario Marín is a particularly unsavoury example of a new crop of governors whose near absolute authority in their territories harks back to the era of regional strongmen, known as *caciques*, who litter Mexican history but had been somewhat controlled under the regime. When it was initially formed in 1929, the ruling party was essentially a stability pact between these *caciques*, many of them generals from the revolutionary era. Once the one-party system was consolidated, the governors were transformed into delegates of presidential power. They had monopolistic control over local institutions, but their ability to exercise it depended on their loyalty to the centre.

The arrangement worked reasonably well for about half a century. The governors, handpicked by the president and often sent from Mexico City rather than born of local leaderships, had too much to lose if they did not toe the line – and much to gain if they did. The federal government not only held the purse strings, but the centralized party determined the career opportunities that might open up for a governor after his (or occasionally her) *sexenio* was over. Corruption and abuse of power were permitted, but the limits were set in the capital.

A well administered term could lead to a powerful position in Mexico City in the party hierarchy, or to a cabinet post. If a governor's loyalty flagged, or if he failed to deliver peace in his territory, he risked being removed from his job and pushed into the political hinterland. 'For better or for worse, the presidents of the PRI had the political resources required to correct the arbitrary use of power by the governors', says Rogelio Hernández Rodríguez of the Colegio de México, author of the 2008 book, *El Centro Dividido* (*The Centre Divided*).

The scholar dates the roots of the new autonomy to modifications in the organization of the regime that took place in the context of economic crisis and growing pressures to relax controls from the 1980s. The initial decentralization of administrative functions in health, infrastructure and, eventually, education was followed by transfers of more cash and by greater discretion over how to use it. At the same time, the opposition gained influence and became more combative in the regions, beginning with the growth of the PAN in the north.

President Carlos Salinas accelerated the decentralization process and allowed the opposition to win its first governorship in 1989. This was one of the strategies he used to neutralize the legitimacy crisis that accompanied his contested election the year before. He was not, however, prepared to give up centralized political control. Over the course of his term, he removed seventeen governors at his convenience.

After he took control of the government in 1994, President Ernesto Zedillo possessed neither the will nor the way to prove that he still called the shots in the states. His one early attempt to do so failed miserably when he sought to persuade party dinosaur Roberto Madrazo to desist from becoming governor of the southern state of Tabasco. Madrazo's blatantly fraudulent election victory had triggered an intense wave of protest led by his defeated PRD rival, Andrés Manuel López Obrador. (The two would meet again as presidential candidates in 2006.) According to the extensive account of the conflict in *Opening Mexico*, by *New York Times* correspondents Julia Preston and Sam Dillon, Madrazo turned down the consolation prize of a cabinet position, and then faced down an attempt to engineer his removal through the courts. His show of defiance revealed not only how deep the splits had become in the PRI, but also how much more independence the governors had accrued.

The federal political transition gathered steam over the rest of Zedillo's term. The strengthening of the Federal Electoral Institute, charged with overseeing national elections and made fully independent in 1996, the loss of control of the Congress in 1997, and a newly aggressive and critical media all set Mexico on the road that would culminate in the democratic transition of 2000. Politics in the country's thirty-one states remained almost as closed as ever.

President Vicente Fox openly embraced the principle of non-intervention in the states, which he argued was a step towards democratizing the country as a whole. The PAN president did break that rule with his manoeuvrings to impeach leftist presidential hopeful López Obrador, who had gone on from the Tabasco defeat to become mayor of the capital (the Federal District which stands as the country's thirty-second state but operates under somewhat different rules from the rest). However, that was a response to national electoral concerns rather than an attempt to impose federal control on local politics.

Fox was also particularly responsive to the pressure exerted by provincial governors to increase the amount of federal funds they received. Much of the additional cash that flowed into the treasury from the boom years of oil production during his administration ended up being frittered away by the governors. The government in the capital is near powerless to control how the money it transfers to the states is used. Oversight powers reside almost exclusively with state-level legislatures, which the regional overlords often control. Even funds earmarked for local municipalities – supposedly merely passing through the state coffers – provide the governors with a mechanism for keeping local mayors in line. While it is difficult for them to use the money, they can easily delay its delivery.

By the time President Calderón took office at the end of 2006, the mutation of the governors into independent political actors was complete. The rising power of organized crime limited the authority of some; but if a governor had a solid support base in his or her own state, there was little the federal government could do to curtail his or her autonomy. Calderón tried desperately to bring the governors into line with his national drug-wars strategy, but beyond the issue of security, he made little attempt to redress the balance. As Hernández Rodríguez writes, 'The governors have obtained so much power, and the freedom to exercise it as they want, that they have converted their states into authentic fiefdoms where the only real authority is their own.'

The extreme cases of feudal-style governors indulging in blatant abuse of power (such as Marín in Puebla) or in the selective repression of dissenters (such as PRI governor of Oaxaca, Ulises Ruiz Ortiz) have received most attention. By and large, however, they exert their control in somewhat subtler ways that block the federal-level institutional advances from filtering into their territories. Their tactics include stalling the implementation of freedom of information legislation and keeping tight control of critical local media outlets in ways that range from cutting off official advertising to sending round the heavies. Suspiciously expensive infrastructure contracts awarded to companies associated with members of the local governor's inner circle are common. Nepotism is rampant, as is the use of public money for such questionable forms of promotion as buying football teams or paying huge amounts to appear on national TV. Several local electoral institutions have been crammed with governor-friendly commissioners, in a way that compromises their ability to guarantee level electoral playing fields. Clientelism is as rife as ever.

'You can find it all,' wrote Jorge Zepeda Patterson in his 2008 edited collection on the 'de facto powers' entitled *Los Intocables* (*The Untouchables*), 'but what all the governors have in common, as well as a galloping fortune, is absolute impunity to indulge their whims and, in the worst cases, their wickedness.'

The most extreme feudal governors of the new era have tended to belong to the PRI, reflecting both their greater numbers (twenty at the time of Fox's victory and the same number a decade later) and a predisposition to employ methods developed within the framework of one-party hegemony. But no party can claim to be blemish free.

The PAN had eight governorships in 2000, and eight a decade later (with two of those won in alliance with the PRD). The most infamous *Panista* governor, Emilio González Márquez in the central state of Jalisco, was dubbed 'El Gober Piadoso' –'The Pious Guv' – for his habit of donating large amounts of public money to the Catholic Church. This included the promise of $9 million for the construction of a sanctuary honouring martyrs of the Cristero War, in which radical Catholics took up arms against the anti-clerical post-revolutionary state in the 1920s. Such crude disregard for the constitutionally enshrined separation of Church and state brought the criticism raining down even in Jalisco, a long-time bastion of conservative Catholicism.

The governor revealed how little he cared about the discomfort his donations caused during a dinner event in 2008 at which he handed over another $1.5 million to a Church-run charity. 'It's not my money, it's the people's money', the clearly sozzled leader almost boasted, waving the cheque in the direction of Cardinal Juan Sandoval Iñiguez, who was guest of honour. 'I couldn't give a shit if some newspapers don't like it', he slurred. 'With apologies, Señor Cardinal, they can fuck themselves. I am here to fulfil a promise to myself.' The arrogance and the language created such a storm around the transfers of public cash to the Church that the cardinal announced he would not accept the donation for the sanctuary.

The controversy eventually died down, and by 2011 Governor González Márquez threw his hat into the ring as a possible presidential candidate for the PAN the following year. He later bowed out, but his ability to even entertain such ambitions indicated that tolerance of governorship transgressions is not exclusive to the PRI.

The PRD controlled four governorships in 2000. A decade later it still held four on its own, along with two in alliance with the PAN. The party's most important bastion has always been the Federal District. Transforming the nation's capital into a personal fiefdom is more difficult than in the provincial states, given the sheer diversity of the political powers based within it. Even so, several working-class boroughs in Mexico City are under firm control of clientelistic organizations led by PRD political operators.

Direct accusations of abuse of authority, particularly nepotism and corruption, are more commonly directed against PRD governors elsewhere. Amalia García Medina filled government positions in the state of Zacatecas with members of her immediate and extended family during her term, which ended in 2010. These included her daughter, with whom she was said to share power.

Whatever party they belong to, the new generation of feudal-style governors has not only helped limit democratization in particular states, but has also impeded coordination of national policy. In the absence of new mechanisms to fill the void once provided by one-party hegemony, each governor is free to act almost as a world unto themselves, able to define how much (or how little) to work with their peers in other states or central government. The governors did form a nationwide organization called the CONAGO – or the National Commission of Governors – but this has no formal institutional status. In the first decade at least, it acted primarily as a lobby group focused on extracting more federal funds.

The governors also exercise more direct influence over the political parties to which they belong than they did in the past. Again this is particularly true of the PRI, where they have taken on a central role in decisions that previously emanated from the president. They have accrued considerable say as to who goes where on the national electoral lists, and consequently which laws do and do not get approved by the legislature. They have also become key players in defining the party leadership and the presidential candidacy.

The feudal governors are not, however, eternal: their terms, like those of presidents, end after six years. The prohibition on re-election (originally enshrined in the constitution to prevent the rise of another dictatorship like the one headed by Porfirio Díaz at the turn of the twentieth century) remains untouchable today. Under the imperial PRI presidency, the next stage in a governor's career depended on his or her relationship with the president in the capital. Now it depends more on a governor's ability to use his or her regional stronghold both as a launching pad for future ambitions and as protection against later fallout from old abuses. Getting a loyalist elected as the new governor is central to both tasks.

Governors who fluff the succession test can consequently look rather vulnerable, particularly if they do not go straight into another elected office and pick up the automatic immunity from prosecution that this brings. This happened to Mario Marín of Puebla after he picked a colourless sidekick to stand in the election to replace him (his choice duly lost to a candidate from a PAN-PRD alliance). But while this stunted his political career and triggered rumours that he would be forced into court, a year later there was no sign of this actually happening.

Occasionally, even former governors who do secure a friendly replacement find themselves under pressure on account of the legacy of their crimes and misdemeanours while in office – particularly if the cases are taken up by the media at particularly delicate political moments.

As governor of the northern state of Coahuila from 2005, Humberto Moreira Valdés became famous for giving full rein to his romantic and familial impulses. He got the local congress to change the civil code to reduce the time that had to elapse before a divorcee could remarry, thus permitting him to take a new wife – a beauty queen – after whom he named an old people's centre and a primary school, eschewing the long tradition of honouring national heroes. His mother had a kindergarten named after her, and his daughter an orphanage. The state was also awash with rumours of the infiltration of organized crime and corruption.

None of this presented any obstacle to Moreira's giving up his term somewhat early in order to become president of the PRI in 2010. Nor did it prevent him ensuring that his brother Rubén won the next governorship elections in July 2011 by a landslide. But everything changed when the media revealed, a few months later, that the state's debt had multiplied from $27 million to $2.8 billion during his term in office. Furthermore, some of the debt was contracted with the help of falsified documents. Moreira denounced what he called a smear campaign, but it soon became clear that the scandal was not going to go away. An astute political operator who had been central to the PRI's strategies for winning the 2012 election, Moreira had become a liability and was eased out of the party presidency at the end of the year.

There was, however, little to indicate that the party had any intention of withdrawing all of its protection from Moreira, as implied by the standing ovation he received when he announced his intention of standing down.

At the same time, the presidential candidate Enrique Peña Nieto had also made sure that he was publicly seen embracing similarly questionable figures from a few years before.

The reappearance in public of Peña Nieto's predecessor as governor of the State of Mexico was particularly striking. Arturo Montiel Rojas' own presidential ambitions had been torpedoed six years before, after photographs of some of his luxurious residences around the world found their way into the media, appearing to prove longstanding assumptions of rampant corruption. During his term as governor, Peña Nieto had done his best never to so much as mention his sometime mentor; but as he launched his presidential bid, he provided Montiel with a platform for a triumphant return. Hailed as a hero, Montiel took his place in the front rows of party luminaries who gathered to anoint Peña Nieto's campaign at several events towards the end of 2011.

The message to the more recent incarnations of the feudal governor phenomenon seemed clear – if you get yourself into trouble, be prepared for a period in the political hinterland, but don't despair, maintain party discipline and your party will never hang you out to dry.

❋ ❋ ❋

Teachers' leader Elba Esther Gordillo Morales seemed both fired up and relaxed during a September 2011 closed-door meeting of the union executive committee (called to discuss strategy ahead of the upcoming presidential elections), a video of which was later leaked to the media. The union, she told her underlings in a tone that oscillated between professorial and confessional, must ensure that it received concrete advantages in return for its electoral support. It must, she added with a wry smile, always be on the watch for potential betrayal. And it was essential – she almost banged the table to drive home the point – that the union maintain its political independence. 'Power is power, señores.' She rolled the words around her tongue for extra emphasis. 'Power is power', she repeated, head nodding in what looked like quiet satisfaction at the certainty that few Mexicans know as much about how power works in their country as she does. Even fewer have accrued anything like as much of it over the years, making this woman – known simply as 'La Maestra', or 'The Teacher', one of the most influential 'de facto powers' of all.

Gordillo's tireless political drive, talent for long-term strategizing, and the Machiavellian sophistication she exudes contrast with the certain sense of decadence that clings to many of the feudal governors. Those with obvious future ambitions, such as PRI candidate Enrique Peña Nieto, treat the governorship as a clear stepping stone to something bigger; but many governors seem infused with a kind of 'milk it while you can' mentality. Most, after all, will never be that powerful again. There is no hint of similar limits in the way Gordillo uses and abuses the power and wealth she has accumulated as a direct result of the demise of the corporatist controls that, like the increased autonomy of the governors, is a spin-off effect of Mexico's democratic transition.

Gordillo has actually fulfilled her formal role as leader of the National Union of Teachers (SNTE) rather well, securing important advancements in pay and conditions for her estimated 1.2–1.6 million members. Her near mythical status, however, comes from the way in which she has used her position to build webs of complicity across ideological and institutional spectrums of the new political plurality. Her interests (and her hand) can be seen behind national, state and municipal elections won and lost, government appointments made, and resignations tendered.

La Maestra's ability to carve out for herself a role as an *éminence grise* also draws on her own brand of political dexterity, forged in an early life of hardship and tragedy that mutated into a grinding, if rapid, rise through the male-dominated ranks of corporatist trade unionism. Her talent would count as extraordinary in any context, but it has blossomed in the post-transition era of more fluid rules and ample rewards for those with the resources and determination to seek them.

There are also structural reasons why Gordillo is in a different league from other union bosses. Most of them have, like her, fended off pressures to democratize and can threaten a political backlash if their fiefdoms are touched. None, however, has a similar national platform in such a key sector, from which to take similar advantage of the weakened state. The decades of receding state involvement in the economy and of globalization have taken care of that.

The SNTE, founded by presidential decree in 1943 in the context of the regime's drive to educate the masses, was bound up with political power from the start. Unionized teachers took up positions of natural local leadership across the nation, from where they helped push a mechanistic pedagogical model designed to produce new generations of Mexicans who could read, write and do simple mathematics, but who were also obedient citizens. The union was also given substantial control over the teaching jobs distributed, which helped contain the kind of radicalism that was particularly associated with the profession throughout Latin America in the second half of the twentieth century.

President Carlos Salinas made Gordillo the head of the union in 1989, at a time when her predecessor, former mentor and lover was struggling to control a wave of dissidence after seventeen years in the job. Gordillo was forty-four at the time. She defused the conflict quickly and efficiently, incorporating the moderates into the leadership and isolating the radicals. Then she successfully neutralized Salinas' plans to modernize education with a reform that included breaking up the union. The educational decentralization of the mid-1990s ended up as little more than a transfer of the administrative control of the budget to the states.

The first time I saw Gordillo in action, she was giving a speech at a PRI campaign rally in 2000, in a sports stadium filled with bored, poor people who had been bussed in to wave little flags and cheer. Despite the apathetic audience, Gordillo paced the stage like a caged animal, the cadence of her voice rising and falling with perfect dramatic timing as she delivered an impassioned defence of the regime's record in education. It was one of the most rousing pieces of rhetoric I have ever witnessed, before or since.

By then, however, Gordillo had also spent years ingratiating herself with the intelligentsia as a budding democrat, as part of her preparation for the political transformations she correctly surmised were coming. Despite her protestations of party loyalty, she did little to get out the vote for the PRI in 2000 and was reputedly delighted when it lost.

The juggling continued into the first years of the post-transition. Gordillo cultivated friendships with both President Fox and his ambitious wife in a way that helped ensure that early promises to democratize the old corporatist unions fizzled out. Fox also poured public money into the SNTE-controlled housing fund, while making no effort to force the union to open its accounts to scrutiny. At the same time, La Maestra secured for herself leadership positions in the PRI that she only lost in 2003, when the double game became too much for even her to handle.

Two years out of the public eye followed, accompanied by rumours that longstanding kidney problems had become critical. But she bounced back in 2005 with a brand new political party of her own.

Developed out of a network of tens of thousands of electoral observers that Gordilla had set up inside the union in the 1990s as one of her first steps towards disassociating herself from the crumbling regime, the New Alliance Party (PANAL) completed La Maestra's transformation into an independent political actor. While still rooted in the SNTE, it has allowed her to participate directly in local and national elections, usually in alliances with whichever of the large parties offers the most favourable deals for her and the union. No dissident challenge to her authority within the union can hope to match that.

The actual number of votes delivered by the PANAL, whose support comes primarily from teachers and their families, is arguably less significant than the army of highly trained operatives deployed at sensitive polling stations, with their ear to the ground. Ricardo Raphael de la Madrid has detailed how it works, in his authoritative political biography *Los Socios de Elba Esther* (*Elba Esther's Partners*). With a national spread that no standard polling company can boast, Gordillo receives fine-tuned and quickly processed information on polling day. This reveals which way the electoral winds are blowing, and allows her to adapt her real-time negotiations with regionally specific sophistication.

In its first foray into the electoral arena in 2006, the PANAL received 4.6 per cent in the congressional poll, while its deliberately limp presidential candidate got less than 1 per cent. Some of the difference between these two figures went to Felipe Calderón. Given that teachers had never traditionally considered voting for the right-wing PAN, this created the impression that La Maestra had tipped the wafer-thin election in his favour.

It was finally too much for the PRI, which expelled Gordillo from its ranks after the election. She had joined the party in 1970. La Maestra was not bothered as she negotiated senior government positions for several sidekicks with president-elect Calderón. These included her son-in-law, who became deputy education minister. In the years that followed, La Maestra's influence was perceived in the shelving of investigations into her unexplained riches and in the tolerance shown towards her manoeuvrings to get herself elected union president for life in 2007. Her position was actually strengthened by the radical dissident union branches that dominate schools in the state of Oaxaca and that have significant presence in Michoacán and Guerrero. The strikes they periodically call can shut schools down for weeks at a time, and provide a regular reminder that at least Gordillo can guarantee that most teachers turn up to work.

La Maestra was also instrumental in the 2009 removal of Calderón's first education minister, Josefina Vázquez Mota, with whom she had a visibly icy relationship. The new education minister, Alonso Lujambio Irazába, took over the job with a speech in which he pointedly referred to the union boss as '*una fina dama*' – 'a fine lady'.

It was a rather surprising epithet to use for a woman who has one of the most negative images in the country – an image that her Louis Vuitton handbags, Hermès shoes, and assumed penchant for plastic surgery only exacerbate.

Time and again Gordillo has been exposed as using classic clientelism to control the SNTE – sometimes taken to extremes, as when she distributed a fleet of brand-new Hummers to regional union bosses in 2008. The move backfired when photographs of the grinning unionists getting into their shiny new cars found their way into the press. With a completely straight face, La Maestra insisted that the vehicles were actually raffle prizes to be auctioned off to raise money for infrastructural improvements in deprived rural schools.

Gordillo has a reputation for distributing gifts to maintain her network of goodwill within the political, intellectual and journalistic elite with considerably more discretion. Former collaborators say her generosity ranges from tokens of esteem, such as designer watches, to the payment of medical bills for treatment by top specialists. And all the gifts, they add, are chosen with a finesse that is matched only by her passion for amassing intelligence.

One particularly trustworthy source told me that he had personally witnessed microphones being placed in flower arrangements for a meeting of regional union bosses at which she was not going to be present. He also recalls a drunken night, during which she boasted to him that she maintained a corps of female spies charged with seducing any associates she suspected of plotting against her.

The most fantastical story told about La Maestra dates from the late 1990s. A former right-hand man (turned bottomless fount of damaging allegations), Noé Rivera Domínguez, claims that Gordillo's desperate efforts to fend off what looked like an imminent attempt to depose her by President Ernesto Zedillo culminated in a ceremony half way up a Nigerian mountain. Rivera says he personally saw local witches skin a white lion alive and dress La Maestra in its pelt, in order to help her 'challenge the leader of her tribe'. A few hours after it was all over, he says, La Maestra received a surprisingly cordial call from Zedillo on her satellite phone. A new arrangement of mutual tolerance began. The tale is retold in detail in a fascinating little book tracing the importance of the supernatural in Mexican politics called Los Brujos de Poder or The Witches of Power by José Gil Olmos.

Whether they are true or not, all the stories add to Gordillo's mystique and aura of omnipotence. They cannot, however, hold off forever the mounting pressure over her role in stifling efforts to improve sub-standard public sector education with her determination to block any reforms that require the union to loosen its hold over teachers. Back in the 1990s, when she so successfully neutralized Salinas' modernization effort, that pressure came primarily from reformists in government. Two decades later it had a broader base, fuelled by a series of new international studies that underlined how urgent a problem inadequate Mexican education had become.

The Programme for International Student Assessment (PISA) started measuring the skills of fifteen-year-old schoolchildren in OECD member countries, and invited partners every three years from 2000. Mexico's position at the bottom of the OECD lists (and near the bottom of the extended lists) could be blamed on the departed regime in the first survey. But the excuses ran out when it remained there in subsequent ones. In the meantime, Latin America's other OECD member, Chile, had leapfrogged Mexico.

The proportion of Mexican pupils surveyed who were unable to achieve baseline competence in reading comprehension fell from 44 per cent in 2000 to 40 per cent in 2009. This slight improvement paled in comparison to the Chilean students, whose below-competency quotient dropped from 48 per cent to 31 per cent in the same period. Meanwhile, the proportion of Mexican students in the top PISA band actually dropped from 0.9 per cent to 0.5 per cent, while in Chile it rose from 0.5 per cent to 1.3 per cent.

La Maestra herself blames insufficient resources – a problem that means many schools do not even have drainage. This may be fair, although education spending has increased sharply since she took over the SNTE, to the point where it accounts for about a quarter of the public sector budget. Absolute amounts per capita compare favourably with many countries of a similar developmental level. Gordillo also argues that the troubles stem from the lack of commitment of the numerous education ministers she has seen come and go. Again, she has a point, although at least some of them have seen their reform efforts flounder in the face of her resistance.

Both President Calderón and Gordillo promised that the situation would be turned around by the Alliance for Quality Education, launched in 2008. But while the introduction of competitive exams for new teaching jobs was promoted by both as a near revolution, new positions make up a fraction of the total teaching force. The Alliance consequently left the SNTE in control of the distribution of most jobs, according to criteria that had little to do with teaching standards.

The majority of the Mexican public describe themselves as satisfied with the education their children receive (itself a legacy of the old conformist model). But a new batch of elite-based non-governmental organizations (NGOs) has emerged in the last few years to up the pressure for more fundamental reform, which inevitably includes reducing union power.

Several prominent businessmen, particularly concerned about the impact of sub-standard education on productivity, sponsor one of the most vocal new groups, called Mexicanos Primero. They have campaigned particularly hard on the lack of transparency within the union. Another group – more associated with the left and called the Citizens' Coalition for Education – demands the repeal of the original presidential decree giving the SNTE a closed shop. It also calls for an end to the 'colonization' of the ministry by union members. There are so many unionists in positions of power within the ministry that it can be difficult to work out where the line is between workers and bosses. This 'atypical symbiosis', to quote UN Rapporteur for Education Rights Vernor Muñoz, is often identified as the origin of Mexico's educational difficulties.

The Calderón government and Gordillo launched a second quality-focused agreement in 2011 that mandated periodic evaluations of all teachers and linked existing merit-based incentives more directly to results in the classroom. These incentives were introduced back in the 1990s, but La Maestra had ensured that the SNTE retained control of the criteria used to define which teachers received them.

While widely welcomed as the most serious reform effort to date, critics still complained about the near absence of debate, let alone active participation of civil society. It is also clear that whatever the plan, what really matters is whether the government can require the SNTE to fulfil it, and that is much harder to do when La Maestra is able to call in electoral favours.

Gordillo's continued power in Mexico's new democracy consequently depends, at least in part, on her ability to be seen to have helped the winning presidential candidate to power in 2012. If her support is perceived as possibly decisive – as it was in the case of Calderón in 2006 – then so much the better.

Gordillo began preparing years in advance, but after years of political flirtations with all the major potential candidates, she eventually negotiated a formal alliance between the PANAL and the PRI, which was announced at the end of 2011. This was hardly unexpected, given the fact that the old party of power had a runaway lead in the polls at the time, with its candidate the former Mexico State governor, Enrique Peña Nieto.

What was more surprising was how much she secured. The deal included near certain seats in the national Senate for one of her daughters and the son-in-law who, at the time of the announcement, was still deputy education minister in the PAN government.

The alliance fell apart after a couple of months, reputedly because of resistance from certain of her old enemies within the PRI (some of whom possess reputations for wheeling and dealing that rival her own). Many observers expected La Maestra to return to the kind of back-room piecemeal electoral deals that had served her so well in the past. Others speculated that (twenty-three years after she took over the union, approaching seventy and with serious chronic health problems) she was finally on the downward slide. Even if this assessment were premature, La Maestra could not go on forever. With no friend or foe coming to mind as an obvious direct successor – certainly none of comparable stature – many predicted that her empire would fragment. That would create the risk of having many mini-Maestras, rather than just one Maestra, unless an acceleration of educational and political reforms altered the context sufficiently to create a space in which new kinds of more democratic leaders could thrive.

Elba Esther Gordillo's metamorphosis from corporatist loyalist to kingmaker in the new political era is mirrored by the transformation of commercial television; only, in the case of the networks, the protagonists are not wily political animals but hard-headed businessmen.

Sharing control of 96 per cent of Mexico's open channels, the country's two commercial TV networks exercise unparalleled influence over public opinion, which they use in both crude and subtle ways to further their corporate interests. The main news programmes of Televisa or TV Azteca often spark a guessing game over what lies behind a particular editorial decision that has no obvious relationship to the newsworthiness of the story, or even the quest for higher ratings. A politician shown in a glowing light raises questions of what favours he or she might be doing the company; another political figure vilified suggests a backlash; a third boycotted also implies vengeance of some kind. If there were several networks competing for different sectors of the market, such editorial machinations would probably be best understood within a framework of questionable journalistic ethics. The domination by just two networks in Mexico means they often appear more akin to political hostage taking.

Televisa is the bigger partner of the so-called *duopolio televisivo*. It holds around two-thirds of the open market, as well as the majority of cable and satellite companies. It is also the older partner and the one that has achieved the most dramatic transformation from regime mouthpiece to powerbroker.

The company's roots stretch back to the 1930s and the nation's first commercial radio network, founded by Emilio Azcárraga Vidaurreta, who went on to lead the development of television in Mexico. After he died in 1977, his son, Emilio Azcárraga Milmo, turned the company into a factory of formulaic *telenovelas* and low grade variety shows sold throughout the region and beyond.

Known as 'El Tigre', Azcárraga Milmo became the richest man in Latin America, at least in part thanks to the protection offered to his business by the PRI. He returned the favour with deliberately mindless entertainment (he once described it as 'television for the screwed') and resolutely pro-regime news coverage. There were periods of tension when PRI presidents sought more control, but the basics of the relationship never changed. When President Carlos Salinas asked business leaders to contribute $25 million each to the upcoming 1994 PRI election campaign, El Tigre reputedly announced that he had made so much money in the previous few years that he would like to give more. Apocryphal or not, the anecdote is consistent with his earlier well documented self-description as 'a soldier of the Institutional Revolutionary Party'.

The picture was far less rosy when the patriarch died in 1997, with the political transition well under way. TV Azteca, formed from the privatization of state-owned channels four years before, had started eating into Televisa's previously captive audience with a more aggressive, sensationalist style. Televisa's credibility was also under sustained attack from the growth of independent critical journalism. The years of coasting had left it ridden with debt and riddled with intra-board feuds.

The company passed into the hands of El Tigre's son, Emilio Azcárraga Jean, who lacked the macho pioneering image of his father and grandfather. This prompted some media observers to predict the network's demise, but the somewhat gormless-looking young business graduate successfully transformed Televisa into a much leaner commercial enterprise. He slashed the number of vice presidents from forty-six to just a handful; introduced more modern entertainment models, such as reality TV; and boosted credibility by instilling a neutral editorial line and attracting a good number of well-known critical voices into the company's stable of commentators.

Distancing Televisa's corporate ethos from the dying regime made sense in terms of competing commercially with other media outlets. It also enabled the company to take full advantage of the large amounts of public money that were being poured into the electoral campaigns of all political parties in the name of levelling the playing field. In an interview with the newspaper *La Jornada* shortly after taking over the company, Azcárraga Jean pronounced that 'Democracy is good business.' It is unlikely that he imagined then quite how good a business it would become.

Mexican media expert Fátima Fernández Christlieb says both Televisa and TV Azteca were preparing themselves for tighter regulations when Vicente Fox was elected president in 2000. The opposite happened, and instead the politicians began bending over backwards to ingratiate themselves with the networks.

The president led the way. Fox's election campaign had relied heavily on well-produced and well-targeted TV advertising, and, once he was installed in Los Pinos, his spokeswoman, future wife and presidential hopeful Marta Sahagún encouraged him to continue courting the media moguls. A 2002 presidential decree slashed the number of free minutes that TV and radio operators were required to offer the authorities for them to broadcast state messages. Although the networks treated the Fox government rather more sympathetically than the print media was inclined to do, they also began exerting pressure for more privileges. Sahagún later admitted that she had been somewhat naïve in her dealings with the networks; but she was far from the only one.

The pinnacle of network cheek came in the run-up to the 2006 presidential and legislative elections, when the outgoing legislature approved a new media law that included measures smoothing the way for the near routine renewal of concessions held by established broadcasters, as well as for their expansion into other services opened up by new technology. Congress – by then famous for being almost unable to agree on anything – approved the bill in just seven minutes. No deputy even questioned the motive behind the proposal to move directly to a vote on the law with no debate at all.

The ensuing scandal, fuelled primarily by the print media, proved highly embarrassing for many politicians and culminated with the Supreme Court ruling that the most controversial parts of the law were unconstitutional. The newly elected legislature, temporarily relieved of pressure to be on good terms with the *duopolio*, decided it was time to make a break for freedom. Legislators from all parties approved an electoral reform that banned paid-for electoral spots and forced the networks to broadcast party political promotions free of charge in election periods.

Both Televisa and TV Azteca hit back. Televisa singled out Senate leader Santiago Creel, President Fox's former interior minister, for special treatment, and made him persona non grata on its news programmes. Not only was he never mentioned, but on at least one occasion his image was digitally smudged out from a report.

Television news programmes on both networks also launched relentless campaigns to expose legislators as lazy, corrupt, inefficient and generally hopeless. There was no shortage of material to justify this, but the vehemence of the message was clearly fuelled by corporate pique. Both networks also went to great lengths to portray the Federal Electoral Institute, which had the task of implementing the reform, as bumbling and authoritarian. The on-screen assault exacerbated the already diminished credibility and authority of the Institute, which was charged with guaranteeing fairness in federal elections.

When, in 2009, I asked him about the campaigns, Ricardo Salinas Pliego, the owner of TV Azteca, painted them as a service to the country:

> These people are thieves, I mean thank goodness I have a lot of businesses and the economic impact of this is not significant, but the principle is. Mexicans are not used to somebody standing up to authority, not used to it. Usually everybody lowers their head and keeps going on the safe road. But we've been kind of a rebel in that respect and we do stand up.

The tension over the electoral reform slowly blew over, and the relationship between the *duopolio* and the political elite settled down. Little by little the networks began once again to accumulate favourable legislative and governmental decisions, albeit in a more piecemeal way. This was aided by a new strategy of persuading different political parties to include candidates with clear connections to the networks high up on their electoral lists. At least fifteen such deputies were elected in the mid-term congressional elections of 2009 – a group dubbed by the print media as the Telebancada, or the Television party. One of the new deputies was Ninfa Salinas Sada, the TV Azteca supremo's daughter.

The sense that the politicians had learned their place was reinforced when Senator Creel was finally invited back onto Televisa for an all-smiles rehabilitation interview in the spring of 2011. The senator no longer even moaned about the news blackout he had suffered in previous years. He could not afford to be boycotted again as he made a second doomed bid for the PAN presidential candidacy in the next election.

Televisa and TV Azteca do not always see eye to eye, and there have been periods of ferocious competition over ratings and incidences of industrial spying. But the networks can be relied upon to cooperate closely when it comes to keeping the political elite docile and protecting their fiefdoms from intruders, as when they saw off a project for a third network that President Felipe Calderón had appeared to be on the point of approving shortly after he took office in 2006. His support was widely perceived as another backlash against the strong-arm tactics used by television in the lead-up to the elections. This time the *duopolio* left the president alone, but set out to demolish the reputation of the pharmaceutical distribution companies owned by the Mexican businessman heading the project, Isaac Saba Raffoul. News report after news report accused his companies of making a fortune from the suffering of millions of Mexicans because of his monopolistic practices. Despite the obvious irony of the situation, Saba Raffoul's plans for a third network faded away.

The *duopolio*, and especially Televisa, meanwhile allegedly developed a new and particularly questionable model for making money out of democracy that amounts to political product placement. The network denies this, but there are plenty of grounds for suspicion, particularly with reference to the PRI's presidential hopeful, Enrique Peña Nieto.

Soon after he took office as governor of the State of Mexico in 2005, Peña Nieto reportedly negotiated a promotion deal with Televisa that amounted to a master plan to build up his popularity. It included slick 'infomercials' shown before, during and after flagship news programmes, as well as extensive and sympathetic coverage on those programmes, regardless of the newsworthiness of what he was actually doing. Peña Nieto was also a stable topic of the gossip programmes, thanks to his carefully managed romance with a Televisa *telenovela* star, which began when she was employed to add a little celebrity to his local promotion campaigns. The couple married in 2010. The blurring between entertainment and politics was epitomized by the infomercials surrounding his annual report in 2009, which took the form of faux interviews carried out by one of Televisa's iconic products, the singer Lucero.

As well as pushing a positive (if rather bland) general image, the narrative constructed around Peña Nieto was structured rather like a traditional *tele-novela*, and included the assumption of a happy ending. His was the story of a dashing and hard-working young governor, destined to become president, whose marriage to a celebrity served as a mid-series ratings booster.

Investigating media journalist Jenaro Villamil got hold of what he claimed was a copy of a contract between a PR company associated with Televisa and Peña Nieto's government, which covered just one year of his term and was worth around $74 million. The amount surpassed the entire declared income from political spots for all parties and candidates during the election year of 2006. Televisa dismissed the claims as ridiculous. A source who attended meetings between top executives in the company and a high-level representative of Peña Nieto confirmed the vaguer allegations of a promotional deal.

In the meantime, it has become clear that several other ambitious political leaders have spent a lot of money getting themselves on the network in ways that are not always explicit. A close aide to Peña Nieto told me in 2009 that negotiating coverage with the *duopolio* was common practice among all presidential hopefuls. His boss was being favoured at the time, he said, but his team was expecting this dominance to fade away as the elections approached and the TV bosses began playing the field of candidates. The governor, he insisted, would prefer more competition in the sector, but, given that he wanted to win the election, there was no choice but to play by TV's rules.

Many experts assume that after the 2012 elections the new president, whoever it is, and the newly elected legislature will once again try to use the window of opportunity provided by being temporarily free from campaigning to rein in the *duopolio*. Some are predicting another serious attempt to push through a third network.

The context also seems more propitious than last time around, given the explosion of new sources of information that are chipping away at the role of Televisa and TV Azteca as Mexico's dominant opinion formers. Internet news sites, social media and subscription TV channels that follow inde-pendent editorial lines have all also called into question the credibility of the networks, whose ratings have begun to fall.

But if the advantages of being on cosy terms with the networks are diminishing, the dangers of picking a battle remain a substantial deterrent, since dirt exposed tends to reach further than gloss applied. According to the networks' journalistic nemesis Villamil:

A good relationship with the *duopolio* can make you popular, but it won't get you elected; but what the politicians fear more are the skeletons in their cupboards that the networks have found out about and are keeping on file . . . The *duopolio*'s real power is extortion, not glorification.

Reining in the 'de facto powers' is one of the biggest challenges facing Mexico in the new political era. The fact that it rarely figures explicitly in political discourse underlines just how tricky the task is.

Of the main presidential hopefuls in the 2012 elections, only Andrés Manuel López Obrador has a history of regularly pointing to the issue, with his pledge to dethrone 'the mafia of power'. But as the campaign approached, the leftist explicitly toned down this side of his discourse. The PAN, meanwhile, is hampered in its ability even to address the problem by the fact that it has so obviously allowed the 'de facto powers' to grow on its watch. The PRI has arguably the most coherent argument that it can set limits on their excessive influence – albeit obliquely, through its claim to be the only party with the strength and discipline to bring coordination and effectiveness back to the presidency.

This is more than mere rhetoric. As the party consolidated its position as favourite to win the 2012 election, important elements within it seemed genuinely to envision the PRI's burgeoning comeback as a modernized version of the way its founding fathers brought order to the post-revolutionary chaos. They apparently included Enrique Peña Nieto himself: one of his top advisers told me that the presidential hopeful believed that bringing about the 'effective state' he promised would include the negotiation of deals with all the different power hubs in order to reinstate the discipline that has gone awry. At least in the case of the governors, the adviser admitted, this would require leaving them with a certain leeway for corruption in the name of governability, just as was the case in the glory days of the regime.

A more democratic vision of how to bring the 'de facto powers' to heel requires not just political will and political strength, but also a complete overhaul of a broken judicial system, so that it no longer allows the rich and powerful to get away with pretty much anything. The problem is not just that those supposed to apply the laws are vulnerable to pressure or financial persuasion. Nor does it stop at the myriad loop-holes always available to astute and expensive lawyers. The whole system is corroded with rules and practices that spiral into a black hole, in which establishing clear responsibilities, innocence or guilt become secondary issues.

The rule of law, as such, does not exist for anybody. The difference is that those with the necessary resources and contacts can take advantage of this, and those without them cannot. Few have more resources and contacts than the 'de facto powers' to ensure that regulation remains weak and malleable, influence-peddling routine and (if needs be) obvious criminality tolerated.

The brief detention of Jorge Hank Rhon in 2011 provided a textbook case. The former mayor of Tijuana is almost a parody of a dirty politician and businessman – from the allegation that he was the intellectual author of the murder of a local reporter in 1988 (for which his chief bodyguard was convicted), to his long-rumoured links to local drug-trafficking gangs. In decades of suspicion, his closest brush with the law had been a run-in with customs agents in 1995, when he was caught with a suitcase full of ivory tusks and waistcoats made from the skins of endangered ocelots.

The son of Carlos Hank González, a former patriarch of the Atlacomulco political dynasty in Mexico State who is said to have coined the phrase 'a politician who is poor is a poor politician', Hank Rhon had branched out to construct his own bastion in Tijuana. This centred on a race track he owned in the city, and extended to hotels, shopping malls and gaming houses across the country. Considered beyond control for years, Hank Rhon's arrest in the early hours of 4 June 2011 sent shockwaves throughout Mexico. President Felipe Calderón was accused of orchestrating the arrest in an effort to derail the PRI's campaign in the elections in Mexico State the following month.

The fifty-five-year-old father of nineteen was detained after soldiers entered his home inside a sprawling complex in Tijuana that stretches up a hill from the race track (and also includes a private bullring and zoo populated by exotic species, imported with dubious legality, including white Bengal tigers). The soldiers said they found eighty-eight firearms on the property, only ten of which were held with valid permits. Ballistics tests linked two of the seized guns to two separate murders in the city.

The case against Hank Rhon for the illegal possession of firearms nevertheless fell apart within a few days. A judge released him because there was little evidence to support the soldiers' claim that the raid had been prompted by the discovery of a crime in the act of commission; that would have removed the need for a warrant, which they did not have.

The Hank Rhon episode was deeply embarrassing to the government, both legally and politically. Going after symbols of 'de facto power' like the former mayor is obviously an essential part of creating a precedent that might deter their peers from assuming they are untouchable and of building a more democratic and equal society. But it is hard to see how this can be achieved if greater efforts are not made to establish a fair and functioning judicial system for everybody. If the federal authorities treated due process in such a cavalier fashion as to ignore the need for a watertight legal justification for searching private property in a sensitive case like this (involving a controversial public figure who could be assumed to have access to a competent and committed legal team), what hope can ordinary Mexicans have that their dealings with the law are fair?

In respect of the rule of law, Mexico is even more stunted than it is in political terms. The political transition established a system in which, for all its problems, the votes are usually counted correctly. When it comes to justice, however, such equivalently basic rights are regularly denied.

The first wave of public activism over Mexico's obviously warped justice system in the new political era focused almost entirely on the authorities' failure to track down and convict criminals, particularly kidnappers. Prior to the explosion and expansion of drug-war violence, kidnapping was the ultimate high-impact crime in Mexico. A poll carried out by Consulta Mitofsky in May 2009 concluded that 72 per cent of Mexican adults feared it would happen to them – only slightly less than the proportion concerned about being the victim of a robbery (even though they are hundreds of times more likely to suffer robbery). The horror and impunity associated with kidnapping turned those who suffered it into symbols of the innocent victim as well as of the state's failure to pursue the vast majority of crimes that affect a broader spectrum of society. A comprehensive study of crime rates in 2010, published by the National Institute of Statistics, concluded that only 12.3 per cent of crimes were even reported to the authorities, and that victims cited such reasons as 'waste of time' or 'lack of trust' for not seeking justice. Of the minority of cases that were taken to the police, less than two-thirds led to an investigation. These official government figures confirmed a number of earlier studies, such as the one carried out by Guillermo Zepeda and published in 2003 under the name *Crime Without Punishment*, which concluded that only 3.3 per cent of all crimes ever led to anybody being charged.

Public anger at the situation brought major anti-crime demonstrations in Mexico City in 2004 and 2008, attended by hundreds of thousands of people. They were led by a generation of activists who were mostly the relatives of kidnap victims. Some had responded to the failure of the system by doing their own investigation and virtually dumping the gang members on the doorstep of the relevant prosecution service. They set up organizations with names like Mexico United Against Crime, SOS Mexico, and Stop Kidnapping, and were treated with great sympathy in the press, on the radio and on television – in part because some of them belonged to the same elite social and business circles as the owners of the media outlets. While they called for an overhaul of the system, their primary concern was the right to justice for the victims of crime. They typically identified corruption and inefficiency as the main obstacles to this, and paid less attention to other distortions that infused investigations, arrests and trials with unfairness and a lack of transparency that encouraged the use of scapegoats. Even human rights activists admitted at the time that they avoided campaigning on the country's failure to respect the presumption of innocence for fear of being accused of protecting criminals.

Gradually, however, the faint whispers denouncing the incarceration of the blameless began to attract more attention. Lawyers from the Mexico City-based CIDE think tank were particularly active. They produced a short documentary in 2006, called *El Túnel* after the tunnels down which inmates walk from prison to the court buildings. They never actually enter the court, but look in on it from behind a barred window. The film emphasized that police officers are often given bonuses for bringing in detainees to be charged, and the way in which prisoners are sucked into a system that is weighted against them at every turn – unless they have money or influential friends. At the time the film was made, some 70 per cent of inmates in the capital's jails had been put behind bars for petty crimes that included the theft of a few dollars or even food. Over 40 per cent of prisoners were waiting out their trials in detention. Around 80 per cent of those convicted never saw the judge who decided their fate.

The revelation of the extent to which the poor, the vulnerable and (not infrequently) the innocent were targeted by a fundamentally unfair system helped persuade legislators to approve a fundamental reform of the judicial system in 2008. It is broadly similar to reforms that have already transformed other legal quagmires in the region – most famously in Chile – and mandates the replacement of document-based procedures (which regularly last for years) with oral hearings in open court. Instead of pondering their decisions in back rooms, usually without even seeing the defendants or the witnesses, under the rules of the reform judges are to reach their verdicts in a matter of weeks, after listening to the cases put forward by the prosecution and the defence. The new system removes the superior value that the other system automatically accords police evidence and confessions (even when there is a credible claim of torture). More weight is also supposed to be given to scientific evidence.

The enthusiasm with which experts greeted the 2008 reform, which was also vigorously supported by the international community, soon turned to concern at the slow pace of implementation, which is supposed to be completed by 2016. Part of the blame for this lies with the governors, who argue that they have not been provided with the necessary resources. It is also related to the priority that the federal government has given to contradictory measures passed at the same time, which increase arbitrary law enforcement powers within the context of the drug wars.

Moreover, the reform has faced credibility problems in the few states where oral trials are up and running – most notably in violence-torn Chihuahua, where the new system has acquired a reputation for almost routinely absolving obvious killers. Some civil society activists complain that it provides too many guarantees for defendants. Prosecutors accuse the judges of a box-ticking mentality that leads them to release defendants on the basis of irrelevant technicalities. In their turn, judges accuse the prosecutors of failing to put together good cases. Experts say the teething problems are rooted in the insufficient training of all those involved and in limited public understanding of what amounts to a cultural revolution in judicial practice – a result of the minimal public debate that accompanied the reform's approval.

The first sign that this, at least, was beginning to change came in 2009, when the case of a mild-mannered indigenous grandmother – sentenced to twenty-one years for kidnapping six highly trained and armed federal law enforcement agents – captured the country's imagination.

I met Jacinta Francisco Marcial in the spartan recreational area of the women's prison in Querétaro, the capital of the eponymous state, about three hours' drive north along a superhighway from Mexico City. It is also about three hours' drive in another direction, along considerably slower roads, to Santiago Mezquititlán, the small town largely populated by indigenous Hña hñu (also known as Otomí) where she had lived all her life.

Jacinta grew up in desperate poverty, wandering barefoot, selling chewing gum and pasturing sheep. Her adult life had been happier, raising her six children along with her husband Guillermo. At the time she was arrested, she had one son still in school. She was proud that the rest had all finished their basic studies and found jobs or formed families nearby, rather than migrating to the US like so many of the children of her neighbours. Satisfied with her life, Jacinta had never really paid much attention to the wider world beyond her community. She had never really had to, and there was little point in watching the news on TV because she did not understand Spanish.

When we talked, one spring morning in 2009, she had been in jail for nearly three years, tried and convicted (along with two other women) of holding to ransom six agents from the Federal Investigation Agency (AFI) and of whipping up the townspeople into a frenzied lynch mob. The forty-seven-year-old woman had learnt Spanish and was also learning to read and write.

'My life was my children and my husband. I didn't know anything about courts and about lawyers. I didn't know what a federal crime was, or state jurisdiction or really anything about all of this', she said. 'I didn't even know what the word "kidnapping" meant when I got here.'

The undisputed facts of the case are sparse. There is no doubt that a group of plain-clothes AFI agents arrived in Santiago in the early afternoon of 26 March 2006 and began confiscating pirate DVDs that were on sale in a part of the regular Sunday market that was some distance from the stall where Jacinta sold the popsicles her family made. Pirate DVDs are a ubiquitous part of the Mexican street-market landscape, catering to the vast majority of the population that cannot afford legal copies. The police usually turn a blind eye.

A heated argument erupted between the stallholders and the police that led to a bizarre agreement, by which the agents promised to pay half the value of the illegal merchandise they had seized – calculated at 70,000 pesos (around $7,000 at the time). The vendors would later claim that the police had been aggressive and reluctant to identify themselves. The stallholders got angry, they said, because they assumed the agents wanted to steal the discs in order to sell them on. They said the police accepted the deal for fear of getting into trouble as a result of their own transgressions.

One of the agents stayed behind to guarantee the agreement, while the others went for the money, at the same time as reinforcements gathered on the edge of town. Once the cash was handed over, the police signed an even odder written promise not to bother the townspeople again. Then they left.

The judicial case started when six agents lodged a complaint at the regional branch of the federal attorney general's office, claiming that they had gone to the market following an anonymous tip-off that a particular vendor was selling drugs, and had started confiscating DVDs only when they found the merchandise being hawked in flagrant violation of the law. They also said they had found a small packet of cocaine at one stall. After that, they claimed, they were taken hostage by the enraged townsfolk and only escaped with their lives after paying a ransom. The subsequent investigation by the authorities identified three women as the leaders of the mob. Two of them, Teresa González and Alberta Alcántara, had been involved in the argument. The third was Jacinta Francisco Marcial.

The women were arrested a few months after the raid. Jacinta says she was bundled into a vehicle by armed police when she came home from a meeting at the local church. She says that, as the agents drove her to the nearest city, they plied her with questions translated by her husband who came with her. They asked her what language she spoke, what religion she professed, and what party she had voted for in the last election. Only after much insistence did they tell her that she was being taken in for questioning over a tree that had been cut down illegally. Jacinta knew nothing about any tree, and so, secure in the knowledge that she was a hardworking and honest woman, she assumed the misunderstanding would soon be cleared up. She laughed at her own naivety as she retold the story, sitting on a concrete bench in the jail that was then her home, her long black plaits reaching all the way down the back of the regulation beige shirt that had replaced the traditional flowered blouse of her community.

Jacinta said that by the time she got to the police station the other two women named in the investigation were already there. All three were photographed by the authorities, who distributed the images to the local press. In the pictures, Jacinta, still in her traditional costume, is seen with her head down, fiddling with a rosary.

That same night they were taken to prison, and a court official took their statements. The other two women were bilingual, but Jacinta struggled to understand what was going on. There was no mention of her constitutionally enshrined right to an interpreter, and none was provided either then or at any stage of the ensuing trial. Confused and frightened, Jacinta signed what she was told to sign and was then taken to a cell and locked up. Eventually, one of her cellmates, who had seen her on the television news, explained that she was being charged with kidnapping, to which Jacinta says she reacted first with bewilderment and then with horror.

The trial began – a two-and-a-half-year nightmare of paper-pushing and po-faced court bureaucrats taking down and ratifying endless declarations from countless witnesses. There was nothing in all those sheets of paper – duly stamped, piled high and moved from desk to desk – that could even establish that there had ever been a hostage situation that day in the market.

The case file Jacinta's lawyers showed me includes evidence that the protestors inflicted minor damage on the agents' vehicles, but nothing more. There is much to support the townspeople's version that the agents were never harmed, were never relieved of their guns, and were never prevented from communicating with their superiors back in the city. And, although everyone agrees that one of them stayed in town to guarantee the compensation deal with the DVD vendors, there is no indication that he was disarmed or prevented from moving about freely as he waited for his colleagues to arrive with the cash.

The only physical evidence that Jacinta was anywhere near the scene is a photograph, in which her face is just visible peeping from the back of a passive-looking small group, observing what appears to be a rather undramatic argument. There are no sticks, stones or machetes in sight, let alone ropes or gasoline (as was claimed in the testimony of one of the agents).

The photograph accords with Jacinta's own version of events, in which she was nowhere near the pirate DVD stands when the agents swooped, and only stopped to have a brief look at the rumpus on her way back to her stall, after buying some medication from the local chemist (who also confirmed her story): 'My father and stepmother couldn't read, like me, and they didn't have any education either, but they taught me that taking other people's things was wrong. They didn't say it was a crime, they said it was a big sin. I never ever imagined that I would be in jail convicted of such a crime because I was a bit nosey on that day.'

At no point in the trial did Jacinta ever see the judge who would eventually convict her just before Christmas 2008. Jacinta was informed of the verdict by a court clerk, who initially resisted telling her because he did not want her to be upset. She says she spent the next few weeks unable to get out of bed, hiding under her blanket at night so that her sobs did not disturb her cellmates.

Jacinta's story is a surreal tale of a woman ripped away from her family and her community, framed for a crime that probably never occurred and that (even if it had) she could not have committed, and then funnelled into a structure that silenced her at almost every turn. But it also contains signs of how the relationship between citizens and state is beginning to change, and hope that this tendency can be speeded up.

At the time of the raid on Santiago Mezquititlán, the AFI was the face of federal power around the country, and so – whatever the real motive was for the DVD raid – it is unlikely that the Agency was prepared to be challenged. The humiliation would have been compounded by the fact that this was a town without a rebellious tradition. It is tempting to see the legal persecution that followed as an effort to teach an unexpectedly uppity town a lesson.

But why target Jacinta? The other two women had at least been involved in the argument over the discs, but she had had nothing to do with even that. Perhaps in such a Kafkaesque system the dynamics triggered within it take on a near arbitrary life of their own as it seeks out a powerless scapegoat. If so, there was a miscalculation. Meek as she seemed, Jacinta had unexpected resources to draw on, beginning with her own tenacious family.

When she was first arrested, the family went to see a lawyer in Querétaro who took money they could not afford and did almost nothing. Then they were let down by a local indigenous activist group that let the case drop, forcing them to rely on the public defender provided by the court, who did no more. But they did not give up. The eldest daughter, a bilingual teacher, eventually found her way to an experienced and combative human rights group in the capital called the Centro Pro Juárez. Here was a woman who might dress in the same traditional costume as her mother, but she had left behind the downtrodden humility of the older generation and was determined to take the democratic discourse of the last decade at its word.

While in jail, Jacinta also went through her own transformation, slowly shaking off the passivity with which she had originally accepted the constant comments from other prisoners of 'dirty Indian', and the way the prison guards regularly ordered her to clean the toilets. As she learned to demand respect inside the jail, so her determination grew to struggle against the conviction, rather than succumb to the fatalism she had grown up with:

> I still cry from sadness and desperation, but sometimes I cry with anger, too. And not just for me, because I know that I am not the only one. I think that in prisons about half the people are guilty and half are not. But lots don't have any hope left because they are frightened or they don't know where to go for help, or because their family doesn't support them. I am very lucky.

The ingredient that really made the difference, however, was the way in which the mainstream media took up the case and how it resonated in public opinion to a degree that took her lawyers completely by surprise. Big-name interviewers tripped over one another to give voice to the tiny, open-faced and quietly dignified indigenous grandmother, whom a judge had convicted for terrifying the living daylights out of some of the hardest police officers in the country. Her case even featured on the main TV networks, which milked the 'schmaltz factor', showing her walking through the prison in slow motion, mood music playing in the background.

The media pressure first led the judicial authorities to order the judge who had convicted her to review the evidence. When the campaigns continued, and when Amnesty International made her a prisoner of conscience in August 2009, the prosecutors suddenly discovered 'reasonable doubt' in the case. Two weeks later her release triggered a media circus. Jacinta had gone to prison an unknown, monolingual, indigenous matron. She emerged a suffering archetype of modern Mexico. She then returned to her home and her popsicle stall in the market, where pirate DVDs were still on sale.

While Jacinta's case broke new ground, it was a documentary called *Presunto Culpable* (*Presumed Guilty*) that really laid the foundations for a broader awareness of how loaded the judicial dice are against ordinary people. The film follows the case of a young, articulate and likeable computer software vendor from Mexico City who was twice convicted of a murder he obviously did not commit.

Antonio Zúñiga Rodríguez was picked up by Mexico City police in December 2005 and, six months later, was sentenced to twenty years for killing a man he had never seen. The prosecution based its case on a single eyewitness, the teenage cousin of the victim. Zúñiga had a long list of witnesses willing to testify that he was elsewhere at the time of the murder, and an initial test for traces of gunpowder had proved negative.

Two committed young lawyers from the CIDE think tank, who had also made the earlier documentary *El Túnel*, got involved and discovered that Zúñiga's public defender had falsified his credentials. This enabled them to secure a retrial. They then persuaded one of the best criminal lawyers in the country to take the case pro bono, and got permission to film the proceedings.

The film they made includes the part of the trial when Zúñiga is allowed to cross-examine the prosecution's only witness, which he does with great style, getting the witness to admit that he never saw him fire a gun. At another point he asks the prosecutor why she is continuing with the charge, to which she responds with a rather sheepish shrug, mumbling 'it's my job'. The police officer who arrested Zúñiga is seen shooting a furious stare at the prisoner through the bars separating him from the court. 'There has to be a reason why you are there', he says.

The retrial judge nevertheless again sentenced Zúñiga to twenty years. The conviction was eventually overturned in 2008, after the campaigning lawyers turned filmmakers persuaded the three judges hearing an appeal they had lodged to watch the videos of the retrial.

Zúñiga commented, around the time *Presumed Guilty* was released in February 2011, that it took him a good while to understand that he was a victim of miscarriage of justice. Initially, he said, he thought of his detention as retribution for bad things he had done in his life, even if he was not guilty of the murder of which he was accused. 'The police needed somebody who was guilty, and I was passing by', he said. 'What happened to me was partly my fault because I didn't know my rights.'

Presumed Guilty became one of the most viewed Mexican films ever made, beating many of the Oscar-season releases that were in cinemas at the same time. Its phenomenal success was aided by a clumsy and doomed attempt by a judge to ban it at the same time as the film took the streets by storm. One pirate DVD vendor called Alberto told me he was selling seventy copies a day; his second-biggest hit – *The King's Speech* – was selling the same number a week. 'I can't remember anything like this', he said. 'Perhaps *Spiderman 3*, but I'm not even sure about that.'

The film resonated so deeply with the Mexican public not just because it tapped into latent public consciousness about the broken judicial system, but also because it spoke to a more general distrust of all authorities. This lack of trust was a problem not just for the state, but also for almost all institutions, including some that had traditionally hovered somewhat above the fray – such as the Catholic Church.

CHAPTER 4

Lapsed Catholics

FROM the millions of pilgrims who visit the Virgin of Guadalupe every year, to the number of footballers who cross themselves before starting a match, the Catholic Church's dominance of Mexican religiosity can seem as solid as the stone churches that dot the urban and rural landscape. A closer look reveals cracks and structural weaknesses, which the hierarchy appears to have neither the will nor the means to repair.

Nearly five centuries after the Spanish conquest of the region, on paper the proportion of Mexican Catholics remains overwhelming. In the 2010 census they accounted for around 83 per cent of Mexico's population of 112 million, giving the country the second-biggest Catholic population in the world, after Brazil. Impressive though this might be, the figure has dropped 4 percentage points in the last decade – and 14 percentage points since 1970 (more than half a lifetime for most people, but a blink of an eye in the history of the Church).

Mexican Catholicism is not only slowly fading at the national level, but it is also breaking up along sociocultural, economic, ethnic and territorial lines. While 94 per cent defined themselves as Catholic in the central state of Guanajuato (in the heart of the religious heartland, Bajío region), in the southern state of Chiapas the figure was only 58 per cent.

The spiritual exodus in Chiapas dovetails with the growing appeal of a long list of Protestant and Evangelical churches that in the last few decades have made significant inroads among the poor, the least educated and the darker skinned. This has triggered further fragmentation and some inter-religious conflicts with converts, expelled from their villages and forced to form new non-Catholic settlements elsewhere.

The Church tends to blame the defection of its flock on a dramatic dearth of priests, which contrasts with the armies of Evangelical ministers ever on call. In 2008, Catholic clergy made up less than a third of the 63,518 religious ministers registered with the interior ministry, and many Evangelical pastors do not even bother to formalize their position.

Mexican Catholic orthodoxy also regularly bemoans the global march of secularism. The proportion of the population professing no religion at all has risen steadily, from 1.6 per cent in 1970 to 3.5 per cent in 2000 and 4.5 per cent in 2010. There may also be some underreporting. The census worker who came to my house tried to persuade a self-professed agnostic living there that he should be noted down as Catholic because he had 'pasado por la pila', i.e. he had been baptized.

The figures for non-believers also ignore how many Catholics now put the demands of modern life above the teachings of the Pope. Mexico City was 82 per cent Catholic in the last census, and yet the population had been notably unfazed by the local authority's legalization of abortion three years before. Perhaps the most noteworthy thing of all is how many people do not even necessarily give it a role in their lifecycle rituals. According to an analysis of the census figures by Javier Flores, only around half of Mexican home-sharing couples were married in church, and the bulk of those are from older generations.

But while the dynamism of many Evangelical churches, particularly the Pentecostals, and the secularizing influence of the contemporary world are important factors in the waning of Catholic dominance in Mexico, they do not explain it all. There are also indirect links to the demise of one-party hegemony, not least the damage caused to the Church's claim to the moral high ground by the rise of a more critical press, and the bishops' inadequate response to the scandals it has uncovered.

The global assault on ecclesiastical probity through sexual abuse scandals has had different effects in different countries. While the US Church was badly shaken by the sheer number of cases aired and taken to court, and by the large compensation payments awarded, in Mexico, the focus has been on the personalities involved and the hierarchy's efforts to shield them from prosecution.

As a magnetic young seminarian in the Bajío, Marcial Maciel Degollado founded the Legión de Cristo (Legion of Christ) in 1941. He went on to direct the order's growth over the following decades into one of the most important in the Church, with schools, universities and seminaries in twenty-two countries.

Based in Rome, Maciel was a particular favourite of Pope John Paul II, who valued his staunch anti-communism, unswerving personal loyalty and his order's continued ability to produce priests just as the current recruitment crisis was really kicking in. In Mexico, the *Legionarios* established close ties with some of the country's richest and most powerful families, who sent their children to the order's exclusive schools, contributed to its charities and were proud to have Maciel personally officiate at their marriages, baptisms and funerals.

The stories of abuse began to surface in the mid-1990s, when a group of ageing former seminarians went public about their ordeals. These had mostly taken place while they studied under Maciel in Spain and Italy in the 1940s and 1950s. The bishops closed ranks around him, and the order's enthusiasts in big business sought to keep the story out of the media. The small Canal 40 was almost closed down by the advertising boycott that followed its decision to give victims a chance to air their grievances in 1997.

After a lull of a few years, the scandal became impossible to contain, as more media outlets took it up in the wake of the political transition in 2000. The Legión de Cristo's clumsy attempts to sully the reputations of the victims as money-grabbing opportunists with dark, hidden agendas were particularly hard to sustain. The most prominent were eminently respectable academics, well into their sixties, who displayed no interest in financial compensation. Instead they insisted on moral contrition from the Church, to which several had dedicated most of their lives. After decades writing letters that got no response, they had filed a case in Latin under canonical law in 1998. For years it got nowhere and Maciel was still revered within his own order and spoken of as a candidate for future sainthood in Rome.

The situation changed with the arrival of Pope Benedict XVI in 2005 and his decision to make cleaning up the Church's reputation one of his top priorities. Within a year, the Vatican called on Maciel to renounce public ministry and to live the rest of his life in 'prayer and penance', although there was no suggestion he would be tried. There was no explicit mention of the abuse allegations, but nobody doubted that they were the reason for his star falling so dramatically. He died in disgrace in Houston in 2008 at the age of eighty-seven.

The controversy trickled on without him and fresh allegations emerged. These included stories that he had abused the two children he had with a woman with whom he had maintained a relationship under a false identity. The original victims also kept pushing for a full apology and an investigation of the networks of complicity that had protected him for so long. They claimed that these had had the knock-on effect of establishing a culture of impunity within the order that encouraged further abuse by (and of) new generations in Legión institutions.

In 2010, the Vatican finally issued a statement condemning Maciel as 'immoral' and appointing a special delegate to lead the order and to review its founding documents. It talked of a 'system of power' created by Maciel and designed to hide 'true crimes' and a private life 'without scruples or authentic religious sentiment'. The top Mexican businessmen who had once publicly defended him turned to avoiding questions and down-playing their former enthusiasm.

Dramatic as it was, the Maciel case did not directly implicate important figures within the contemporary Mexican hierarchy, since the abuse had mostly taken place outside the country. A separate scandal, which broke in 2006 and touched Cardinal Norberto Rivera Carrera, brought the issue closer to home.

The archbishop of Mexico City and the highest-profile religious leader in the country at the time suddenly found himself accused of helping to cover up for Father Nicolás Aguilar Rivera, who had allegedly sexually assaulted dozens of boys in different Mexican parishes in the 1980s and 1990s. Cardinal Rivera arranged for the priest's transfer to California in 1987, when he was already being pursued by complaints from his parish-ioners. He was back in Mexico in less than a year, avoiding US warrants for nineteen felony counts of committing lewd acts on children. Even so he was still given churches to run.

The case came to light when a young man called Joaquín Aguilar Méndez, one of the priest's more recent alleged victims, gave up on his efforts to seek justice in Mexico and teamed up with campaigning US lawyers. They filed charges in a Los Angeles court, alleging that Cardinal Rivera's facilitation of the priest's move to the US was motivated by the desire to calm the waters back home, and consequently contributed to his ability to continue committing crimes.

The Los Angeles court ruled in 2007 that it did not have jurisdiction to try the cardinal, but the efforts of Rivera's media relations team to spin the news as a vindicating absolution in the face of false accusations hurled by 'enemies of the Church' were only partially successful. The case faded from the news, but not before leaving the impression that clergy at all levels, like politicians and union leaders, could do almost anything they liked without fear of ending up in court. The hierarchy did promise to stamp out abuse in the Church, but its public actions were largely limited to periodic rhetorical condemnations.

The Church's image also suffered from evidence of a widespread association with drug traffickers and half-hearted efforts to deal with the problem. The first high-profile case dates back to 1994, when Papal Nuncio Girolamo Prigione confirmed reports leaked to the press that he had received Tijuana cartel bosses Benjamín and Ramón Arellano Félix in his residence in Mexico City. He said they wanted him to pass on a letter to the pope, distancing them from the death of Cardinal Juan Jesús Posadas Ocampo, killed during a gun battle in an airport car park the year before. The nuncio said he had met the *capos* at the request of a Tijuana priest called Gerardo Montaño. Montaño had long ministered to the family and admitted to reporters that he had accepted money from them to refurbish his church. He claimed he had never asked where it came from. The scandal over, the case faded from view and Father Montaño continued to work as a priest until his death in 2010.

Latent accusations that such practices were common bubbled to the surface again in 2005, after Pope Benedict XVI expressed concern about drug money in the Mexican Church. The reaction of the then head of the Episcopal Conference made it clear that many in the Mexican Church were not similarly worried: 'When Mary Magdalene washed the Lord's feet in very expensive perfume, Jesus didn't investigate. He didn't say "where did you buy that perfume?". He didn't say "Where did the money come from?" No. He simply received the homage', said Bishop Ramón Godínez Flores. 'There is no reason to burn money just because its origin is evil. You have to transform it. All money can be transformed, just as corrupted people can be transformed.'

In subsequent years the bishops learned to be more circumspect. They took to issuing periodic statements abhorring the acceptance of dirty donations, but there was little evidence of an active clean up.

In 2010, Mexican newspapers published a picture of a bronze plaque on the side of a newly remodelled church in the deprived neighbourhood of Tezontle on the outskirts of Pachuca, the capital of the central state of Hidalgo. The plaque thanked Heriberto Lazcano Lazcano for the donation that had made the work possible. At the time, Lazcano, a native of Hidalgo, was the leader of the notoriously bloody Zetas drug cartel.

Both the local diocese and the federal attorney general's office sprang into damage-limitation mode and announced that they would open investigations into the donation. A year later, neither investigation had borne public fruit.

I have seen no quantitative or qualitative study of the impact such scandals have had on ordinary Mexican Catholics, but it can hardly have boosted the Church's moral standing in their eyes. The hierarchy, however, does not seem all that bothered.

Sitting in sparkling new offices decorated with impeccable modernist taste, Father Hugo Valdemar Romero, the spokesman for the Mexico City archdiocese, chuckled at the memory of how the bishops and cardinals initially mishandled the new scrutiny that came with the political transition. 'They went into crisis. They got frightened. They were used to being nearly invisible, except when they were treated with great respect', he said. He was confident that the scandals would diminish now that a new generation of media-savvy clergy like himself had taken the reins of public relations but stressed they would not disappear. They were, he explained, an unfortunate but inevitable side effect of the Church's successful efforts to increase its political influence in the context of the weakening of the centralized state.

> The truth is that the Church today has more opportunities than ever to have its opinion heard and to even enter into the political dynamic. The Church has come out of the shadows and all of a sudden, like the presidency and the army, it is open to attack. This is the price to be paid.

The long history of tight restrictions placed on the Mexican Catholic Church's political influence is atypical for Latin America. Liberal leaders won wars against their conservative enemies all over the region in the mid-nineteenth century, and immediately set about separating Church and state, and confiscating ecclesiastical property. But while conservative victories a few years or decades down the line would at least partially turn the tables in most other countries, in Mexico the liberal dominance was absolute. Mexico developed a jealously guarded secular state tradition that at times lay uneasily with the intense religiosity of the culture.

When the victors in the 1910 Revolution tightened the screws on organized religion still further, they triggered an armed uprising of radical Catholics in the Bajío heartland. The Cristero rebellion between 1926 and 1929 was brutally quashed by government forces – but it also instilled in the political powers-that-be the realization that the Church could not be completely subjugated without a backlash.

The 1917 constitution remained blatantly anti-clerical, but the relevant laws were left largely unapplied. They remained on the books primarily as a reminder of what could happen if the hierarchy got too bold. In practice, the regime reached an accommodation with the episcopacy that started off as mutual tolerance, but soon developed into complicity, giving the Church a corporatist aura. Bishops were allowed a certain limited autonomy and social privileges, in exchange for supporting the regime, or at least refraining from open criticism. This ensured that while state-promoted family planning was anathema in many Latin American countries, in Mexico it was easily implemented and slashed the number of children per woman of fertile age fell from 6.8 in 1970 to 2.8 in 2000. The PRI could also often rely on local priests to help control signs of political dissidence.

The rolling back of formal anti-clericalism began in the late 1980s, in tandem with the initial stages of the country's transition to democracy. The weakening of the PRI's monopoly on power opened the possibility for a renegotiation of the old modus vivendi to make it more favourable for the Church. The bishops did this by lobbying within the PRI, but also by accompanying the growing influence of the PAN, founded in 1939 as a peaceful offshoot of the Cristero rebellion. The gathering momentum behind a more general human rights discourse also strengthened the case for greater religious freedom.

The pressure eventually led to constitutional changes promoted by President Carlos Salinas in 1992 that removed most of the strongest anti-church provisions. The reforms recognized church organizations of all kinds, removed the prohibition on the public celebration of services, and allowed the clergy to vote. Restrictions remaining included the ban on running for elected office, intervening in electoral politics and owning media outlets. The Salinas reforms, which also led to the establishment of formal diplomatic relations with the Holy See, constituted a watershed in Church–state relations. Vicente Fox's victory for the PAN in the 2000 elections and the consolidation of political pluralism marked another.

Not only had Fox openly sought ecclesiastical support during his election campaign, but he paraded his Catholic faith in a way no other modern Mexican president had ever done, arguing that it was time to bury the hypocrisy of the old regime, in which Catholic presidents were forced to hide their beliefs. Fox seemed to revel in the controversy he caused when he visited the Basilica of the Virgin of Guadalupe on his way to his inauguration ceremony in Congress. Later that same day, he accepted a crucifix from one of his daughters on the stage of the National Auditorium, shortly before swearing in his cabinet. He chose a deeply devout labour minister, who exhorted union leaders to pray to the Virgin, and was said to have given key posts in his government to members of a secretive political organization of right-wing conservative Catholics, known as El Yunque (The Anvil). He even kissed the papal ring when he welcomed John Paul II to Mexico in 2002.

Fox's explicit religiosity was not always advantageous for the Church, as it was often also tinged with controversy, particularly in his personal life. The president married his spokeswoman, Marta Sahagún, while in office and before either of their original church marriages had been annulled by the Vatican. And while Mexican bishops close to the family helped lobby these through a few years later, confidential documents obtained by the investigative online site Reporte Indigo revealed that Fox's annulment included an embarrassing reference to a personality disorder.

As president, Fox had also baulked when his openness encouraged the Church to launch a clumsy direct assault on the secular state in 2002, attempting to get the government to ban a film about a wayward priest. *The Crime of Father Amaro* starred the rising Mexican film actor Gael García Bernal as a young cleric who persuades his pregnant schoolgirl lover to have the back-street abortion which kills her. The couple are shown having sex under a cloak emblazoned with the image of the Virgin of Guadalupe, and Father Amaro's superior (who is also having an affair with the girl's mother) is seen trying to cover up the scandal and taking money from drug traffickers.

'Freedom of expression has its limits, which is the right not to be attacked for our convictions, and the immense majority of the Mexican people are Catholic', said Bishop José Guadalupe Martín Rábago, the then head of the Conference. Outrage at the failed attempt to force the government into censorship turned a rather mediocre melodrama into the most successful Mexican film ever and proved that the lay state tradition was well rooted. The 5.2 million people who saw the film in cinemas set a record that remained unbroken a decade later.

Incidents like these persuaded the Church that it needed to pick its battles more carefully and to wage them with more subtlety and patience. Over the years, it has acquired a better understanding of how to play the new fragmented political environment, which requires new degrees of tolerance in some areas, but also provides fresh opportunities to apply behind-the-scenes pressure in others.

A more measured approach was also encouraged by the election of Felipe Calderón. Another *Panista*, Calderón is rather less brazen about his Catholicism than his predecessor, but is both closer to the conventional Catholic ideal, and has provided more effective, if more discreet, support for the hierarchy's socially conservative agenda. Throughout the Calderón *sexenio* this has focused on abortion.

Abortion had long epitomized the habit of sweeping controversy under the carpet that had characterized Church–state relations in the PRI regime. It falls under individual state jurisdiction, and under the PRI all Mexican states permitted it in restricted situations, primarily when pregnancy was a result of rape or represented a threat to the mother's life. The laws, however, were largely ignored, and almost nobody received legal terminations. The authorities preferred to turn a blind eye to the practice in upmarket clinics and insalubrious back streets alike, while the Church contented itself with nominal illegality.

The case of Lucila, a twelve-year-old with cognitive disabilities who fell pregnant after being raped by her father in 2001, exemplified the absurdity of the situation. When I visited her in the shack where she lived with her mother and siblings, in the northern city of Los Mochis, she giggled shyly when I asked her about the changes to her body. 'I am getting fatter because I am eating too much', she said.

Her mother, who worked as a maid, had sought help from state sector doctors, who told her they would not perform an abortion without an order to do so from the prosecutor's office. The prosecutor's office told her they would not determine the legality of any termination until after it was performed.

Such cases prompted feminists around the country to begin campaigning to turn legal abortions into a reality. At the time, the most visible face of the feminist movement, Marta Lamas Encabo, told me that the broader aim was to open the debate, but that directly calling for abortion on demand risked triggering a popular backlash.

Things moved quickly. In 2007, Mexico City's left-controlled legislative assembly approved reforms to permit all adult women free first-trimester terminations in city health facilities with no questions asked. Minors received the same treatment if they had the permission of their parents. The ease with which the legalization was proposed, approved and implemented surprised many and demonstrated how secular the capital had become, and how distinct it was from the rest of Mexico. A poll carried out by Parametría in Mexico City, shortly before the legislation was passed, found that in the capital 44 per cent of people supported the reform and 38 per cent opposed it; in the rest of the country 58 per cent opposed it and only 23 per cent approved.

Opposition everywhere, however, was rather soft. Only small groups of eternal anti-abortion diehards responded to church calls for mobilization against the reform when it was being debated extensively in the press.

The whole process was a rare example of Mexican democracy working as it was supposed to – from the use of the left's majority in the local legislature, to the openness of the discussion in the press that accompanied it, and the freedom that opponents had to express their discontent. This was rounded off by a Supreme Court ruling rejecting the federal government's attempt to get the legislation declared unconstitutional.

But while the Church decided it had no choice but to cut its losses and accept the new situation in the capital, it turned its attention to generating a countermovement elsewhere. Provincial bishops began a discreet, but intense, effort to get state-level politicians to criminalize all voluntary abortions. They had a remarkable degree of success. One by one, local legislatures passed local-level constitutional reforms enshrining the 'right to life' from conception until a natural death. By the end of 2009, the clause had been included in the constitutions of seventeen of Mexico's thirty-two states. By 2010, cases were coming to light of women imprisoned (often on a charge of infanticide) after alleged abortions, some of which at least appear to have been simple miscarriages.

The surreptitiousness of the pro-life reforms contrasted dramatically with the openness that characterized the liberalization of abortion in Mexico City. The strategy of whipping the bills through with very limited public debate seemed designed to avoid raising secular hackles too directly. The discretion also encouraged the PRI to support the reforms, casting to the wind those decades during which it had set itself up as the embodiment of the lay state.

Pollsters point out that abortion has never been a major electoral issue in Mexico, and few analysts expect it to become one any time soon. The direct electoral advantages of supporting the provincial crackdown were consequently unclear. Rather, the politicians who voted for it seemed intent on obliquely currying favour with religious leaders who might, in the future, help nudge their congregations to vote for them.

The success of the anti-abortion reforms around the country consolidated the Church's position as a back-room political player of considerable influence. Its new status as a 'de facto power' was confirmed by signs that political leaders were stepping up their efforts to court the approval of the Church's hierarchy in the run-up to the 2012 presidential election.

President Calderón's decision to attend the beatification of John Paul II in Rome in summer 2011 was interpreted by some as a sign that he was trying to make up for the irritation he had caused by his work with Evangelical churches active in drug-addiction treatment programmes. PAN congressional leader and presidential hopeful Josefina Vázquez Mota, who had similarly annoyed the hierarchy during an earlier stint as education minister, facilitated the gift of eighty-four iPads to the Episcopal Conference, in the name of a charity supposed to assist elderly Catholics living in poverty.

While he was governor of the State of Mexico, The PRI's candidate, Enrique Peña Nieto, had gone to particular lengths to be on good terms with as many bishops as possible. He was particularly associated with Onésimo Cepeda Silva, the bishop of Ecatepec, with whom he regularly played golf.

Cepeda is one of the most colourful figures in the Church. A former stockbroker and banker with ties to some of the richest families in Mexico, he was ordained as a priest in 1970 and became a bishop in 1995. In 2009, he was formally accused of tricking a rich old lady out of her impressive collection of art works shortly before she died. The collection included paintings and lithographs by Mexican stalwarts Diego Rivera and Frida Kahlo, as well as works by Marc Chagall, Francisco de Goya, Amedeo Modigliani and more. The case – which was dismissed on technicalities in the summer of 2011 – did not prevent the bishop from holding his traditional spring birthday party that year. On that particular occasion, the guest list included the federal health minister and several deputies. Peña Nieto was seated at the bishop's table, along with Carlos Slim, the world's wealthiest man.

Only the left – and not all of that – seemed prepared to get into extended run-ins with the Church. Mexico City Mayor Marcelo Ebrard Casaubón followed up his support for abortion on demand with the promotion of new legislation allowing same-sex marriages, and got into a legal spat with a cardinal who accused him of taking bribes.

The Mexican Church's decision to use its new influence to push an extreme, socially conservative agenda fits with global trends emanating from the Vatican, but risks distancing the hierarchy from its flock. The Mexican public tends towards social conservatism, but not in a particularly aggressive way. This is, in part, a legacy of the long tradition of the separation of Church and state, but it also reflects the fact that more pressing problems, such as poverty and insecurity, tend to take precedence in public opinion. The bishops make regular pronouncements on these and other, more general, topics; but their actions to back the rhetoric pale in comparison to the energy they displayed in their back-room moral crusade against abortion.

On one visit to the Basilica in 2010, I talked to about a dozen female pilgrims from various parts of the country. They were all, in principle, against abortion but I found none who thought women who aborted should be put in prison, as the church-sponsored reforms around the country directed. The majority said abortion was a matter for each individual and her conscience, and they all thought it should be allowed in cases of rape. While hardly scientific, this did suggest that the religious leadership was out of touch with many active Catholics.

A small but committed minority of nuns, priests and the occasional bishop seek a much greater engagement with the day-to-day struggles of their flock; but these are the exception that proves the rule, rather than a challenge to that rule. Most are survivors of the liberation theology movement that grew out of the Second Vatican Council and that flourished in Latin America in the 1970s, the 1980s and part of the 1990s. The movement focused on the poor, and was less concerned about their individual sins than about the immorality of the oppressive political, economic and social contexts in which they lived.

Compared to other countries in the region, liberation theology's influence in Mexico has always been limited, but it has produced some prominent figureheads. The most famous was Samuel Ruiz García, bishop of San Cristóbal de las Casas in Chiapas from 1959 to 2000. Bishop Ruiz's insistence on putting social justice at the centre of his teachings earned him many admirers on the left and many enemies on the right. By the time he retired, the movement had become distinctly marginal. Bishop Raúl Vera López, who had been Ruiz's adjunct in Chiapas but was moved to the northern diocese of Saltillo, emerged as a powerful anti-establishment voice in the new century. He began speaking out against the government strategy in the drug wars and accusing it of failing to protect tens of thousands of Central American migrants victimized by the traffickers and the authorities as they travelled through Mexico towards the US. Outspoken as he often is, even Vera has shied away from criticizing the hierarchy. Vera and clergy like him do not suffer the pressures Ruiz was under to tone things down; but nor are they encouraged. 'Those of us in the Church who do this kind of work are a small minority, and there seem to be fewer of us all the time,' said Father Oscar Enríquez Pérez, referring to his work with the victims of violence in Ciudad Juárez and activism against the Calderón government's drug-war strategy. 'Most of the bishops, they don't understand things in the same way; they don't get involved with the real causes of the pain, with the abuses of the army or anything like that. They don't support us, but they don't ask us to stop, either.'

It seems logical to assume that the hierarchy's general lack of interest in generating the sense that it understands the needs of the faithful has added to the scandals and has directly contributed to fading public confidence. Although Mexicans still trust the Church more than almost any other institution, good will is flagging considerably faster than the rate of formal defections to other denominations would suggest.

Opinion polls indicate that, although 70–80 per cent of Mexicans still say they trust 'the Church' a bit or a lot, more specific questions reveal that they do not feel the same about its leaders. While a Demotecnia tracking poll found that in 2007 50 per cent considered the cardinals and bishops to be doing 'a good job', by 2011 approval had fallen to 34 per cent.

The hierarchy, it appears, is widely perceived as just another self-interested elite that has little or no moral authority. This gulf between Catholic leaders and their nominal congregations has created a propitious context for the rapid expansion of several cults that contradict some of the Church's most basic doctrines. It allows concerns about these transgressions that are expressed within the clergy to be relegated by followers to the status of insignificant background grumbling.

The fast-growing and, in some ways, deeply disturbing cult of the Santa Muerte or Saint Death is the most extreme example of this phenomenon.

The almost two-metre Santa Muerte that stands in a pavement-facing glass case set into a ground-floor apartment in a low-income housing estate on Alfarería Street in Mexico City wears a fancy frock and an abundant black wig over her skeletal frame. Hundreds of candles and offerings lie at her feet.

When a formidable local housewife called Enriqueta Romero (otherwise known as Doña Queta) set up the shrine in 2001, only a few dozen people attended the monthly 'mass' she began organizing on the first night of every month in her image's honour. Doña Queta, like all Santa Muerte devotees I have ever talked to, considers herself a Catholic.

The first time I went to the ceremony, in 2004, the crowd filled half a block. Five years later, on a night when Mexico was playing a key World Cup qualifying match, it had become a tightly packed throng that extended a full two blocks.

On that occasion I got a little lost on the way through the labyrinthine back streets of Tepito, the capital's infamous and celebrated *Barrio Bravo*, where Alfarería Street lies. During the day, the area is filled with a vast street market, and at midnight it buzzes with mopeds, which the police say are central to drug distribution. But at this hour, just after dark, it was empty – aside from the piles of rubbish rustling in a warm spring breeze. There was an air of dubious legality. It felt rather like a rite of passage into another world.

One of the most striking things about this – and many other – Santa Muerte shrines is that almost all believers carry their own personal images of the skeletal power (also known as La Niña Blanca, La Flaca or La Santíssima – 'The White Girl', 'The Skinny Girl' or 'The Über Saint'). Many are dressed in long, silky, gaudy gowns, adorned with cascades of cheap jewellery. A few sport white bridal veils, crowns and tiaras. On this particular night, two young men stood beside an adult-sized, translucent, purple Santa Muerte sitting on a great throne of black skulls and wielding a sword. Another held an equally large papier-mâché model with a scythe in one hand and an orb in the other. Less flamboyant androgynous figures were clothed in dark, hooded robes. A few carved wooden images had no ornamental additions at all.

Towards the end of the 'mass', a disembodied voice, emanating from loudspeakers fixed to electricity poles, instructed the crowd to hold hands and pool their mental and spiritual resources in order to summon the presence of La Santa herself. 'Relax, concentrate and visualize the Santíssima Muerte in your mind', the voice droned with monotone solemnity. 'Visualize the problem that you have and put it in the hands of the Santíssima Muerte, so that she can solve it for you.'

The ceremony culminated with devotees holding their statues aloft, creating an eerie forest of deliberately unnerving figures against a backdrop of urban decay. Even the most vacant-eyed adherents, with solvent-soaked rags pressed to their nostrils, managed to raise their images in celebration of the power of the inevitable, in the hope of keeping it at bay.

Devotion of the Santa Muerte mushroomed around 2000, after several decades as a minor fringe cult. The claim that there were 5 million devotees by 2010 was almost certainly an exaggeration, but nobody denies that new centres of worship are springing up all the time. Doña Queta's shrine is just one of the most popular: others range from personal altars in living rooms to towering monuments in public places. The most famous of these in the capital is a twenty-metre fibreglass statue built by a young man nicknamed 'Commander Panther' in 2007. He was shot dead in 2008.

The phenomenon has also extended out of deprived city *barrios* into the countryside – as well as out of Mexico altogether. In 2009 I saw Santa Muerte images on sale at a market in a mountain village in the southern state of Guerrero, and cult paraphernalia has become standard in some Mexican American-run supermarkets in the United States.

Religious scholar Bernardo Barranco Villafán of the Center for the Study of Religions in Mexico identifies three main components to the Santa Muerte mix. The strongest influence, he says, comes from Baroque Catholicism and its exaltation of pain, exemplified by the gory seventeenth-century crucifixes still displayed in churches all over Spain and Latin America. Another obvious root stretches back to the fascination with death that infused the civilizations of pre-Hispanic Mesoamerica. The third stems from black Caribbean witchcraft traditions. Crystallized in the 'Santeria cults', these are particularly strong in the Mexican Gulf Coast state of Veracruz, where many say the Santa Muerte cult originated in the middle of the last century.

The Santa Muerte is, nevertheless, very much a work in progress, developing before our eyes largely in the absence of charismatic leaders to impose their vision from above. For all its sinister undertones (and overtones), the Santa Muerte is rather a democratic cult.

Doña Queta's hour-long monthly 'mass' centres on a specially adapted version of the traditional rosary prayer. The ceremony dedicates each Mystery to La Santa's powers, with a built-in silence in which individual worshippers can invoke them. These powers include the Santa Muerte's reputed ability to help prisoners to freedom and provide protection from enemies. She is also regularly credited with answering appeals for riches, as well as helping drug addicts to self-control and the terminally ill to health. An additional catch-all slot tacked on at the end of the prayer allows for 'any other petition not already mentioned'.

The rosary provides the structure, but the ritual power of the service relies on the inventions of those who attend it. The extraordinary variety of the images that most of the congregation hold contrasts dramatically with the standardized way in which the official saints are represented and underlines the individual basis of the cult. Sometimes, however, fashions spread and a particular style of figure begins to dominate.

The same goes for the forms of worship. At the Alfarería Street shrine, participants bring bags of sweets, trinkets and flowers to exchange with others. Lollipops or paper sunflowers thrust in one direction might cross with marshmallows coming the other way. Some hold bottles of alcohol with which to anoint the statues of others that meet their approval. Many whip out aerosol cans decorated with pictures of the Santa Muerte and spray sickly smelling blessings. Queues form behind marijuana-puffing followers, who exhale smoke over statues in another substitute for incense.

The constant exchange of small gifts and tokens of shared religious identity was already in evidence when I first went to the shrine in 2004; but by 2009 there were other rituals I had not noticed before. Every so often, a cry would rise from somewhere in the crowd – 'allí va una manda' or 'here goes a promise'. A canyon-like passage would then open up through the throng to make way for a believer walking on his or her knees towards the shrine. As these individuals shuffled through the human chasm, sweat pouring from their brows and statues hugged to their chests, they received offerings and blessings from the people making up the human wall. All these offerings were finally deposited at the foot of the main image.

The Santa Muerte's rapid growth is a modern phenomenon, but it is also firmly rooted in a long tradition of dynamic popular faith within the Catholic Church that has always existed partly outside institutional control.

The most striking popular religious cults over the centuries have mixed Catholic directives with pre-Conquest beliefs, but at the same time they have proved remarkably able to incorporate more modern influences as well. The famed Day of the Dead celebration loosely intermingles with the Catholic All Souls' Day, but it is a true hotchpotch of belief and practice from past and present, and varies enormously from place to place. In the Mayan town of Pomuch in the Yucatán peninsula, the community congregates in the cemetery to exhume the bones of dead loved ones and give them a brush-up for the year to come. In Mexico City, many families set up altars in their home with a vague sense that the spirits of their departed relatives will pop back to visit, while their kids roam the streets 'trick or treating' over several days, as Halloween is absorbed into the tradition as well.

Right from the time of the Conquest 500 years ago popular religiosity has presented the hierarchy with a dilemma of how best to handle the balance between encouraging its vitality and limiting its potential to challenge ecclesiastical authority.

A relatively tolerant faction within the drive to evangelize the new subjects of the Spanish crown interpreted the spiritual zeal of indigenous religion as a natural expression of deep, if uneducated, Christianity. The bishops and priests who followed this proto-noble-savage vision of belief argued that it could be appropriated into the Church with little more than a baptism. A harder line insisted that the Indians were incapable of conversion. The conviction that this meant the conquered peoples were not fully human, or at least not fully rational, provided theological justification for extreme exploitation in the mines and haciendas.

The influence of the two currents ebbed and flowed over the centuries that followed, but the space for communities to define how they practised their nominally Catholic faith was never completely closed off. Even when that was the aim, it was unrealizable, given the chronic shortage of priests even in colonial times. Imposing conventional doctrine on such a large, diverse and territorially dispersed population was simply not possible.

The limitations on directed religion that came with the consolidation of anti-clericalism in the nineteenth century provided a further measure of protection for popular beliefs. The tacit live-and-let-live arrangement with the PRI encouraged the bishops and priests to maintain a pragmatic tolerance of doctrinal transgressions, although the soft authoritarianism of that period perhaps made it harder for these to spiral out of control.

The Mayan Indian liberation movement of the Yucatán Caste Wars in the mid-nineteenth century provides the most dramatic historical case of a popular religious rebellion. The movement's surprising resilience, despite its military weakness, was partly attributable to the cult of the Talking Cross, which urged the flagging Maya army to continue fighting. The war continued sporadically for decades.

Examples of smaller explicit mutinies are legion. In the spring of 2002, a new priest assigned to the parish of Santa Clara de Asis on the outskirts of Mexico City banned the local tradition of taking an image of Christ down from his cross during Holy Week and manipulating its arms to bless the faithful. The congregation ran the priest out of town. The local bishop, Onésimo Cepeda Silva, was furious. 'The Church is not a democracy', he told the villagers, before he shut the village church down until they were prepared to bow to his authority. They did, but only for a while: a few years later there was a new priest, and the crucifix was once again dismantled annually.

The Santa Muerte takes such defiance to a new level, in terms both of the numbers involved and its territorial spread. Given this, the Church can seem remarkably unconcerned. 'It has become an important social phenomenon that, of course, worries the Church', I was told by Mexico City archdiocese spokesman Father Romero, who did not look worried at all. 'On the other hand, we are also convinced that it is a devotion of fashion that will pass. It has no basis, no real root, and we hope it will not last much longer.' He made it clear that there were no plans to exert any real pressure on believers to change their ways.

The reluctance to crack down on a cult that is viewed as anathema by doctrinal teaching – death enters the world via Satan and is overcome by Christ – suggests a certain pragmatic realism. Any effort to discipline the followers would probably be embarrassingly ineffective – or worse, might trigger an exodus of devotees from the lists of nominal Catholics. 'If our devotion bothers them [the bishops] that's their problem', a cobbler called José once told me, as he lifted his shirt to show off Santa Muerte tattoos all over his torso. 'The truth is that the Santa Muerte is closer to God than anybody, and she is closer to Jesus Christ, too, because she was with him at the crucial moment.'

The rapid expansion of the Santíssima is often linked to, and blamed on, the explosion of drug culture in the context of the drug wars. Busted safe houses and hideouts have revealed shrines that suggest the skeletal divinity is used to sanction the most terrible of crimes. The museum of drug trafficking, which is maintained by the ministry of defence as an educational tool to teach soldiers what they are up against, includes several guns gilded with Santa Muerte reliefs. Rumours of human sacrifice are rife.

On Palm Sunday 2009, around a hundred Santa Muerte followers marched around the capital's great Zócalo plaza to protest against the automatic association of their beliefs with the drug cartels. A few days before, the authorities had bulldozed dozens of shrines along roads near the northern border, in what appeared to be psychological warfare directed against traffickers in the area.

The march was organized by David Romo, the head of a congregation he formed in the capital in 2003 and registered with the interior ministry under the name of the Traditionalist Church Mexico-USA. The registration was withdrawn in 2005. Romo's claim to be a 'bishop', and his active search for media exposure, led some to treat him as a kind of spokesman for the Santa Muerte cult as a whole. Some stories even described him as the 'high priest' of the cult. From this perspective, the scant participation in his march was a sign of weakness, but it probably said more about his weakness as a leader. Santa Muerte followers, it seems to me, tend to think of their faith as so far beyond institutional control that they do not respond when it is directly targeted.

Romo's demonstration was, nevertheless, both colourful and symbolically charged. All the protestors carried their own images, and the march was brought up in the rear by several Santa Muerte idols strapped to car roofs. One stood upright in a long, flowing bridal dress, a crown on her head. Another sat nursing a crucified Jesus Christ on her bony knees. As they passed the cathedral, shouting slogans about religious freedom and tolerance, their voices were drowned out by the great bells that began to peal. 'Sure there are some narcos who believe in La Santíssima', middle-aged, cross-dressing cook Isidro told me as he walked along with a scythe in one hand. 'Our faith is much bigger than them.'

Most serious observers agree that, while the Santa Muerte's association with drug violence is real and fearsome, this represents the crudest expression of a much broader phenomenon. The cult did not originate within the drug cartels, and it stretches far beyond them. Nor are all drug traffickers Santa Muerte devotees. Several of Mexico's most ruthless *capos* profess and practise much more conventional Catholic beliefs.

The Santa Muerte phenomenon first gathered real momentum inside Mexico's jails, where it appealed to all kinds of inmates, not just killers or even drug users. 'I would say most people in prison worship La Santíssima', a gentle-faced man called Rubén told me during the protest. He was carrying a wooden image he had carved himself while behind bars. He insisted he had never committed the car-jacking for which he was imprisoned. 'Nobody else helps you when you are on the inside.'

The power of the cult in the prisons is another reminder of how irrelevant institutions are to the followers of the Santa Muerte. Mexican jails are the ultimate expression of state control in theory only. Day-to-day survival behind bars often has less to do with playing by the official rules, overseen by wardens, than with the ability to navigate the unofficial regulations, enforced by the gangs that are really in charge. It amounts to a particularly acute version of life for many Mexicans who have neither the chance nor the inclination to seek solutions to their problems through formal authorities.

An estimated 30–60 per cent of the economically active population in Mexico work in the informal economy, at least to some degree. There are entire *barrios*, such as Tepito, where it certainly feels as though only a minority are plugged into formality. While some do rather well out of not paying taxes and managing their businesses without state interference, the majority barely scrape by. These communities live and breathe the disadvantage and insecurity that comes with the knowledge that there are few official safety nets worth speaking of either for themselves or for their children. Few hold out hope that there will be any more in the future.

Widespread informality in the context of the Mexican transition has been a perfect environment in which the cult can grow. Political change at the top soon showed itself unable to offer those on the margins powerful reasons to feel that they had a stake in the system, and many perceive things to be getting ever more precarious. As drug war-related violence has spun out of control, the economic and social status quo has altered little, while the unjust and arbitrary machinations of the justice system have become ever more obvious.

The Santa Muerte offers those inclined to fill the void with otherworldly powers an option that responds more directly to this situation than do the traditional saints, or the platitudes of the clergy. She helps Mexicans on the edge explain, alleviate and even take advantage of the crudeness of their reality, and the raw choices they face every day.

Prostitutes at Santa Muerte shrines have told me that they invoke her to protect them from aggressive clients and extortion by police patrols. A butcher credited his Flaca with curing his wife of cancer, getting his son out of jail and saving him from being injured in a shootout he happened upon one day. A debt collector said he only escaped dying in an assault when the bullet meant for him ricocheted off a Santa Muerte medallion hanging in his car. A desperately poor couple recalled one anxious night when they had no money to feed their small children, but pieces of chicken miraculously appeared in their kitchen. A grandmother was convinced that the Niña Blanca was keeping her grandchildren in school and out of trouble. A taxi driver said he appealed to the saint whenever he went into a rough neighbourhood and needed to hone his senses in the face of danger. A policeman said the Santa Muerte was fast gaining followers among officers, who felt insecure in certain parts of the city. A toilet cleaner said his devotion had helped him keep his job when the 2009 economic crisis set in and his workmates, who did not share his beliefs, were fired.

The Santa Muerte is not alone in recruiting from this demographic. The cult of Saint Jude Thaddaeus, known as the Saint of Desperate Causes, has also grown phenomenally in recent years. The monthly pilgrimage to the colonial church where the central image is kept in central Mexico City has swelled in the past decade, a phenomenon that has been fascinatingly chronicled in the work of photographer Keith Dannemiller. Disenfranchised youths are particularly drawn to the saint, who, they say, often protects them while they carry out illegal acts.

Even so, San Judas is generally considered relatively tame. Incongruous as it might seem to have people smoking spliffs or sniffing glue as they queue up to get their images of San Judas blessed by a priest who does nothing to try and stop them, it is still the case that an ordained priest is involved. As one young self-confessed thief told me outside the church one day, 'The people who follow San Judas are tough, but those who follow the Santa Muerte are tougher.'

In-depth studies of Santa Muerte beliefs are still few and far between, but what immediately jumps out is the way the faithful bypass the need to worry about righteousness by dispensing with the distinction between good and evil altogether. Santa Muerte followers often comment on the relief they feel at not having to pretend to live up to moral standards they know they cannot meet (and are not so sure they really want to, either). Gabriella, an orange-haired transvestite with evening stubble visible beneath his make-up, described his discomfiture at the looks he used to receive while sitting in church:

The Santa Muerte is different. She accepts you for who you are. She doesn't discriminate. She doesn't discriminate now, and she doesn't discriminate when she comes for you either. Rich or poor, it doesn't matter. She comes for everybody in the end. So we embrace her before she does. She is beautiful.

The Santa Muerte has no interest in the moral qualities of the favours she grants. She sees no difference between a plea to cure cancer and a petition for help in robbing a bank. She does not care if the request comes from a teetotal grandmother or a substance-abusing murderer. The crux of the cult is to be on good terms with death, because death comes to everybody, whatever they may look like, whatever kind of life they may have led, and whatever their intentions may be. The Santa Muerte becomes not only a representation of destiny, but a possibility of negotiating a stay of execution.

The flip side of all this equanimity is that the Santa Muerte demands absolute devotion, backed up by the threat of vengeance against those who do not keep their side of the bargain. 'You can ask absolutely anything, and if you ask it with your heart, she will help you', said a drug dealer called Beto. 'If you don't keep your promise and you don't keep up your devotion, she can get angry. She can hurt you or your family.'

In this, she recalls the powerful and capricious Tío, said to both protect and threaten Bolivian tin miners. As interpreted by Michael Taussig in his 1980 book *The Devil and Commodity Fetishism in South America*, El Tío helps peasants-turned-miners grapple with the spiritual contradictions created by leaving behind a culture based on relationship with the land to become cogs in the wheels of capitalist production. In a similar way, the Santa Muerte helps Mexicans mediate the empowerment that came with more democracy and the risks of life in the dog-eat-dog world of informality.

Aside from its fear that the cult may push followers to leave the Church altogether, the hierarchy's nonchalant response to the growth of Santa Muerte is also rooted in the confidence that comes from the large number of other expressions of popular religiosity that appear to strengthen the Church as a whole.

Drive along a secondary road and you will frequently get stuck behind caravans of pilgrims on their way to a particular holy place that has the explicit backing of the Church. Turn up in a small town on the local saint's day and you will be in no doubt about which is the most important community event of the year. In both examples, it is ordinary believers that direct the show, which has as much to do with social cohesion as with piety. Even so, the framework helps reaffirm institutional, Catholic identity.

And then, of course, there is the Virgin of Guadalupe, who, with her offer of maternal love, comfort and gentle help for the humble, stands as the one true beacon of conventional Catholicism.

The avenue that leads to the basilica where her image is kept in northern Mexico City is difficult to miss. It is long and wide, and on most days of the year has a steady stream of people making their way along a pedestrian walkway in the middle. For the last few hundred metres before it delivers the pilgrims to the centre of their devotion, the walkway disappears into a tunnel of stalls selling religious kitsch.

The old, colonial-era basilica stands directly across a great plaza. Behind it rises the small, steep Tepeyac hill – site of some older chapels and the spot where, believers hold, the Virgin appeared to a Christianized Nahuatl peasant called Juan Diego in December 1531, just a decade after the Conquest. First she commanded him to go to the local bishop and ask for a shrine to be constructed on the hill in her honour. After the sceptical cleric had twice dismissed her messenger, she sent him back a third time with his cloak filled with roses that had miraculously appeared in the arid landscape, where normally only cacti grew.

The image of Guadalupe, the sacred centre of the cult, hangs behind the altar in a huge new basilica to the left, a circus-tent-like orange and brown 1970s extravaganza where the vast majority of pilgrims first head. It is said to be the same image that appeared on Juan Diego's cloak as he unfurled it before the bishop, driving the point home even more forcefully than did the roses, which tumbled out at the same time. Below the image, four moving walkways slowly transport worshippers, their heads tilted back, from one side to the other.

Some come just to pay their respects; many bring a specific problem; and others give thanks for favours granted. Yolanda, a housewife from the central state of Michoacán, was so grateful for her daughter's recovery from a serious illness that she made the final approach on her knees. 'Doctors are necessary, but sometimes they can use a little help', she told me. 'And for us Mexicans, nobody helps like Guadalupe.'

An obvious amalgamation of the Virgin Mary and the Aztec earth and fertility goddess Tonantzin, who had her own shrine on Tepeyac hill before the Conquest, some say Guadalupe was a useful tool in the original evangelization of the country – a dark-skinned figure of solace, who helped bridge the gap between the conquering and the conquered, whose defeat extended beyond military overthrow to the subjugation of their gods as well. 'I will always be here to listen to your cry and your sadness', she tells Juan Diego, rejecting his plea that she find another, higher-status spokesman, to whom the bishop might be more inclined to listen. 'To purify and cure your different miseries, your troubles and your pain.'

Other scholars place more emphasis on the idea that Guadalupe empowered the local population in the face of foreign domination; that she provided the current of latent defiance that grew with time, until she was taken up by the *Criollos* (locally born people of Spanish descent who were denied the privileges of the Spanish-born *Peninsulares*) who headed the independence movement in the early nineteenth century and who went to battle under her banner. This helped the cult spread across the country and also turned Guadalupe into a symbol of identity in the newly created Mexico, which had little else to hold it together.

This process continued after the Revolution. The nominally anti-clerical PRI regime not only tolerated the cult of Guadalupe, but at times encouraged it in the name of knitting together a fractious nation under one-party rule. In an effort to defuse the tensions exposed by the pro-democracy student movement of the 1960s (brutally put down in the Tlatelolco massacre of 1968), President Luis Echeverría Alvarez helped finance the construction of the new basilica.

This overlap between religious and national identity ensured that the Virgin became rather secularized around the edges. In the latter years of the twentieth century, it was common to hear Mexican agnostic intellectuals pronounce that, while they might not believe in God, they were most definitely 'Guadalupana'.

The church claims that every year around 19 million people visit the basilica, a large proportion of them over the December anniversary of the visions. No other devotion can ever hope to reach its heights, but the fact that even here the veneration is not fully directed by the hierarchy, and never really has been, calls into question the Mexican Church's claim to speak for the nation's spiritual health as a whole. This was demonstrated by the failure of Juan Diego's canonization to achieve its stated aim of bolstering institutionally channelled, popular Catholicism.

Juan Diego's elevation to sainthood was one of the last and most elaborate of the 458 canonizations that John Paul II performed during his twenty-five years at the helm of the Vatican. All the other twentieth-century popes put together had performed just ninety-eight, but Karol Józef Wojtyła was convinced that popular devotion to saints would help the Church confront the challenges of secularism and alternative religions around the world. He was also particularly fond of Guadalupe and appreciative of the zeal of Mexican religiosity. All this ensured that Juan Diego sailed through the investigation into his saintliness, despite questions raised over whether he had ever actually existed. The abbot of the basilica, Guillermo Schulenburg, had caused a scandal in 1996, when he described Juan Diego as 'a symbol, not a reality'.

The ailing eighty-two-year-old pontiff travelled to Mexico in 2002 to make Juan Diego a saint, in a ceremony held inside the basilica that was jazzed up by dancers in feathered costumes to recall the new saint's Aztec ancestry. For good measure there were also large amounts of confetti and a symphony orchestra. In his homily, the pope lavished admiration on the 'humble Indian' and stressed that, by making him a saint, the Church was showing that it was close to people going through 'difficult times'.

The magic faded almost as soon as John Paul II's plane disappeared into the distance, accompanied by a final twinkling homage of mirrors raised to the sunlight to say goodbye. The visit would be fondly remembered as a triumphant and emotional farewell to the rock star pope, obviously nearing his death, who had visited the country five times – more than any other country bar Poland. But Saint Juan Diego would be all but forgotten.

On one recent visit I stood beside his official statue, placed just inside the entrance to the old basilica. A steady stream of people came through the door and walked straight up the aisle without so much as turning their head for a look. Some even skirted the image to study an anti-abortion exhibit, which showed models of foetuses at every stage of intrauterine development.

The few that did stop made it clear that they saw Saint Juan Diego as an appendage of Guadalupe, rather than as a figure of importance in his own right. 'We always come to see San Juan Diegito when we come to see the Virgin', said sixty-five-year-old Margarita, on the arm of her husband. 'It's sad he's been forgotten. All the saints should be important.'

A figure that is not linked to a specific community, and whose claim to sainthood is based on his subservience, was never likely to resonate with modern Mexican Catholics, disinclined to accept that it is their destiny to be tossed about by disadvantage. Those looking to supplement their devotion to the Virgin with new additions were actually more likely to turn to the Santa Muerte cult that was taking off at just about the same time as efforts to promote Saint Juan Diego were falling flat. In some ways the skeletal power is a kind of anti-Virgin, or a figure that complements her in the shifting morality and complexities of a harsh modern world.

'I went to see the Virgin last week to help my son study for his exams', I was told by Ivette, a street vendor, at the Tepito shrine in 2004. 'Tonight I've come to see my Flaca to help my other son with a problem he has with the law.' A female boxer called Angélica, whose crooked jaw testified to years in the ring, had transferred her allegiance almost completely:

I say to her 'look, I have done this and I've done that, and I need help with this or I need help with that', and she listens. She doesn't care if I use swear words and she doesn't care what I've done. She understands. I still respect the Virgin, but recently I find that the Santíssima is more effective.

Roberto Blancarte Pimentel, a key figure in the study of Mexican religious sociology, believes the hierarchy's lack of understanding of how it fits into the wider transformations in society hampers its ability to respond to challenges to its authority, such as the one represented by the Santa Muerte. 'It's not that the bishops today are not intelligent. They are very good at criticizing things outside of the institution', he says. 'But their own organization, methods and pastoral action are beyond criticism. They just don't see that they are part of the problem.'

Other scholars, like Bernardo Barranco, emphasize a more deliberate world-wide strategy by the Vatican to consolidate a core around conservative doctrine in order to ride out troubled contemporary times. The idea seems to be, he says, that at some point this core will be strong enough to resume a more missionary ethos and bring wayward believers back to the fold. The Catholic Church, he notes, is used to thinking long term.

The Catholic Church in Mexico has ridden out many crises over the centuries, giving it reason to assume that it will do so again. But it is one thing to survive intense bouts of anti-clericalism by appeal to the baseline religiosity of the population, and another to stave off slow-burning indifference to the leadership in a context of defiant plurality, unprecedented media scrutiny and institutional fragmentation.

The inability of the hierarchy to provide nominal Catholics with reasons to trust in its spiritual guidance illustrates the general narrative of institutional weakening in post-transition Mexico, and runs parallel to the failure of the political elite to generate a sense that it can solve the enormous challenges facing the country. But the potential consequences of the waning legitimacy of the bishops are by no means equivalent to those associated with the limitations of the governing classes. There is, after all, no reason for Mexicans to fret about a future in which Mexico is no longer describable as essentially Catholic. But they have every reason to shudder at the governability crises triggered by the drug wars in some states. While these crises might stem most directly from inter-cartel rivalries, they are also associated with the vulnerability of institutional life exacerbated by a security strategy focused primarily on force.

CHAPTER 5

A Bungled War

Felipe Calderón will go down in history as the drug-wars president. As the end of his term approached, he claimed that his determination to go after the cartels was halting Mexico's otherwise inevitable slide towards becoming a narco state. Some of his harshest critics accused him of propelling the country towards just such a fate. Others predicted that the government offensive's failure to bring the violence under control was creating the kind of conditions that might lead to a full-on authoritarian solution.

The situation did not look anything like as portentous when the offensive began with a series of piecemeal military-led shows of federal force in parts of the country where inter-cartel rivalries were already disturbing the peace. The president ordered the first of these, to his home state of Michoacán, just days after his inauguration in December 2006. Dramatic as it undoubtedly was, few people at the time predicted that the crackdown would dominate the rest of Calderón's term. Up until then, there had been little to suggest that the *Panista* was particularly concerned about the cartels – he had fought the presidential campaign with the promise to become 'The President of Employment'.

Calderón later said that, as president-elect, he had received intelligence that revealed the seriousness of the situation and forced his hand; but the move inevitably seemed like an attempt to exorcise the aura of weakness and illegitimacy that accompanied his contested election. The president came close to admitting this in an interview with the *Financial Times* in January 2007. 'The message we wanted to put out, not specifically with that image but in general, was that we were taking control of the presidency', he said, responding to a question about an early photo opportunity, in which he dressed up in a military jacket and cap to inspect some troops in Michoacán. In the same interview he claimed that the strategy was already producing very encouraging results and talked of his hopes that the tranquillity it brought would trigger new investment. A bright new future already seemed to be twinkling in the presidential mind's eye.

The country had not been clamouring for a crackdown, but once Calderón began talking and acting tough, the overwhelming majority thought it was the right thing to do. Bereft of an automatic honeymoon period, he had created his own.

The initial strategy on the ground mirrored the buoyant simplicity of the early rhetoric. It seemed based on the assumption that a committed show of state force would intimidate the *capos* into taking their power struggles back underground. As well as sending convoys of soldiers and federal police to trundle around trouble spots, the government also extradited some of the country's top jailed kingpins and negotiated a taboo-breaking US financial and technical support package. It all added up to the message that Calderón, unlike his predecessor, was serious about tackling the problem.

The president always stressed that reining in the cartels would 'take time, money and human lives', but it was clear that he never imagined how much or how many. One very senior law enforcement official told foreign correspondents during a background briefing in autumn 2007 that he expected the murder rate to start dropping by the following spring, as the cartels realized that it did not make sense to defy state power. The exact opposite happened. Though a *capo* peace deal did reduce the murder rate for a few months, it soon broke down and the escalation of the violence began in earnest in 2008.

President Calderón started tacitly admitting that things were more complicated than he had at first thought; but rather than rethinking the force-focused strategy, he plunged deeper into it. He began comparing himself to a surgeon who sets out to extract an appendix but, with the patient already under the knife, discovers a malignant cancer that requires more aggressive treatment. His stated objective moved from the reimposition of law and order to total destruction of the cartels; a crusading zeal crept into his tone; and he began to dismiss the mounting criticism of his strategy as tantamount to complicity with the traffickers.

By the end of 2009, Calderón's constant assertions that 'there is no turning back' hinted at anxiety as well as commitment. A classified cable sent from Washington to the US embassy in December detailed Secretary of State Hillary Clinton's specific interest in how the Mexican president was 'dealing with the stress'. Another, this time originating in the embassy in the same month, noted that the president had seemed 'down' in meetings.

Calderón rebounded in 2010, with a new, more confident and open way of justifying why he was sticking to the strategy in the face of evidence that it was triggering more violence, and despite polls showing a decline in popular support for it.

This was partly rooted in the offensive's growing success in bringing down major kingpins, beginning with the operation by the navy's special forces that resulted in the death of Arturo Beltrán Leyva in December 2009 (see Chapter 1). By January 2011, the government was boasting that nineteen of the thirty-seven 'most wanted' criminals it had identified less than two years before had been either captured or killed. Much of the intelligence that led to these 'hits' came from US sources, as was revealed later in the Wikileaks cables. Even so, it was clear that the Mexican forces were now both better able than they used to be to persuade US agencies to trust them with such delicate information, and more capable of using it in a way that produced results.

The substantial number of Sinaloa cartel leaders on the list also helped Calderón minimize the damage from widespread accusations that the offensive was biased in favour of Joaquín 'El Chapo' Guzmán and his close associate Ismael 'El Mayo' Zambada.

The president had initially claimed to be going after all the cartels with equal determination, but it became common to hear and read claims that the whole offensive was little more than a front to cover up a government deal with the Sinaloa cartel to help it eliminate its rivals. I never found such conspiracy theories particularly convincing, as they required a degree of neatness that always seemed absent from both the strategy and the way the drug wars developed. Even so, there was considerable evidence that the offensive was somewhat softer on Chapo and his associates than it was on other groups, including overall arrest figures that appeared to hit his competition harder.

Protected witness testimonies leaked to the media suggested that Sinaloa-linked traffickers had developed more extensive corruption networks to protect themselves. Investigative journalist Anabel Hernández also cited unnamed former officials who talked of Mexican government efforts to persuade Chapo to tone down the violence in exchange for lenient treatment. At the end of 2011, President Calderón himself changed his rhetoric to promise that federal forces would pay particular attention to going after the most violent organized criminal groups, such as the Zetas, though he was careful to insist that this did not mean any cartel could relax.

Furthermore, court documents that emerged during the 2011 Chicago trial of Vicente Zambada Ziebla, El Mayo's son, suggested at least some degree of US tolerance of the Sinaloa cartel in previous years. Zambada's defence argued that the young trafficker had negotiated an immunity deal with the DEA that protected him from prosecution. While the DEA denied any such deal, it did admit that agents had met Zambada in a Mexico City hotel in 2009, shortly before his arrest and subsequent extradition. The meeting, the agents testified, had been set up by an informant who was a close adviser to Chapo and El Mayo. The implication that neither kingpin was particularly troubled by having an informant within their inner circle certainly suggested that, at least for a time, there was some form of mutually beneficial relationship.

All this ensured that accusations that the offensive was deliberately aiding Chapo, the single most important symbol of cartel power and impunity, never went away. But it was also true that, once the *capos* started to tumble with some regularity in 2010, it came to seem possible that he, too, might one day be taken down.

President Calderón's new optimism of that time also drew heavily on the vision of Joaquín Villalobos. This one-time leading military strategist of the Farabundo Martí National Liberation Front (FMLN) insurgency in El Salvador in the 1980s had since transformed himself into an international consultant and drug-war ideologue. In the words of one Los Pinos insider, the baby-faced former guerrilla became 'somebody the president relied on a lot to help him make sense of what was going on'. At a meeting with Mexican ambassadors, Calderón personally handed out copies of an essay that Villalobos had published in the monthly magazine *Nexos* in January 2010 and instructed them to use it to explain the offensive around the world.

The argument emphasized that Calderón had inherited a problem which previous administrations had allowed to grow to the point where it posed such a serious threat to national sovereignty that it could only be combated with the full force of the state. This, continued the argument, inevitably triggered a violent response from organized crime that was not an indication of the state's failure, but rather a measure of the size of the problem. It was also an indication that the cartels were hurting, because gangsters typically prefer to work within a context of complicity. The fact that they were now prepared not only to go to war, but to continually escalate that war, was viewed as evidence of the difficulty they were having in securing government protection. Fragmented, weakened, involved in territorial disputes with rivals, and yet still under pressure from the federal forces, they began recruiting inexperienced, marginalized and particularly violent youth to replace the fallen, and that only accelerated their own process of self-destruction. Victory would come, Villalobos and the president argued, when local law enforcement was strong enough to consolidate the successes of the federal forces by ensuring that wounded cartels did not have the space to recuperate and that new cartels were denied the space to grow.

'An important part of Mexican society refuses to accept the idea that Mexico is in a war, and for as long as it does not accept that reality it will never be able to understand the violence in the country', wrote Villalobos. 'Violence is an inherent part of a war and is not, in itself, a sign that things are going wrong.' The president was rather less crude in his own rhetoric, but the same message peppered the long speeches he began to give that frequently directly lifted quotes from Villalobos. The bristling 'with me or with the cartels' retorts of the previous years had been replaced by a concerted effort to convince Mexico and the world that there was rhyme, reason and hope behind the pain.

In line with this thinking, the government stopped trying to minimize the violence, and at times even stressed how bad things were. The official database of 'deaths because of criminal rivalry' released in January 2011 exemplified the new thinking. The figures were marred by confusion, mistakes, lacunae and contradictions; but to have any official numbers at all was a sea change. The fact that they were significantly worse than the newspaper counts that had filled the earlier data vacuum also lent credibility to the government's new claim to transparency.

The database classified the deaths as either 'executions' (defined as killings where the murderer and/or the victim were associated with the cartels), or 'shootouts and assaults' (described as confrontations or attacks involving criminals). This fed into the argument that the government had a constitutional obligation to go after the cartels with all the force it could muster.

By refocusing attention on who was doing the killing, the classification also sidestepped the thorny issue of who was being killed and allowed the government to quietly drop its (by then) thoroughly discredited original claim that 90 per cent were associated with the cartels.

But if the president had found a narrative that convinced him, he failed to persuade the rest of the country. Approval for 'the offensive launched against organized crime by Felipe Calderón' was at its peak (of 88 per cent) in June 2007, and was still high (74 per cent) at the end of 2009, according to a GEA-ISA tracking poll. But by the end of 2010, it had dropped to 50 per cent, and active *disapproval* had risen to 45 per cent. The proportions remained similarly uncomfortable for most of 2011, during which time the president's commitment to his core strategy was tested even further by a newly active and innovative peace movement that intensified pressure on him to pay more attention to the impact of the violence on ordinary people and on society in general.

A deeply religious, chain-smoking, left-leaning poet called Javier Sicilia sparked the Movement for Peace with Justice and Dignity after the torture and murder of his own clean-living son in their home city of Cuernavaca in March. In the early months, the poet possessed an uncanny ability to articulate the pain, anger and frustration that pervaded Mexico at the senseless killing and the state's inadequate response to it. His credibility was further bolstered by his personal loss, and by the fact that he was obviously not motivated by any desire to obtain political office for himself. He headed large marches in Cuernavaca and the capital, and toured some of the worst-hit parts of the country, providing a platform for victims to come forward with their own stories. These *Caravanas de Consuelo* (best translated as Caravans of Solace) became magnets for mothers, fathers, daughters, sons, sisters and brothers of victims. At each stop, they would take the microphone to tell their stories of terror and loss – and of courageous (and usually fruitless) pilgrimages around bureaucratic offices in search of justice or, in some cases, just a body to bury.

Sicilia and the other spokespeople blamed the strategy for not only exacerbating the violence, but also for taking the country to the brink of institutional, social and moral collapse. 'There are 40,000 dead people and we don't know the names of most of them', Sicilia told me in the spring of 2011 in the garden of the church in the capital where he was staying temporarily.

They are dismissed as criminals or collateral damage, but the truth is that most of these nameless victims are humble people ignored because their families don't have the resources to bring attention to their cases ...

Things cannot go on this way and I believe this is the last chance that we have as citizens to change things. If we lose it, I don't know what will happen. Either the politicians will find themselves governing a nation of cadavers and terrified people, or there will be a coup or the country will explode. Either the politicians take this opportunity or they will lead us to something even worse than the national emergency we are already living.

The Movement for Peace with Justice and Dignity bore some similarities to the movements of relatives of victims of the military dictatorships in other Latin American countries in the 1980s and 1990s, including the demand for a truth commission. Unless he wanted to risk being lumped together with the barking generals of that era, Calderón had to show that he was listening. He did this in dramatic fashion, by holding public meetings with members of the movement in Chapultepec Castle in Mexico City, where he reformulated the reasoning behind the strategy as an effort to contain the bloodshed. 'The violence is not the result of the presence of the federal forces. The federal forces are there because of the violence', Calderón told Sicilia during the first meeting in June. 'Violence that the local authorities could not control. A violence that overwhelmed them.'

President Calderón claimed that the offensive had been hampered by the insufficient support it received from other political and institutional forces. It was true that most national opposition leaders had mouthed support for the strategy when it was popular, but they had done very little to back this up in practice. And while many had since jumped on the bandwagon of discontent, they remained notably vague about what they would do differently, were they in power.

It was also true (as the president insisted with increasing vehemence) that local governments had shied away from their particular security responsibilities and were often unable to fulfil them even when they willingly stepped up to the plate. During the early years of the offensive, state-level authorities had largely hidden behind the formalistic argument that organized crime did not fall within their jurisdiction. If things got out of hand, they might appeal for federal help, but even then they often seemed reluctant to offer active support to the federal forces once these arrived.

By 2011, several governors had thrown their weight behind the offensive, but they did not necessarily have the same priorities as the president. Some state governments were particularly prone to the kind of clumsy criminalization of victims that Calderón had already discarded. This damaged the president's efforts to counter accusations that the offensive was predicated on a callous disregard for the suffering of ordinary people caught up in the violence.

When thirty-five bodies were dumped on a main road near a shopping mall on the edge of the Gulf port city of Veracruz in September 2011, the state government not only removed them within fifteen minutes, but within hours was claiming that almost all of them were known criminals. It later turned out that almost none had been identified at that time. When they were, it emerged that only a few had criminal records, and these were not for organized crime.

But while President Calderón was right to complain that a good many other political leaders got off rather lightly in the blame game over the death toll, his 2011 reinvention of the federal offensive as an effort to reduce the violence was disingenuous. It brushed over the fact that the escalation of the killing only really began *after* the deployments of federal forces, and was also often associated with the fragmentation of cartels that this prompted. The new official line also directly contradicted the previous efforts to argue that the increased murder rate was a sign of cartel desperation and consequently amounted to an unfortunate, but necessary, step in the right direction.

The rethink was not entirely superficial, as many critics claimed, and was accompanied by a quiet reorganization of the operational strategy that explicitly prioritized actions aimed at containing the bloodshed, rather than going after the *capos*. It was far from the full-scale rethink that many demanded, but it did amount to a sign that the government was finally beginning to learn from at least some of the mistakes in a strategy that had been plagued with errors from the start.

In many Latin American countries, the sight of soldiers in the streets conjures up images of coups and coercion. In Mexico, the military has long enjoyed an essentially benevolent reputation, born of the legitimacy provided by the Revolution and the army's subsequent willingness to submit itself to civilian authority.

The 1968 massacre of students in Mexico City and a subsequent dirty war against the dissident left blotted the army's copybook, but the brutality never approached the scale of elsewhere in the region. Efforts by the military to clean up its image by assuming a key role in disaster relief also helped limit the damage. Mexican soldiers became associated in the popular imagination primarily with rescue rather than repression.

The political transition in 2000 was, nevertheless, a worrying time for the top brass. According to military expert Raúl Benítez Manaut, who was a security adviser to the Fox government in the early years, it feared both the return of the ghosts of the dirty war and the imposition of a civilian defence minister. These concerns faded during Vicente Fox's lacklustre presidency, and went out of the window completely when Felipe Calderón sent the army out to fight organized crime.

Benítez says the generals were also rather pleased with their performance. They usually came out on top in skirmishes with cartel commandos and also started taking down important *capos*. 'As far as they are concerned, they are winning the war', he told me in 2010.

By then, however, it was clear that the offensive also carried a downside for the army, in the form of mounting accusations of human rights abuse. From the start, human rights groups had warned that this would happen, arguing that an institution designed to eliminate the enemies of the nation is simply not suited to chasing down criminals, whose personal lives and organizations are often knitted into the social fabric of the territories where they operate.

The complaints ranged from soldiers stealing food from a fridge (after raiding a house without a warrant) to forced detention, tortured confessions, enforced disappearances and extrajudicial assassinations. The accusations came out in a rather piecemeal fashion until a report by the US-based group Human Rights Watch, based on two years of research in five areas of the country and released in November 2011, provided a bigger picture of widespread abuse. Up until then, the type of violations attracting most attention stemmed from a lack of clarity in the rules of engagement, which placed civilians in danger, and a tendency to try to cover up the tragic consequences.

In March 2010, two young men died during a gun battle between cartel hit-men and soldiers on the campus of the private Tecnológico de Monterrey University in Monterrey. The army immediately issued a statement claiming they had been gunmen. A subsequent report by the National Human Rights Commission concluded that the victims had been exemplary scholarship students who were beyond suspicion of cartel links. It also found that somebody had placed weapons beside them in an attempt to suggest otherwise. Evidence later emerged that at least one of them had recent bruises on his face and had died by summary execution, with a shot to the head.

Hints were also growing of systematic violations of the rights of people identified by the offensive as legitimate targets. Though the context of the conflicts made these very difficult to investigate at the time, they lurked in the background as potentially large scandals for the future. Most were associated with the army, although neither the federal police nor the navy was exempt.

It was at least odd, for example, that two navy raids on Zeta training camps in Tamaulipas in February 2010 should have left dozens of gunmen dead when only one marine lost his life. Given the amount of firepower reportedly at the Zetas' disposal, it might have been assumed they could do more damage if, as the navy said, they had resisted. It might be standard special forces procedure to maximize the kill rate among the enemy, but in theory the navy's role was to supplement police work, not eliminate rivals. By mid-2011 there were also reports of a take-no-prisoners policy in some border cities in the same state, at the same time as rumbling hints of a slide towards officially backed paramilitaries.

Respected security analyst Eduardo Guerrero told me at the end of 2011 that he thought it likely that the navy was allowing a Sinaloa cartel-linked group called the Matazetas – 'Zeta killers' – to operate freely in the port city of Veracruz. It seemed to be, he said, part of an attempt to run the Zetas out of town.

The government's initial attempts to discredit the stories of human rights abuse with counter-accusations that branded activists as apologists for organized crime was difficult to sustain in the face of mounting evidence to the contrary. The alternative strategy, of admitting to occasional 'excesses' but insisting that these were always fully investigated by military courts, was no more successful. It was hard to imagine that the armed forces would violate their own *esprit de corps*, and the minimal amount of information released about prosecutions in progress did not help. At a background briefing with foreign journalists in 2009, supposedly to herald a new era of transparency, the general presiding insisted that human rights groups were wrong to claim that not a single soldier had been convicted of a serious violation against a civilian. He had, however, omitted to bring with him any details of any such case.

The pressure from local and international human rights organizations and institutions, including the Inter-American Court of Human Rights, eventually pushed the government to propose a partial overhaul of military jurisdiction in 2010. This was branded as cosmetic by activists and military experts alike. The following year, the Mexican Supreme Court ruled that military jurisdiction in all human rights cases should end, but how this would play out in practice remained unclear. Meanwhile, the number of complaints about the army submitted to the semi-autonomous National Human Rights Commission almost quintupled between 2006 and 2011, when there were 880 in the first half of the year. For its part, the navy saw the insignificant number of complaints against it in 2006 soar to 205 in the first six months of 2011.

The fear of future prosecutions was reputedly one of the reasons the generals became deeply unhappy with the woolliness of the legal framework behind the military deployment, which was based on little more than requests for help by local authorities. The Wikileaks cables revealed that, in 2009, Defence Minister General Guillermo Galván Galván actively pushed for a state of emergency to be declared in certain areas, notably Juárez, but that the government was reluctant. Such a move would have hinted at desperation, and would also have required congressional approval, which was by no means guaranteed.

By then General Galván was also publicly urging federal legislators to approve a constitutional reform that would both clearly mandate the military's new domestic security role, and give it greater powers within that framework. The president sent an initial reform proposal to the legislature in 2009, but it was held up both by activist opposition and by the internal congressional machinations that have paralysed so many pieces of legislation in the new political era. Signs of frustration in the military hierarchy mounted.

The spectre of infiltration by organized crime is also closing in. Calderón had initially entrusted much of the offensive to the armed forces because they are generally considered cleaner than the police. Soldiers (the argument goes) are moulded into more honest stuff by their codes of honour, their strict discipline and the controlled environments in which they live. The genuine opportunities for advancement offered to disadvantaged people by the army are also singled out as an incentive to institutional loyalty and honesty. Defence Minister Galván stood out in any photograph of Calderón's cabinet as much for his dark skin as for his uniform. Less flatteringly, top-ranking officers are said to be plugged into a complex system of kickbacks that considerably reduces the attraction of a few briefcases full of cash.

Reduced vulnerability to cartel infiltration is one thing; immunity to it quite another, particularly given the increased exposure that has come with the drug wars. The Zetas – originally formed from a core of ex-soldiers from a special operations unit set up by President Ernesto Zedillo who were lured into the ranks of the Gulf cartel – provide chilling proof of that. Though the drug wars had not produced a corruption scandal on the same scale by the end of 2011, many believe it is just a matter of time.

All this has been compounded by a growing perception of ineffectiveness in the face of spiralling violence. Opinion polls show the army is still the most popular institution in the country, and anecdotal evidence in a variety of trouble spots suggests that most people still prefer it to the local police; but the shine is clearly wearing off. A national poll, commissioned by a group of established security experts called the Colectivo de Análisis de la Seguridad (CASEDE) and released in October 2011, found that overall 72 per cent approved of the job the army was doing 'a bit' or 'a lot'. The breakdown of the figures, however, showed that in Chihuahua, where the soldiers have been deployed in large numbers since 2008, approval was just 47 per cent. One woman in Acapulco told me in 2011, 'I trust the army. I have to. It symbolizes Mexico.' She then went on to list the reasons why, as far as she was concerned, it was not going to help.

President Calderón had always stressed that the heavy reliance on the armed forces was an emergency measure to cow the cartels and buy time to clean up and strengthen civilian police forces, to the point where they could take up the mantle. Over time, his insistence on this point became ever greater. 'What the armed forces are doing today is to confront the criminals with superior force, more discipline and better weapons, in order to make them retreat. The problem is that when the operation is over and the federal forces withdraw, there is nothing to take their place', he said in summer 2010. 'The day we have local police forces that can do the same will be the day that we have really turned things around.'

The problem has been that this is not happening – or at least is not happening fast enough. While a lot of this may not directly have been the government's fault, it was certainly predictable, given the fragmentation of political authority that was already in evidence before Calderón took office. Some critics have argued that steps should have been taken in advance to lay the foundations for better policing, instead of rushing in with a military-led offensive and just assuming that everything would fall into place before the credibility of the armed forces came under strain. There have also been signs that the increase in the number of drug war fronts is beginning to stretch the federal forces in human resources terms, adding further urgency to the plea for local forces to step up to the plate.

❋ ❋ ❋

Corruption in the Mexican police has a long tradition. It extends from traffic cops offering to turn a blind eye to a minor offence in return for a tip, to a deep-rooted association with organized crime. A number of the country's biggest kingpins – past and present – began their careers in the police.

The phrase *plata o plomo* – silver or lead – has long stood as shorthand to describe the choice facing police officers, made all the easier because of pitiful salaries, lack of institutional support and a bad public image. While still used, it has lost its accuracy in the context of the drug wars, which make officers in the pay of one cartel targets for its rivals – something that can change the equation to silver and lead. When officers are killed – and over 2,000 of them were in the first four years – it is rarely clear whether it is proof that they had turned down temptation or evidence that they had not.

Evidence of corruption in the federal force is particularly worrying, given the enormous efforts made to turn it into a model of patriotic probity, as well as a sign that improvements in civilian law enforcement will eventually allow the army and navy to return to their barracks.

President Zedillo originally created the Preventative Federal Police (PFP) in 1999, with many of the original members recruited from the army. It replaced a whole battery of different, smaller national-level police forces with a bewildering array of different-coloured uniforms, bizarrely demarcated remits and subtly different reputations for corruption. Two years later, the Fox administration set up the Federal Investigation Agency (AFI), which was promoted as Mexico's answer to the FBI. Both the PFP and the AFI were deeply corroded by the time they were abolished in 2008 and replaced by the Federal Police (PF), with the drug wars already well under way.

The latest mutation included a recruitment drive among university-educated, technologically savvy young people, and a propaganda offensive, complete with a publicly funded prime-time soap opera called *The Team*, accompanied by the slogan 'They know that good overcomes evil'. The PF also has a state-of-the-art command centre in Mexico City, pretensions to develop intelligence capabilities second to none in the country, and an information-sharing database that promises to help coordination across the nation over such basic issues as whether a gunman arrested in one state has a criminal record in another.

By 2010 these new *federales* were already taking over the lead role in the struggle against organized crime in some parts of the country, though this was accompanied by a rapidly growing number of accusations of abuse. That July around two hundred officers beat up their own commanders in Ciudad Juárez, complaining that they were being forced to run extortion rackets. Local rights activists suggested that the violence was actually prompted by a row over how to divvy up the proceeds.

The Juárez rebels were among the 10 per cent of the entire force (of 35,000) sacked a few weeks later. The government promoted this purge of suspicious elements as proof of its commitment to keeping the force squeaky clean. Even so, it hardly boded well for efforts to reform local forces if the crème de la crème of civilian policing was curdling so quickly.

There are an estimated 400,000 police officers in Mexico. The fact that the number is an estimate indicates how little control there is. Aside from the Federal Police, there are thirty-two state-level forces, as well as some kind of police presence in most of the country's 2,438 municipalities. The ratio of officers to population is actually significantly higher than in the US and much of Europe, but this theoretical strength is more than cancelled out by complicity with criminals.

It took only a few leading questions to get the former builder I met in the border city of Tijuana one afternoon in 2008 to begin boasting that he had gone to school with several of the biggest gangsters in town. He was particularly proud of sharing a classroom with 'El Muletas', or 'Crutches', who had gone on to become notorious for smuggling, killing and kidnapping (as well as for getting 200 uniforms made up for his men – printed with a skull and cross-crutches). His old buddy had recently promised him a job in the police.

It was, the new cartel recruit said, the perfect solution for people like him who were attracted to drug smuggling and keen on increasing their incomes, but not ready to take on the risks associated with life fully outside the law. As the conversation wound up, I asked if he would give me his name to use in an article. 'I like the guns and the adrenaline,' he mocked my naivety, 'but I'm not suicidal.'

Stories of local police involvement with organized crime are the bread and butter of the daily news – from reports that officers studiously ignore convoys of killers driving through their beat and tip mafia bosses off before a raid, to evidence of their direct participation in kidnappings and executions. There have also been stories of municipal police forces disintegrating as officers walk off the job in fear of their lives. The interior ministry reported in 2010 that around four hundred municipalities had no police force at all.

At the start of the offensive, the military deployments to trouble spots cruised in and took over local security functions with little regard for the local police force, which, on occasion, was formally taken over but in most cases was simply ignored.

Security expert Fernando Escalante Gonzalbo has argued that suddenly dismantling corrupt local police operations actually made things worse, because it destroyed the only local structures that were (at least in some way) setting limits on lower-level criminal activity – even if these were associated with complicity.

The Calderón government's first attempt to improve local policing – rather than merely to override it – centred on a project to subsume local forces within a single national police, which would theoretically be easier to monitor, as well as better coordinated. The plan foundered in the face of the reluctance of governors and important mayors to give up control of their law enforcement apparatuses.

The government then pinned its hopes on new legislation in 2008, which required local authorities to 'certify' all officers by subjecting them to lie detector, toxicology and other 'trust tests'. A federal government report released in February 2011 revealed that only 13 per cent of municipal-level officers, and only 12 per cent of state-level officers, had undergone the promised vetting. In this context, the 60 per cent of federal officers who were tested seemed like something to boast about.

In the meantime, a more pragmatic reform idea emerged: to absorb municipal forces, in all but the biggest cities, into new, super, state-level police corps. Several governors publicly embraced the proposal, which was submitted to the legislature in October 2010, only to be caught up in the political paralysis of the legislature until at least 2012.

Calderón's police strategy consequently relied ever more intensely on back-door militarization of civilian policing, via the appointment of retired colonels and generals to top local law enforcement positions wherever the local civilian authorities could be persuaded to cooperate. The former army men brought with them a determination to impose discipline on the civilian police under their command, and were always willing to coordinate closely with local military commanders. In several cases, this strategy also included the incorporation of soldiers on loan from the army into those forces.

The model claimed one major success story in Tijuana, where high-impact violence dropped significantly after the appointment of retired Lieutenant Colonel Julián Leyzaola Pérez as municipal police chief in

December 2008. Even if the success was due to the iron grip with which he managed the force under his control, it carried with it worrying implications for human rights, starting with the way he was protected from accusations of forced detention and torture of suspected dirty cops.

Leyzaola was also far from alone in delighting in tough-guy theatrics, which, while they were locally popular, fanned the controversy over the wider militarization strategy. General Carlos Bibiano Villa Castillo, a direct descendent of the revolutionary Pancho Villa, was even more extreme as he boasted about how he maximized 'enemy' casualties. He held several different civilian security posts from 2009, but when I interviewed him in November 2011, he was head of public security in the state of Quintana Roo and had a brief to ensure that the Caribbean tourist paradise did not get dragged into the kind of violence that was besetting Acapulco at the time. During our conversation, he recalled his response to a recent death threat against his family, made on his personal phone: 'I told the guy that if anything happened to my family, I would make sure that he was put in jail; and then I would look for him there and tear him to pieces. Him and all his descendants.' After that, the general assured me he held 'an exaggerated' respect for human rights.

Meanwhile, it was never clear whether soldiers on loan to police forces and accused of abuses fell within the jurisdiction of military or civilian courts. One case in Monterrey in 2011, in which a twenty-nine-year-old newly-wed called Jorge Otilio Cantú was shot dead on his way to work by trigger-happy soldiers in police uniform, ping-ponged between the two for months. Activists pushed for a civilian trial, although this, too, was no guarantee of fair and swift justice.

The impunity rate for all crimes that fall within civilian jurisdiction is usually estimated at around 95 per cent. A 2011 Human Rights Watch (HRW) report quoted data, much of it obtained under freedom of information legislation, suggesting that things were as bad in cases related to the drug wars. The authorities in the state of Chihuahua told the New York-based group that 212 individuals had been found guilty of murder in the state between 2009 and the middle of 2010 – a period during which there were more than 5,000 deaths. The federal judiciary revealed that it had achieved convictions for just twenty-two homicides tied to organized crime between the start of the offensive in December 2006 and January 2011.

President Felipe Calderón regularly appeared to lay the lion's share of the blame for the dysfunctional judicial system in the context of the drug wars on corruption among judges. But while undoubtedly a serious problem, there are many other factors also involved in ensuring that justice is so rarely done.

One is lack of clarity of jurisdiction between the state and federal levels. All murder investigations traditionally go first to state authorities, with the federal attorney general's office empowered to take over the investigation in cases of organized crime. The drug wars mean that there are dozens of such murders around the country nearly every day, but the federal authorities rarely muscle in and take charge, although they say they regularly offer support to state investigations. Many serious crimes consequently hang in jurisdictional limbo, with the different institutions passing the buck between each other and the case getting nowhere.

When we talked in 2009, Saúl Trejo Torres, a criminal lawyer from Juárez, admitted that, when defending a drug war-related case, knowing which palms to grease was important, as was knowing how to play the jurisdictional ambiguities. Nevertheless, he put most emphasis on the poor quality of the prosecution cases he faced. 'They are good at torturing confessions out of people, but lousy at putting together the legal case', he said. 'Any good lawyer can pick holes in them.' Trejo said that this significantly reduced the considerable risks involved in defending cartel members, who would get angry if convicted: 'Guilty or innocent, it isn't difficult to get people off.'

A dramatic shortage of detectives does not help either. This was particularly acute in Juárez up until 2011, when there were some serious efforts to improve investigations. Before that, there were just two federal detectives based in the city, and around fifty-five state investigators. Even imagining that they were all incorruptible, worked in perfect coordination, and only worked on homicide cases, it would have been impossible for them to deal effectively with an average workload of around eight murders a day.

Juárez provided an unusual context, not just because of the sheer scale of the killing, but also because it was one of the earliest places to complete the transition from the paper-based labyrinthine inquisitorial model into an accusatory system, with open oral trials, as mandated in the 2008 judicial reform. The change could hardly have happened under greater pressure. The oral trials were more transparent, and new demands for evidence beyond police confessions obtained under suspicion of torture provided more guarantees for the rights of the accused. Even so, lack of adequate training for all involved and, presumably, fear and corruption too, mean judges routinely let obvious killers off the hook.

Marisela Escobedo was one of the activists who regularly complained that the new system made people like her particularly vulnerable. That was before she was shot in the head, in December 2010, at a protest camp she had set up to pressure the authorities into pursuing the man she was convinced had killed her teenage daughter but who, despite confessing to the murder before three judges and under no apparent pressure, had been released on a technicality.

Even the alleged mass murderers the authorities regularly paraded before the cameras upon their arrest were not necessarily put behind bars for any length of time – men like Juan Pablo Castillo López, whom I saw standing handcuffed, shackled and expressionless between two rifle-carrying soldiers in the central patio of the Juárez army barracks one chilly October morning in 2009, prior to being handed over to the civilian authorities. The prisoner had been through a similar ritual a year before, when he was detained in connection with twenty-three murders. He had been released by a state-level court a few days before his re-arrest and, the assembled reporters were told, had killed at least two more people in the interim.

This time the authorities said Castillo López, who was wearing a regulation lime-green fluorescent jumpsuit that conjured up images of the orange-clad alleged Islamist terrorists held at Guantanamo Bay at the time, had been arrested after a car chase. We were allowed to scramble over his vehicle and try out three secret buttons that opened three even more secret compartments. One contained a 9mm pistol and another a Kalashnikov rifle. A third released nails from under the back bumper. The nails were on display, too, spread neatly on the ground beside the car for additional effect.

Castillo López also illustrated how difficult it could prove to keep even convicted criminals in jail. He was finally sentenced to nine years for a federal charge of weapons possession, but was free again within a year, after a commando ambushed the vehicle driving him back to prison following a medical appointment. Two prison guards died in the attack. The escape was too minor to figure in the count of prison breaks kept by the El Universal newspaper, which traced the rising number of such events from six between 2008 and 2009 (freeing thirty-one inmates) to sixteen in the following two years (which liberated 463).

The credibility of the judicial system was also called into question by the number of prisoners whose guilt was genuinely in doubt. The habit of slapping people in jail with little regard for hard evidence and due process was particularly prevalent in the lengthy, paper-based trials of the old inquisitorial system, still in force in most of the country and in the federal courts as well. Some said it even tainted the highest-level federal investigations into corruption.

Operación Limpieza, or Operation Clean Up, brought down around twenty-five high-level members of the federal police and the special anti-narcotics unit of the attorney general's office towards the end of 2008. The government promoted the cull as irrefutable evidence of its commitment to root out narco influence everywhere. Few doubted that such rotten apples existed, but the cases against at least some of this batch of detainees appeared to rely almost exclusively on protected-witness accounts, some of which were leaked to the national media.

Samuel González Ruiz, a fervent critic of the Calderón offensive, was personally convinced of the innocence of former anti-drug tsar Noé Ramírez Mandujano, who was accused of receiving at least one bribe of $450,000 from the Beltrán Leyva cartel. González, a former anti-drug tsar himself and an acquaintance of Ramírez, stressed that no money had been found. Three years after his arrest, I failed to obtain any information about the case from the authorities, beyond the fact that Ramírez was still awaiting sentence in a high-security jail.

The deep crisis of the judicial system in the context of the drug wars meant that rather than strengthening the rule of law, the Calderón offensive against organized crime exacerbated the impression that innocence or guilt was less important in determining whether a suspect would be caught, convicted and kept behind bars than were money, power, connections and political convenience.

The failure to systematically go after criminal influence within politics was another major flaw in President Calderón's strategy. Indeed, some said it was the biggest problem of all.

Mostly the offensive against the cartels simply ignored the issue. The one time it made the top of the agenda, with the mass arrest of thirty-five mayors and other public officials from the state of Michoacán, in May 2009, the effort backfired dramatically. This was despite the fact that few doubted that the local La Familia cartel could only operate with the freedom it did thanks to political protection. To begin with, the operation, in a state controlled by the opposition PRD just ahead of the mid-term congressional elections, reeked of political opportunism. Then the cases against those detained fell apart. All thirty-five were released within two years.

The government was not alone in sweeping evidence of political complicity under the carpet. The rest of the political elite did the same, unless accusations of narco links could be usefully employed to score points against rivals. National leaders were particularly reluctant to acknowledge that all political parties were not just vulnerable to infiltration, but were already deeply affected by it.

Local political assassinations began to take off from around 2010. They included the near certain winner of the governorship elections in Tamaulipas of that year, about one mayor a month from around the country, and a coterie of high-level local government officials. As with the police, it was rarely publicly established whether they were killed because they were a threat to cartel interests, or because they were identified with them.

Beyond the assassinations, the rivalry between different cartels clung to political life on the most intense fronts like a thick mist. The PRI candidate in the governorship election in Sinaloa in 2010 was repeatedly accused of links to kingpin Ismael 'El Mayo' Zambada. The evidence presented was rather slim – a photograph of the two together at a party in the 1970s and the candidate's own reluctance to deny the charge. This was taken as a tacit confession, though it could equally be seen as an effort to appear stronger than he was.

In the end, the election was won by the candidate of a PAN-PRD alliance, who benefited from an unpredicted surge in turn-out. Many observers interpreted this as a sign that the people of Sinaloa were beginning to stand up to the cartels, but an investigation in the weekly *Río Doce* concluded otherwise. The paper's sources said that El Mayo had secretly operated in favour of the PAN-PRD candidate in several key voting districts. The new governor then filled his cabinet with a good many figures who had long been suspected of narco links.

Such situations, repeated in key drug-war states across Mexico, rarely generate any degree of noise at the national level. That is, unless they are associated with efforts to avoid blame for the rising violence, or to pin it on others.

In June 2011, President Calderón publicly explained a surge in killing in the port city of Veracruz by saying that the state had been previously overrun by the Zetas. He hinted heavily that the PRI former governor was directly implicated in allowing this to happen. There was no indication that any judicial case was being built. The presidential accusation hung in the air, just like the ones levelled at members of his own inner circle by investigative journalists, convinced that corruption went almost right up to the very top.

The lack of any significant action beyond the rhetorical condemnation of narco politics was widely interpreted by Calderón's fiercest critics as evidence of reluctance to break a kind of pact of mutual impunity agreed by the political class. It could also be because the president did not consider it strategically very important. At least that was the line of Joaquín Villalobos, at the time when he was a key presidential adviser. 'It is obvious that a culture of corruption is useful for the drug traffickers', he wrote in *Nexos* in January 2010. But, he added, 'It is naïve to think that to improve security in the short term you first need an ethical reconstruction that will end the codes of corruption. The issue is where to start in an emergency.'

Edgardo Buscaglia, a Uruguayan-American academic based in Mexico, who became something of a guru figure for many on the independent Mexican left, argued the exact opposite right from the start of the offensive. He claimed that his studies of criminal processes – from Naples to Kabul via Colombia and Russia – showed that any force-focused strategy was always doomed to be counterproductive, unless it was accompanied by an equivalent assault on narco influence in politics. Otherwise, he said, the cartels simply respond to the military and police pressure by devoting more money and effort to penetrating ever deeper into the institutions in search of protection.

Buscaglia argued that the Calderón offensive had been neutralized in large part because the different pieces of what he called the 'jigsaw' of Mexico's federalized political system had been 'captured' by different criminal organizations, which ensured that they often found themselves working against each other. He further claimed that competition between the different criminal groups to secure or increase their political possessions was at the centre of the escalation of the inter-cartel war.

The only way out of the mess, he told me in 2011, was for the political elite to recognize the magnitude of the problem and to begin a genuine purge of its own ranks by means of a cross-party pact, ideally with international monitoring. This would come, he predicted, when the violence had begun to directly affect not just provincial politicians, but national ones as well. And, he added, when the highest levels of the country's economic elite were also beginning to feel the pain: 'This is a monster, and sooner or later they will have to combat it. The pact will happen, but only when the core of the political and economic elite in the capital really begins to suffer. They will respond, but only when there are massacres inside their exclusive clubs or car bombs in the business districts.'

Around the time of President Calderón's annual state of the nation address in September 2010, a slogan filled the airwaves proclaiming that the struggle against organized crime was 'worth it'. The strategy on the ground, however, appeared more focused on pushing the cartels to decide that the drug wars were not 'worth it' for them, without any obvious success.

A government report released around the same time boasted that the amount of suspected dirty cash seized in the first three and a half years of the offensive was twelve times greater than the quantity secured in the equivalent period at the start of the Fox administration. It omitted to note that this $412 million amounted to a tiny fraction (between 0.3 per cent and 1 per cent) of the total drugs proceeds repatriated to Mexico, estimated at around $10–40 billion.

Almost half the record haul came from a single extraordinary bust in March 2007, when police discovered over $205 million stuffed into the closets of a wealthy home in Mexico City. The raid was ordered because the tenant, a Chinese-born pharmaceuticals businessman called Zhenli Ye Gon, had been importing very large quantities of the restricted chemical pseudoephedrine. The authorities said they suspected Ye Gon, who was considered a novice in the business, of selling them on to the Mexican cartels producing methamphetamines.

The results of efforts to track the cash once it gets inside the legal economy have been even less encouraging: no major money-laundering prosecution came to light in the first five years of the offensive. An AP investigation in 2011 revealed that federal prosecutors had seized just $65 million in money-laundering proceeds between 2008 and mid-2010. A new law allowing the seizure of the properties of drug traffickers had not affected a single property in the two years since it was passed in 2009. Nor is there any sign of a concerted effort to go after companies that appear on the lists of suspected drug money-laundering hubs drawn up by the US and European authorities.

President Calderón himself admitted that the results were disappointing. His efforts to improve this – such as new restrictions on cash dollar transactions and proposals to outlaw cash purchases over about $8,000 – were condemned by critics as mere tinkering around the edges of a massive problem and a nuisance for many legitimate businesses.

The most conspiratorially minded blame the government's limited efforts on reluctance to take action that might end up affecting well-established business figures with political clout. Others suggest nervousness about the consequences of taking a major source of cash out of the economy. More sympathetic analysts point out that, small fry aside, tracing the bulk of drug money sloshing around a globalized financial system is beyond the competence and the jurisdiction of the Mexican authorities.

Major drug seizures are more common, but they still do not happen frequently enough to make a major dent in the wider context of drug smuggling through or from Mexico.

In late 2007, the navy discovered nearly 24 tonnes of cocaine on board a container ship in the Pacific port city of Manzanillo. It was one of the biggest recorded hauls of that drug anywhere in the world and contributed to a significant overall rise in Mexican cocaine busts, in comparison to the Fox years. Even so, according to the UN's 2010 World Drug Report, the proportion that this represented of global interdictions actually fell from just under 8 per cent in 2001 to 4 per cent in 2008. This decline has more to do with the huge drug hauls registered further south in Latin America than with any failing of the Calderón offensive; but the figures are not much to shout about either.

Record marijuana busts, meanwhile, such as the 142 tonnes found in the border city of Tijuana in October 2010, mask the embarrassing reality that production has ballooned in the context of the offensive, which took resources away from eliminating plantations. According to the US justice department's 2010 National Drug Threat Assessment report, Mexican marijuana production more than doubled between 2005 and 2008 – to 21,500 tonnes. The same report estimated that Mexican heroin production tripled – from thirteen to thirty-eight tonnes – between 2006 and 2008, while seizures were minimal.

In August 2009, the army seized the biggest methamphetamine manufacturing facilities ever seen. Located in the Golden Triangle, the complex extended over 240 hectares and was said to be able to produce a hundred tonnes of pure 'crystal meth' a day. Even so, seizures of the drug by the US authorities on the border continued to rise, which was interpreted as a sign of greater production, rather than greater success on the part of the authorities.

If the Calderón offensive amounts to little more than a nuisance when it comes to drug smuggling within Mexico, there is also evidence that the Mexican cartels are playing an ever greater role in distribution within the US. This, presumably, means that their share of the final street price is greater than it has ever been before. Or at least that this compensates for a certain fall-off in US consumption of some drugs, such as cocaine.

The growth of Mexico's domestic drug-user market, the retail value of which was estimated by the government in 2011 at around $8.7 billion, also provides additional profits for the country's cartels. I know of no serious financial quantification of the wider criminal business interests also at stake, such as extortion rackets, pirate DVD production, people trafficking and kidnapping.

Waging wars with various rivals obviously brings additional costs for the cartels. The kinds of arsenals that are on display on some drug-war fronts do not come cheap, and protected witnesses regularly quote astronomical corruption premiums. Government and independent experts alike say this is one of the reasons behind the dramatic expansion in criminal side lines, such as extortion and kidnapping – to keep the cash flow going. But is this really something to celebrate?

The drug wars also require the *capos* to continually recruit new low-level members, in order to replace those who die. There are other very personal costs as well. Chapo Guzmán lost a son and a brother in his battle with the Beltrán Leyva cartel. The authorities have also arrested several alleged traffickers they claim were close to him. His movements are reputedly restricted almost exclusively to the mountains of the Golden Triangle, which implies that he has few opportunities to fully enjoy his wealth, even if he is worth the $1billion that *Forbes* magazine attributes to him.

But even if – for the sake of argument – Mexico's kingpins do find themselves wondering whether they have made the right career choice, five years into the offensive the US-born trafficker La Barbie was the only *capo* said to have given himself up under the pressure. For the moment at least, drug trafficking remains financially attractive enough, and the desire for freedom basic enough, to keep on fighting.

It is also reasonable to speculate that, as the drug wars drag on, some of the biggest *capos* might start negotiating truces with each other that have a better chance of holding than those of the early years. A fall-off in inter-cartel violence could, after all, be expected to bring with it a reduction in the pressure from the offensive, and that would provide a more favourable environment for drug trafficking. Even in this case, however, the process of fragmentation associated with the conflicts has spawned many smaller armed groups without the capacity to traffic large quantities of drugs, whose survival consequently depends on violent control of the territories where they operate.

The extent and impact of the US government's influence on the course of the drug wars is particularly difficult to evaluate, not least because it is routinely downplayed by officials on both sides of the border in deference to Mexican nationalist traditions. It is no less real for all that. According to Mexican military expert Raúl Benítez, the US does not dictate Mexican strategy, but it is an important voice that seeks to nudge it in certain directions. As the drug wars continue, that voice appears to be getting louder.

The newly inaugurated President Calderón immediately set about negotiating a security aid package with President George W. Bush. The Merida Initiative, worth $1.4 billion over three years, was unprecedented and taboo breaking.

The package was less controversial than many at first predicted it would be. This not only reflected a certain waning of anti-imperialist sensibilities, but also the impression that the driving force behind it was actually Calderón. The Merida Initiative, signed in 2007, was also soon dwarfed by Mexico's own ballooning security budget and the sense that Washington was not all that interested in what was going on in Mexico anyway. The release of funds was held up in Congress, and US attention was clearly focused on the wars in Afghanistan and Iraq, as well as on the looming financial crisis and the upcoming US presidential election.

The US only obviously started taking notice of the escalating violence across its southern border after the election of Barack Obama, in November 2008. A series of worrying reports bombarded Washington with catastrophic potential scenarios, including one from the Joint Forces Command, in January 2009, that put the potential instability of Mexico on a par with that of Pakistan, and talked of a risk of 'rapid and sudden collapse'.

Several angry public outbursts from Calderón initially prompted the Obama administration to replace the rhetoric of alarm with mollifying showers of admiration. Both Obama and Secretary of State Hillary Clinton not only extolled Calderón's 'heroism', but repeatedly and publicly acknowledged that the Mexicans were right to complain that US demand for drugs and ready supplies of guns were fuelling the bloodbath. The new spin culminated with Obama himself standing on the Los Pinos lawn (painted bright green for the occasion) in April 2009, gushing about his host and setting the stage for a more active US role, encased in the language of co-responsibility and partnership.

The new US administration redirected the Merida Initiative funds (which were finally beginning to flow) away from hardware and into efforts to improve Mexican intelligence capabilities, strengthen the Federal Police, and move judicial reform forward. Confidential cables from the US embassy in Mexico City, released by Wikileaks, also revealed US enthusiasm for the Mexican navy's growing role in the offensive, reflecting the fact that the navy had always been more responsive to working with US agencies than the traditionally more nationalistic army.

The new US ambassador for the new era, Carlos Pascual, took up his post in August 2009, with his reputation as an expert in troubled states before him. He initially engaged in velvet public diplomacy, but his confidential musings – later revealed in Wikileaks – were a different matter. He reserved some of his most scathing analysis for the lack of coordination within the offensive. This, he said, had compromised numerous operations because different federal institutions 'would rather hoard intelligence than allow a rival agency to succeed'. Mexican use of strategic and tactical intelligence was, he said, consequently 'fractured, ad hoc and reliant on U.S. support'.

Pascual resigned from his post in March 2011, after President Calderón publicly insulted him and said that he had lost his trust. Anthony Wayne replaced Pascual that September. Wayne's previous posting as deputy ambassador in Afghanistan suggested that the names might change, but the focus remained the same.

While the tension over Pascual was obviously uncomfortable for the US, sometimes officials appeared almost deliberately to provoke President Calderón. In September 2010, Secretary of State Clinton described Mexico as 'looking more and more like Colombia looked 20 years ago where the narco traffickers control, you know, certain parts of the country'. Clinton went on to suggest that the solution could lie in a version of the major US involvement in the Colombian counter-narcotics and counter-insurgency effort known as Plan Colombia, which began in 2000. 'I know that Plan Colombia was controversial', she said. 'I was just in Colombia, and there were problems and there were mistakes, but it worked.'

This time President Calderón was joined by politicians across the political spectrum in his strident rejection of the possibility that Mexico

The mood was both festive and full of hope on 1 December 2000, when Vicente Fox was inaugurated Mexico's first PAN president.

Vicente Fox (left) with Felipe Calderón in September 2006; Calderón owed his July 2006 election victory the support of outgoing President Vicente Fox, but even before his inauguration that December there re signs that the second PAN president was determined to distance himself from his predecessor.

3 Leftist Andrés Manuel López Obrador's efforts to prevent Felipe Calderón taking office after the disputed 2006 elections were already beginning to run out of steam when he had himself symbolically inaugurated as 'Legitimate President of Mexico' on the anniversary of the 1910 Revolution, 20 November 2006.

4 President Felipe Calderón put the army at the centre of his drug war strategy; he is seen here with Defence Secretary Guillermo Galván Galván during the Army Day celebrations at a base near Monterrey, February 2009.

5 The campaign that eventually overturned Jacinta Francisco Marcial's conviction for kidnapping helped put patent miscarriages of justice on the Mexican agenda. This image was released to the press by the federal authorities immediately after her arrest in August 2006.

Parents of the 49 small children killed in a fire at the ABC day care centre in Hermosillo on 5 June 09 started a protest movement that began as a call for justice in their particular case, but developed o a wider symbol of public pressure for greater political accountability.

7 A woman puts flour on the road to soak up blood left after the murder of a young man in Ciudad Juárez, August 2009. There were 2,754 murders that year in the city, which has suffered acutely in Mexico's drug wars.

8 Culiacán, January 2009. The luxurious mausoleums constructed in the Humaya cemetery on the outskirts of the state capital of Sinaloa stand testament to the power and deep roots of drug trafficking in the area.

9 A young man holds an image of the Santa Muerte, or Holy Death. Veneration of the unofficial saint has exploded among Mexicans who live on the margins of institutional life.

10 The erosion of Cancún's famous white sand beaches through a mixture of overbuilding and extreme weather has exposed the unsustainability of Mexico's tourism policy, which prioritizes mega coastal resorts.

11 The diverse social uprising that paralyzed Oaxaca city for several months in 2006 before it was repressed by federal forces towards the end of the year illustrated how closely radicalism bubbles beneath the surface in some parts of Mexico.

The relationship between the extraordinarily powerful teachers' leader Elba Esther Gordillo
(left) and Education Secretary Josefina Vázquez Mota was never easy. Gordillo won that battle and
pushed Vázquez Mota out of the ministry, although the latter went on to secure the PAN's presidential
candidacy for 2012.

Former Mexico State governor and PRI candidate Enrique Peña Nieto was the early favourite to win
2012 election. His popularity was built on a carefully crafted telegenic image and the continued mus-
of a party machine still largely intact after twelve years in opposition.

14 This photograph of the Interlomas area of Mexico City by Adam Wiseman starkly illustrates the division between rich and poor.

might tolerate intervention on a similar scale, prompting Obama himself to deny any comparison with Colombia. After that the controversy faded away, but it is hard to imagine that Clinton did not expect the idea of a Plan Mexico to get shot down. This suggests that she may have set out to see just how fervent the reaction was. It was certainly hard not to assume that there were at least some people in the State Department, the Pentagon, the DEA and the CIA arguing that only something similarly dramatic could get things under control.

As more parts of the US government have got more interested and more active in the drug wars, it has become clear that they do not all think the same way. While the diplomats and politicians seem most concerned about the parts of Mexico slipping towards ungovernability and general institutional weakness, others have focused on operational successes against the cartels. One high-level US official waxed lyrical to me in summer 2011 about Mexico's success in taking down *capos*; he called it the Kingpin Strategy, and still considered it to be at the heart of the offensive – and, indeed, the only strategy possible. This was despite the fact that by then President Calderón had begun to insist in public that the main aim was to reverse the violence.

The US official argued that taking down kingpins was a very effective way of disrupting trafficking organizations, because when a top trafficker fell, his immediate subordinates tended to take more communications risks as the organization adjusted to the loss of its boss. More communication means more information about drug shipments, as well as about the people involved, he insisted.

It was abundantly clear in almost everything he said that, as far as he was concerned, things were going pretty well in Mexico:

> When you look back at the past two years, the things that the [Mexican] security forces have pulled off have been tremendous. The unfortunate thing is that you know you've got this increasing violence that they've got to get their arms around; but when you look at the cartels themselves it's been tremendous . . . I mean the pace that they are going down is really impressive.

As evidence of increasingly direct US involvement continued, it emerged that some of it was going on at the edges of Mexican law, which places tight limits on what foreign agents can do on Mexican territory. Most of the revelations came from US media investigations, much of it in the *New*

York Times. In March 2011, the paper reported that unarmed US surveillance drones were flying deep into Mexico. In August it revealed that CIA operatives and civilian military employees were posted at a Mexican military base, advising on operations. The paper said the idea was modelled on the 'fusion intelligence centers' set up by the US in Afghanistan and Iraq to keep an eye on insurgent groups. By the end of the year, another story emerged, quoting DEA agents talking about how they routinely laundered millions of dollars in drug money in an effort to get to high-level operators and so as not to blow their cover. It was not clear whether the Mexican government knew about this or not.

All of these stories were controversial, but none compared to the revelation in the US media, also in 2011, of a secret gun-tracking operation – codenamed Fast and Furious – that was run out of the Bureau of Alcohol, Tobacco, Firearms and Explosives (ATF). Beginning in November 2009, the ATF field offices in Arizona and New Mexico deliberately allowed 'straw buyers' to stock up on weapons from US dealers and deposit them in safe houses. The operation was supposed to track the guns and see what happened next. The blindingly obvious problem with this was that the ATF lost sight of the marked guns once they had crossed the border, and only began to catch up with them again when they turned up at crime scenes. Thousands of firearms were allowed to 'walk' in this way.

The operation came to light after one of the weapons was linked to the shooting of a Border Patrol agent in Arizona, prompting whistleblowers to reveal both the operation and the way their concerns had been overridden by superiors. There followed congressional hearings, during which a string of high-level officials denied all knowledge. The officials also confirmed Mexican claims that the Mexican authorities had not been informed of what was going on. It appeared that not even the US embassy in Mexico had known what was going on.

The US ambassador might moan about the lack of communication, coordination or efficiency within the Mexican authorities that was hampering the Calderón offensive, but growing US inter-agency involvement was hardly a beacon to follow. Nor did it appear to be of any great assistance, and it certainly did not help President Calderón's efforts to convince the Mexican public that he was taking Mexico down a road that would ultimately deliver security. As he himself acknowledged several times in interviews, the struggle against organized crime was also a matter of perception, and that was obviously not going very well. One of the problems was that the government not only had to contend with the fallout within public opinion from its failure to contain the violence, the vocal critics of the strategy in the media and in organized civil society, and the backlash from clumsy US support. It also had to cope with cartel propaganda, and it struggled to do this in an effective way.

The tendency to display victims and leave messages beside them is the most basic form of cartel propaganda. Particular types of brutality, from the chopping off of fingers to the positions in which corpses are left, can be infused with specific meanings. Whatever the subtleties, however, the choreographed horror of the drug wars always contains some version of the claim by the killers to be able to do whatever they like, whatever the president says.

From around 2008, the government began urging the media not to publish or broadcast graphic images or direct cartel messages, on the grounds that this was playing into the hands of the criminals. As the years went on, many major outlets, including the two big commercial TV networks, complied. By 2011 some were also responding to appeals to pay more attention to offensive successes and general good news stories about Mexico.

The cartels, however, also get their messages across through the internet. Set up in March 2010, El Blog del Narco became the most famous of many sites dedicated to the drug wars. Its anonymous administrators uploaded endless videos and photographs of the cartels in action, motivated, they said, by the mainstream media's reluctance to cover what was really going on. One of them told me in an email interview in 2010 that the blog sometimes received 4 million visits in a week.

Sometimes material posted on the blog broke important news. This happened in July 2010, with a video of a beaten, dazed and soon-to-be-shot policeman telling an off-camera Zeta interrogator that the director of a local jail in the northern city of Torreón periodically let out inmates linked to the Sinaloa cartel to carry out hits using the prison's guns and vehicles. Surreal as it sounded, the authorities later confirmed the story.

The saga continued days later, when four journalists working in the same area – three of them for national TV networks – were kidnapped by a Sinaloa commando, which demanded that the networks air their narco videos. They released two of their hostages when their demands were partially met. The remaining two were let go a few days later, under pressure from a closing circle of Federal Police.

Then it was the turn of the government propaganda machine. It pressured the freed journalists to attend a press conference that exaggerated the police's role in their rescue. The following year the US gave one of them asylum: cameraman Alejandro Hernández Pacheco successfully argued that the police had turned him into an unwitting government spokesman, making him vulnerable to further attack.

The events in Torreón highlighted the risks to journalists caught in the middle of cartel and government efforts to control information, as well as the absence of serious efforts by the authorities to protect both them and freedom of expression. The US-based Committee to Protect Journalists reported at the end of 2011 that at least twenty-seven journalists had been killed in Mexico since the start of the drug wars in 2004, probably because of their work. A further eleven had disappeared in the same period. Countless more are frightened into manipulating their coverage – either because they have received direct threats or because they know what can happen.

Reporters employed by the big national titles who make short reporting trips or who base their stories on leaked documents are the most secure. Some have done extraordinary work. Journalists in local outlets are particularly vulnerable, although the degree and type of pressure depends on the region and the particular dynamic of the wars there. The pressure facing local journalists is further compounded by the fact that newsrooms – as indeed any place that is of interest to the cartels – are subject to infiltration. Some reporters who have been killed are suspected of narco links, but by no means all.

Only a tiny number of provincial papers continue to do investigative reporting, among them the small and dedicated team of reporters at *Río Doce*, in Sinaloa. They push the limits week after week, although they admit that they publish only a fraction of what they find out. 'When you write, you think about the narcos first, and then you think of your reader', the editor, Ismael Bojórquez Perea, told me in 2009. 'You can't publish anything about their families, or their properties, clandestine landing strips, ranches or businesses; but there are no clear lines defining what you can or can't do. You have to go by instinct, so you never really know and we do get frightened.' The following year someone threw a grenade at the paper's offices.

In Ciudad Juárez, local media outlets fill their pages with stories and images of the violence, but tend to avoid going beyond basic details. The boldest is the *Diario de Juárez*, but it lost two staff members in two years. After the second murder – of a novice photographer called Luis Carlos

Santiago, in October 2010 – the paper published a deliberately provocative editorial. 'Señores of the different organizations fighting for the Ciudad Juárez plaza,' it began, 'we'd like you to know that we are communicators, not mind readers, so we ask that you explain what it is you want from us, what you'd like us to publish and what not to publish, so that we know what is expected.'

In Tamaulipas, the local media have almost no freedom left. A news editor with a major newspaper in the state capital Ciudad Victoria (I will call her 'Dora') did not rush to beat rival media to the story when two car bombs went off one summer morning in 2010. Instead she sat back and waited for instructions from the press attaché of the Zetas, the cartel that controlled the city at the time. Eventually she was told to ignore one of the events completely and to refer to the other as 'an explosion' rather than a 'car bomb'.

The feisty single mother, who has overcome countless obstacles in the past to pursue her career, refrained from fuming or even joking about the situation, as she suspected some of her colleagues were on the cartel payroll. She just did as she was told – just as everybody else at the paper did when asked to cover a particular child's birthday party for the society section, talk up one politician and talk down another, or abort plans to interview an irate circus owner who was complaining about being denied a permit to put up his big top. 'They are the editors now', Dora told me.

For a while, Dora had used the social networking service Twitter to reveal some stories that she knew would otherwise never be aired; but later she got too nervous to do even that. This was more than paranoia: in autumn 2011, María Elizabeth Macías Castro's decapitated body was dumped near a monument in the border city of Nuevo Laredo. Headphones had been placed on the severed head, and there was a message, signed by the Zetas, threatening social networking sites. Macías Castro had regularly posted information anonymously on a local crime-monitoring site. She also worked at a local paper, which did not even report her death.

While most of the terror stems from organized crime, there are also cases of intimidation by the authorities. The first Mexican journalist to win asylum in the US, Luis Aguirre, left Ciudad Juárez in 2008 after receiving death threats, which he attributed to his reporting of alleged abuses by the Mexican military.

The authorities in the Gulf state of Veracruz imprisoned a maths teacher and a radio host in September 2011 after they allegedly caused panic across the port city of the same name with unfounded rumours on Twitter and

Facebook about attacks on schools. They were initially accused of terrorism, but the charges were dropped following an international outcry. In the meantime, the local legislature changed the law to introduce a crime of disrupting public order that could be applied in similar cases in the future. By then most of the media in Veracruz was publishing or broadcasting very little about the violence other than officially sanctioned statements.

The official side of the propaganda war is perhaps most obvious in the use of detainees to push the impression that the offensive is moving forward. This goes beyond the tired, old, traditional, trophy-like presentations of shackled prisoners to the media. From 2010, the Federal Police became particularly keen on releasing videos of informal interrogations of important detainees answering questions about their activities. The videos, however, have no value in a court of law, and many of the alleged traffickers featured have clammed up in their formal statements before investigators or judges. It is also not really clear whether it has been a good idea for the government to give traffickers such a platform. Several have given the impression of being rather ordinary guys who just happened to be confessing to killing hundreds of people.

※ ※ ※

With President Felipe Calderón's anti-cartel offensive clearly struggling to even contain the escalation of organized criminal violence, the obvious question became what should be done differently. A significant number of people, particularly in drug-war states, appeared to nurse a certain nostalgia for the days when the cartels coexisted with everybody else in relative peace.

A computer engineer from Reynosa, Tamaulipas, whom I will call 'Pedro' (and who I very much doubt had any criminal links at all), told me in August 2010 that he believed the only way out of the terror was for the *capos* to negotiate a truce with each other. The government, he said, should act as a kind of referee to make sure they stick to it:

> Before, when the traffickers had a deal with the authorities it wasn't great, but it was much better than this. They didn't kill as many people; they invested their profits in the local economy. They ate in local restaurants, set up little shops that employed local youth, and mostly they kept their rivalries to themselves. The offensive has made things intolerable.

While driving home from work a few weeks before, Pedro had got caught up in a terrible shootout between gunmen and the army that had set him combat-crawling along burning tarmac to escape the bullets and grenades. While he was showing me a video of the event that somebody had uploaded onto YouTube, his two-year-old daughter appeared in the room to ask what the noise was. 'Popcorn in the microwave', his wife lied, before turning her face away to hide her tears: 'You try so hard to stay out of trouble and to live an upright life and stick to your principles but it means nothing in the end.'

Pedro's family was not alone. The October 2011 study carried out by the Collective for Analysis of Security with Democracy (CASEDE) mentioned earlier found that 27 per cent of Mexicans agreed with the statement 'The next president should negotiate or make a deal with the drug traffickers.' The figure in the beleaguered state of Chihuahua was 45 per cent. The study did not give a figure for Tamaulipas.

President Calderón dismissed such approaches as not only immoral but doomed. The cartels' criminal portfolios were now so diverse, the control they exercised over their own structures so loose, and the general organized criminal stage so fragmented that the idea of workable deals should be dismissed as fantasy. Many independent experts – and even fervent critics of the strategy – agreed, although other forms of tacit cohabitation were more accepted, and little by little seemed to influence the president himself.

Momentum grew in the *comentocracia* (the intellectuals and academics who have regular spaces in the media to air their opinions) behind the argument for forgetting about trying to dismantle the cartels, and instead focusing on combating the crimes that impact most directly on ordinary people, such as kidnapping and carjacking. It was a strategy that, some proponents admitted, included a tacit agreement to let the traffickers alone, so long as they kept their tendency to violence in check.

The president's announcement of a 'second stage' of the strategy at the end of 2011, in which he promised to pay particular attention to going after the most violent cartels, seemed like a nod in that direction at least, though he insisted no gang would be tolerated. By that time, the decriminalization lobby – which argued that a simple change in the legislation could slash the profit incentive that kept the cartels fighting – had also grown substantially. Legalization of drugs had been dismissed for years as pie in the sky, on the assumption that the United States would always oppose it. But a document circulated in February 2009 supporting the idea in the case of marijuana, and signed by former presidents Ernesto Zedillo

(Mexico), Fernando Enrique Cardoso (Brazil) and César Gaviria (Colombia), catapulted the debate into the mainstream. The vote on marijuana decriminalization in California in November 2010 – which was only narrowly lost – even made it seem possible.

President Calderón initially condemned the idea as 'absurd'. It would, he said, trigger a drug consumption boom in Mexico and would fail to deal with other lucrative branches of organized criminal activity. By the autumn of 2011, however, the president seemed to be quietly changing his mind as he began urging developed nations to explore 'alternative market solutions' to the drug problem.

Other proposed methods for combating the violence stressed the need to undermine the cartels' ability to exploit pervasive poverty by placing social development and the reduction of inequality at the very top of the political agenda. The media paid particular attention to young people who neither worked nor studied – dubbing them Ni Nis. These were epitomized by the gang members in Juárez who were so easily recruited into the bloodbath there. A government report in 2010 identified nearly half of the city's population of 13–24-year-olds as Ni Nis.

Vulnerability to being sucked into organized crime was also evident in the countryside. One former security official from the Guerrero state government that left office in 2010 told me the authorities were regularly bombarded with requests from rural communities to help find alternatives to growing opium poppies in the mountains there. The problem was that while it was easy to suggest growing avocados or setting up ecotourism centres, it did not make economic sense even to try in isolated areas where roads were often impassable in the rainy season.

President Calderón became more sympathetic to such stories as time progressed, and took some steps to increase public spending on social programmes in drug war-torn areas. But he also stressed that the fruits of poverty alleviation and the new economic opportunities that provided young people with a stake in society would take time to grow.

His one-time ideologue, Joaquín Villalobos, provided a cruder explanation for why the offensive largely ignored the social side of the equation, unless pushed by the local population. He argued in 2010 that it was wrong to assume that a pool of disenfranchised young people provided criminal organizations with an infinite capacity to regenerate. Ever younger, less experienced and more brutal assassins who rose quickly to positions of control actually accelerated the demise of the cartels, he claimed. In terms of the objectives of the force-based focus of the offensive, then, it did not actually make much sense to put too much effort into poverty alleviation.

Apart from some fiddling around the edges, President Calderón seemed determined to maintain his strategy broadly unchanged until he left office in 2012; but the all-important question of what the next president might do differently was very difficult to answer.

As the campaign approached, the possible candidates from the governing PAN party were clearly less bellicose personalities than the outgoing president; but then again, Calderón himself had rarely mentioned drug cartels until after he donned the presidential sash. Andrés Manuel López Obrador, once again set to represent the hopes of the left, promised to put the issues of poverty and inequality at the centre of his policies, as well as to strengthen the judicial system; but what such a strategy might look like on the ground was still vague.

Many Mexicans assumed that the PRI would seek to return to some kind of live-and-let-live arrangement with the cartels, reminiscent of the way things had worked in decades gone by; but the PRI candidate Enrique Peña Nieto denied this. He tended to emphasize the need to improve the efficacy of the offensive, without really explaining how to achieve this in any detail.

The anti-war movement, led by victims of the violence, was meanwhile suffering from internal divisions over the usefulness of seeking dialogue with the authorities. Its poet leader, Javier Sicilia, began to appear tired and drained by the controversies surrounding the way he called on Calderón to apologize for submerging Mexico in tragedy, at the same time as he hugged and kissed the president and offered him gifts of rosaries. The movement was also hit by a series of assassinations of local activists. Even if it faded away, however, it was hard to see how the next president could disregard the victims of the violence in his or her strategy, as Calderón had done in the first four years of the offensive.

Most observers, myself included, tended to incline towards pessimism for the future, combined with a nagging sense that things could surely not really be so apocalyptic. Mexico's not so distant past was littered with acute crises that had seemed insurmountable but that had nevertheless somehow faded away, without ever really being solved.

In 1994 there was an assassinated presidential candidate, a six-decade long regime subsumed in infighting, a new guerrilla with post-modern appeal, a financial collapse and an economic crisis that nearly wiped out the middle class. And what happened? The economy slowly returned to an even keel, politics reconfigured and the institutions were put in place to guide Mexico to a remarkably smooth democratic transition.

But even if the drug wars were brought under control, it seemed hard to imagine how so much bloodshed, cruelty and injustice could simply be forgotten and the institutional weakness and disarray it exposed patched up without trouble. Even the best scenario posed serious challenges for any country – let alone for a young and deeply fractured democracy like Mexico, with an economy that steadfastly refused to grow at more than mediocre rates.

CHAPTER 6

Not Good Enough

ONE of the world's fifteen largest economies, Mexico's muscle is obvious in everything from its sheer physical size to the frenzy of activity at its international airports. Most major cities are ringed by a sophisticated network of highways, flyovers and tunnels, and are dotted with modern multi-screen cinema complexes. The bank buildings are shiny, credit cards are used widely, and a temporary breakdown in BlackBerry services in 2011 was important news. Multinational car manufacturers churn out vehicles, locally owned factories produce global beer brands, and few places in the world have anything like as many different international trade agreements.

Bountiful natural resources – from oil to gold to timber – abound in a nation of extraordinary biodiversity that attracts over 22 million foreign tourists a year. The majority might flop on beaches, but a good few trek off to view well-preserved colonial cities, while rock stars perform against a backdrop of pre-Hispanic pyramids surrounded by neatly mown grass. The occasional restaurant wins a prestigious international prize. Mexican contemporary artists and filmmakers command a world following. A sprinkling of top universities, internationally recognized intellectuals and scientists, and economists at the head of international organizations all show that this is a country that knows it has the potential to be a force to be reckoned with.

And yet Mexico is also a land of deep disadvantage. It has one of the most extreme indices of wealth disparity in the most unequal region of the world. In 2008, the income of the top 10 per cent was twenty-six times that of their counterparts at the bottom of the pile (the OECD average was 9:1).

There was a gradual reduction in inequality between around 1995 and 2005, but this has since levelled off and, even if it gets no worse (which many expect it will), the income distribution in Mexico is still significantly more unequal than it was in 1985.

The *Forbes Magazine* rich list in March 2011 contained eleven Mexican billionaires. This is more than in many major European countries, and includes the wealthiest person on the planet. Carlos Slim's fortune, at $74 billion, beat Bill Gates' by $18 billion and is roughly equivalent to 7 per cent of Mexico's GDP. Rooted in telecoms, the magnate has acquired important interests in mining, infrastructure, banking and retailing. For many Mexicans, a day would not be a normal day if they did not hand some money over to a Slim-owned company.

Slim is famous for disdaining ostentatious luxury, aside from his voracious appetite for classic European art, and even then much of his collection is on free public display in a Guggenheim-style museum in Mexico City. He is not the norm. The rest of the Mexican rich tend to wallow in conspicuous consumption and to lord it over lesser classes. They exist within a bubble of aggressive convoys filled with bodyguards that hog the roads, extensive plastic surgery, and uniformed servants who know their place. The bad taste hidden behind their walled mansions was exposed by photographer Daniela Rossell's 2002 book *Ricas y Famosas*, which pictured the pouting women of the extremely wealthy posing like tigers about to pounce. There is little to suggest that the coming of democracy has changed the prevailing ethos.

In the meantime, about half the population lives in poverty, with a third struggling to cover its basic nutritional needs. In remote indigenous villages, large families live in mud-floored shacks, cramming into one or two beds at night. Their lungs labour under the daily inhalation of smoke from wood-fuelled cooking stoves, as they try to stay healthy without running water, drainage or sufficient protein – let alone a nearby qualified doctor. The biggest treat that many children receive is junk food, bought with anti-poverty handouts.

The misery around major cities often mingles directly with the trappings of privilege. In Cancún many a chambermaid leaves behind air-conditioned hotel towers to go home to a metal-roofed box that doubles up as a mosquito-infested oven. Some of the communities who live in the warrens of dusty social decomposition that stretch into the desert around Ciudad Juárez have a nice view of the order and security on the other side of the border. When a luxury car fell into an open sewerage canal during a rainy season downpour in Mexico City, the family of the watchman who lived next to it barely escaped with their lives as their home flooded in minutes.

Beyond extreme poverty, inadequate public services make life a struggle for many more. State sector education does not provide most children with the skills required even to apply for jobs that promise social advancement. The number of places available in state-subsidized universities falls far short of demand, and there are minimal opportunities for vocational training. Despite significant advances in health coverage in recent years, the health system remains fragmented and partial. Filling a prescription from unreliable state stocks can turn into an odyssey of dawn rises and hours of queuing. Appointments to see specialists for life-threatening conditions within the state system are often for months ahead. In most major cities, public transport is slow and crowded, with no provision for the elderly or the disabled. Aside from superhighways that charge considerable tolls, rural road connections are often tortuous and slow.

From around 2009, some leading members of Mexico's influential *comentocracia* began insisting that the country should stop focusing on the extremes and start thinking about the middle classes. Some say these sectors have grown so much that Mexico should now be defined as a middle-class nation. They cite the rising proportion of people with possessions that improve quality of life: the number of families with a fridge rose from 68 per cent in 2000 to 81 per cent ten years later; the number with a washing machine from 52 per cent to 65 per cent; and those with a car from 33 per cent to 52 per cent. Ownership of mobile phones had exploded to 80 million by the end of the decade.

Well-known economists Luis de la Calle and Luis Rubio published a book about it called *Clasemediero: Pobre no más, desarrollado aún no,* or *Middle Class: No longer poor, not developed yet.* 'Mexico is turning into a middle-class society', they wrote. 'The consolidation of this sector is perhaps the most important issue for the future development of the country and the most important historical event of the last decades.' They identified two types of middle class with different sources for their relative material comforts. The traditional Mexican middle class, they argued, grew up within the corporatist state and owed its relative privileges primarily to jobs in the bureaucracy and unionized labour. They also identified an emergent middle class, typically made up of hard-working and hard-studying poor people who have dragged themselves up the ladder. They credited falling birth rates since the 1970s with being the main factor driving this new development, as it had led aspirational families to invest more of their assets in fewer children.

The middle-class definition is stretching things a bit. The increased proportion of women in the workforce (often used alongside consumer durables as a sign of socioeconomic transformation and new opportunities) reflects low wages as much as any social advancement. For a working mother in a low-income household, a washing machine becomes as basic a need as the availability of public transport, as there is simply no time to do the family's laundry by hand. The new Mexican middle classes also lack the voice and influence associated with such a status in more developed regions of the world.

Nevertheless, bringing the middle classes into the spotlight does show that the Mexican economy is more complex than merely a combination of a few haves and a lot of have-nots. There are also millions who, while they still struggle to get by, are acutely aware that there are many who are worse off than them. With more security and real routes for their aspirations, this sector could become a motor for further change that begins to address the deprivation and inequality that continue to hold Mexico back a hundred years after its Revolution.

The regime that grew out of the chaos of the Revolution initially dedicated its efforts to political and economic stability and basic reconstruction. The one-party model began to take shape under President Lázaro Cárdenas in the 1930s. He cemented the new regime's hold at the top by developing rules that provided for a peaceful transfer of presidential power every six years (*sexenio*), and so dissuaded the generals and regional power bosses from continuing their habit of periodic rebellion. Cárdenas, whose 'socialism' was developed against the backdrop of the Great Depression and the New Deal north of the border, also created organizations that incorporated the masses into the project. His major distribution of land to the peasants was plagued with problems, so that few ended up with fertile plots and the support needed to farm them. Even so, it ensured rural loyalty to the regime for decades. In the rest of the economy, Cárdenas rebuilt the transport infrastructure and a functioning banking sector. With known oil reserves low at the time, the economic impact of the nationalization of the country's oil reserves then appeared to be less important than its role in consolidating the idea of a national economic project.

Cárdenas left office having laid the foundations of the industrialization drive that brought GDP growth averages of over 6 per cent between 1940 and 1970, within a context of general stability in macroeconomic indicators from public debt to inflation.

The industrial expansion took place within a paradigm of import substitution, which protected the Mexican private sector from competition from foreign imports by way of high tariffs. At the same time, the state invested in infrastructure, as well as spearheading a drive to increase agricultural production through irrigation and the mass distribution of fertilizers and pesticides.

Each president stamped his personal seal on his *sexenio*. The exuberant era of Miguel Alemán Váldes was marked by a personality cult, the rise of the nouveau riche and considerable corruption. This was followed by the austere gravitas of Adolfo Ruiz Cortines, replaced in turn by the playboy charm of Adolfo López Mateos. Overall, however, these were the glory days of the PRI, in which the regime not only provided jobs and stability, but also created and expanded education and social services.

When the Revolution broke out in 1910, Mexico's population of around 15 million was overwhelmingly rural, illiterate and vulnerable to death from preventable causes. By 1940, there were still fewer than 20 million Mexicans, and two-thirds still lived in the countryside, with little access to education or health. Thirty years later, the population had shot up to 48 million and the rural/urban balance had almost been reversed. Illiteracy now dogged only around a quarter of the total, and decades had been piled onto life expectancy.

The mid-century was also a period of cultural effervescence that ranged from the monumental public art of the likes of Diego Rivera to the melancholy of Juan Rulfo's novels and the existential deliberations on the national character epitomized by Octavio Paz. The golden age of the national film industry produced such legendary figures as María Félix, while Hollywood stars gave the new resort of Acapulco a touch of international glamour.

The underbelly of misery was always there, and there were periods of conflict between the government and workers, resolved with bouts of selective repression whenever co-optation failed. Relations with the private sector were also prone to periods of tension, as when the quotas skimmed off by government officials were deemed by business leaders to have become excessive. Even so, as the economy kept growing, the regime never seemed even close to losing control – until the late 1960s, when pressures to democratize were brutally quashed by the hard-line President Gustavo Díaz Ordaz.

President Luis Echeverría took over in 1970 and responded to the political pressure by upping public spending under a populist leftist banner and by building an international progressive reputation that contrasted with his repression of domestic dissidence. But many of the projects ended up as badly planned 'white elephants', riddled with corruption. A wave of nationalization also left the regime's formerly cosy relationship with the private sector teetering on the edge. It all put government finances under strain at a time when the import substitution was running into problems because of the rising cost of capital imports. Echeverría also broke the tradition of leaving macroeconomic policy to the economists. He left office in 1976 with Mexico labouring under an exchange rate and debt crisis, as well as high inflation and unemployment.

President José López Portillo took office promising stabilization but threw this to the wind almost immediately following the discovery of one of the richest oil fields ever found anywhere in the world. The Cantarell fields were named after a fisherman who noticed a gurgling oil slick in the sea. It was a geological freak, perhaps caused by the meteorite that crashed into the Yucatán Peninsula 65 million years ago and that many people believe led to the extinction of the dinosaurs.

López Portillo pronounced that the extraordinary reserve meant Mexico's economic problems were over. All that was required, he said, was to 'learn how to administer abundance'. The president did not take his own advice. His government borrowed huge amounts from international banks to finance a frenzied and badly thought-out modernization drive. When the export of oil began to bring in the dollars at the end of the decade, it spent those as well. Corruption reached new heights, while the self-confessed macho president indulged his ego with a personality cult and rampant nepotism.

When interest rates increased and the oil price began to fall in 1981, the government continued to borrow and continued to spend. The president ignored his advisers, who urged him to devalue the peso: he did not, he said, want to devalue his presidency. This intensified capital flight, putting yet more pressure on the currency. By 1982, Mexico had to tell the world that it had no money to pay its debts amid a multiple and dramatic series of devaluations. López Portillo left office, a tragicomic figure who epitomized the decadence of the regime and who had transformed a tale of incredible luck into a story of heart-breaking waste.

The administration of the more demure President Miguel de la Madrid Hurtado brought a painful stabilization programme and the promise of 'moral renovation'. The social costs were huge, but the macroeconomic indicators were brought back into line – until things got knocked off track again by the 1985 Mexico City earthquake. Another peso devaluation was accompanied by rampant inflation. The misery belts around the major cities grew, and the flow of migrants north increased.

Mexican migration to the US goes back well over a century, although its impact was limited until the Bracero Programme began in 1942, designed to offset labour shortfalls in the US created by the Second World War. Bracero migration, focused on seasonal agricultural jobs, reached a peak in the 1950s, when around half a million people migrated under the programme each year. By the time the US ended the arrangement in 1964, there were already well-established routes for migrants not within the programme. They crossed the still highly porous border with relative ease to find work in the fields and, increasingly, the cities with few questions asked.

The phenomenon was circular. Migrants saved up their wages of a season or a few years and then went home to Mexico. Nationalism, as well as emotional ties to families left behind, still acted as a powerful deterrent to their moving permanently away, and those who did were viewed almost as traitors. These taboos began to relax with time, as the end of the Mexican economic miracle and the arrival of the crisis years prompted ever more to head north, to a greater range of states, and to do a broader assortment of jobs. In 1986, one-off legislation formalized the position of some 2.3 million Mexican immigrants already in the USA, and many more were allowed in through family-reunification programmes.

When he left office in 1988, de la Madrid had once again brought things under control in the domestic economy, this time by moving towards a free-market model. Joining the General Agreement on Tariffs and Trade (GATT) in 1986 brought cheap imports that helped keep price rises down. Up until the 1980s, foreign goods were available only to the rich in exclusive shops, or on the black markets of a few notorious *barrios*. The rest of the people turned on their Zonda televisions to watch pro-regime news and mind-numbingly frivolous entertainment.

The economic opening ran parallel to the development of major cracks in Mexico's cultural isolationism. By the end of the decade urban youth were not only eyeing Adidas trainers in the shops (even if they could not afford them), they were also listening to British rock bands on new and trendy radio stations. For decades the regime had kept international rock stars out of Mexico, nervous about large crowds of young people. The watershed moment there fell to the hardly revolutionary figure of Rod Stewart, and a concert he gave in the city of Querétaro in 1989.

But if the regime's willingness to break nationalist taboos helped it stay afloat, it also sowed the seeds of its own destruction. The final years of the de la Madrid *sexenio* were marked by a political struggle within the PRI that led to the departure of Cuauhtémoc Cárdenas Solórzano. The left-leaning son of President Lázaro Cárdenas opposed both the shift to the economic right and the lack of democracy, and his decision to abandon the party of power left the regime in the hands of the technocrats and the dinosaurs. The technocrats were US-trained economists, steeped in the then-fashionable idea that the free market solved all problems. The dinosaurs were the unscrupulous political operators, forged in the regime, who seemed to have been around since time immemorial. President Carlos Salinas de Gortari, who took office in 1988, was both.

Salinas accelerated the liberalization process to breakneck speed, negotiating the North American Free Trade Agreement (NAFTA) with the US and Canada. He also stepped up the closure or privatization of over a thousand state-owned companies that ranged from the telecommunications monopoly to fishing fleets, mines to a famous nightclub. He used income from the privatization and inflows of additional cash, attracted by government bonds in dollars, to fund a major government anti-poverty programme called Solidaridad, which conveniently doubled up as personal political promotion in every corner of the country.

Salinas, who had started his term under the shadow of the obviously dirty 1988 elections, became immensely popular at home, and was lauded as a near prophet abroad. A master of persuasion, he sold the idea that Mexico was poised to become part of the first world in a way that glossed over evidence that his administration was also riddled with cronyism and corruption. It was under him that Mexico joined the OECD.

The bubble burst just minutes after NAFTA officially kicked off, on New Year's Day 1994, with the sudden appearance of the Zapatista indigenous guerrilla army in the southern state of Chiapas. This was followed by a series of high-level assassinations. The murders of Luis Donaldo Colosio, Salinas' chosen candidate for the 1994 presidential election, and the PRI's Secretary General José Francisco Ruiz Massieu amounted to a political earthquake and revealed intense divisions within the party. They also exposed Mexico's economic fragility, as the government's dollar bonds came home to roost. Salinas left his successor an acute public and private debt problem and an obviously overvalued peso that he had refused to do anything about.

Ernesto Zedillo fell into the presidency almost by accident. An earnest, Yale-educated economist from a poor background, he had entered the bureaucracy – and then high politics – with the rising wave of technocrats in the 1980s. He ended up with the presidential candidacy in 1994 because the death of Colosio with the campaign already in full swing meant that it was too late, legally, for more obvious candidates to take up the mantle.

As president, Zedillo subordinated politics to a single-minded insistence on putting economic stability first. He did, however, make an unprecedented and dramatic move to draw a line under the Salinas years with the decision to go after the former president's brother. Raúl Salinas was imprisoned on murder charges and an investigation opened into his alleged laundering of millions of dollars derived from the drugs trade. For the first time in the PRI regime, former presidents and their families were no longer beyond reach.

In economic terms, Zedillo's administration began with yet another disastrously mishandled devaluation (although the new president could not be blamed for the inherited conditions that made it necessary) and a deep recession. Over $50 billion in emergency loans from the US government, facilitated by President Bill Clinton, averted collapse. Even so, the economy still contracted by 6.2 per cent in 1995, unemployment ballooned and disposable income all but dried up as the poverty rate jumped from 52 per cent to 69 per cent of the population.

Loan defaults, meanwhile, left banks near bankruptcy. López Portillo had nationalized the banks in 1982, and Salinas had re-privatized them a decade later, leaving the new owners to indulge in a few years of binge lending, including a fair amount of insider lending, before it all went 'belly up'. By 1998, the government had bailed the banks out to the tune of $60 billion. It was either that, Zedillo said, or let the entire financial system go under.

The austerity regime that Zedillo imposed on other government spending, at the same time as the controversial bailout of the rich bankers, was sharp and painful. The economic travails also triggered a major crime wave. Public sector cuts left law enforcement agents on the streets, and several of them found their way into organized crime, beginning with the kidnapping gangs that began to flourish in this period.

Difficult as the mid-1990s were, the economic discipline did clean up public finances and laid the foundations for a more solid recovery, this time rooted in booming exports under NAFTA. By the turn of the century, GDP was growing at over 6 per cent again and the mood was sufficiently upbeat to allow a traditionally risk-averse electorate to take a leap into the unknown with the election of Vicente Fox in 2000. Always the economist above all else, Zedillo did little to halt the political demise of the regime – and much to ensure a smooth transition away from PRI rule.

Over the first decade of Mexico's democratic experiment, the optimism about the economy began to fade and the pessimism to grow, until they more or less cancelled each other out. On the positive side, macroeconomic stability continued and was consolidated under the PAN. Between 2000 and 2010, inflation fell steadily, international reserves climbed to record highs, exchange rate devaluations determined by the market were relatively painless and the current account deficit remained manageable throughout.

The benefits of the new stability were most obvious during the Fox administration, when consumer credit ballooned, leading to a housing construction boom, as well as fast-growing sales of cars and consumer durables. Aided by high oil prices, the first PAN government was also able to expand a targeted anti-poverty programme (originally set up by Zedillo), which tied direct cash transfers to the very poor to school attendance and preventive medical visits. The Fox government also developed a new state-subsidized health insurance (the Seguro Popular) aimed at those outside the limited social security system. President Calderón followed much the same economic policies as Fox, encouraging the expansion of home ownership and consumer credit, as well as intensifying efforts to widen health care and anti-poverty programmes – always within the context of a commitment to keeping public sector borrowing tight.

The horizon, however, was clouded by a plodding annual average GDP growth of under 2 per cent throughout the first decade of the new millennium. NAFTA might have sparked an export boom that had quadrupled exports to the US to $280 billion a year by 2008, but the model had also proved itself unable to trigger a broader dynamism in the wider economy.

Some of the problems are associated with the rules of the agreement, which has encouraged an emphasis on Mexico's unskilled labour and a subsequent focus on 'assembly for export', usually involving imported inputs. This means that NAFTA has done very little to generate knock-on economic development, particularly local chains of production. It has even dismantled some that already existed. A high-tech enclave in central Guadalajara was promoted as a model for the future. But the big manufacturers that set up there preferred to rely on their global suppliers, so killing many local firms that had previously done well out of providing parts for the international companies that had been producing in the city before NAFTA.

NAFTA has also cemented pre-existing dependence on the US. Mexico might claim more trade agreements than any other nation, but 80 per cent of its exports still head to the US. Domestic consumption also remains a relatively minor factor in determining growth. Moreover, Mexico does not just depend on US consumers buying Mexican-made products; it also needs US employers to employ Mexican migrants, and US tourists to visit Mexican beaches. In the good times, this has proved enough to keep the economy ticking over quite nicely, but insufficient to kick-start the kind of growth rates required to make a real dent in poverty rates. In the bad times, it has made the country particularly vulnerable to economic problems over the border, breathing new life into the old adage about Mexico catching pneumonia when the US catches a cold.

Dependence on the US was the main reason why the world financial crisis of 2008 and the subsequent global recession hit Mexico particularly hard. The Mexican economy contracted by 6.1 per cent in 2009 (which was three times worse than the average for Latin America and the US). Of the world's major economies, only Russia's shrivelled more.

Aside from export industry workers and areas where export industry dominated, the crisis sliced into the incomes of the poor, particularly in regions dependent on migrant remittances. Remittances had ballooned from $6.6 billion in 2000 to a peak of $26 billion in 2007, only to fall back again to $21.2 billion at the end of the decade.

Most worryingly for many, the success in reducing poverty – from 54 per cent of the population in 2000 to 43 per cent in 2006 – was reversed, and poverty was back up to 51 per cent by 2010. Extreme nutritional poverty had likewise dropped from 24 per cent to 14 per cent, only to creep back up to 18 per cent. It would have been much worse had the government not prioritized targeted anti-poverty programmes, but it was hardly much to celebrate.

President Calderón boasted that Mexico had endured the knocks rather well because stability had kept all major macroeconomic indicators (aside from growth) steady and the financial sector sturdy. The government had done this by keeping anti-cyclical spending notably modest, at a time when much of the world was doing the opposite. It even pushed through a VAT hike in the middle of the recession. The recovery that began in 2010 was hampered by renewed troubles in the US and Europe, but Calderón could justifiably claim credit for steering Mexico away from the meltdown scenarios that by 2011 were playing out in countries like Greece, Italy and Spain.

But if the 1995 crisis had revealed how desperately Mexico needed financial discipline before the NAFTA motor could kick in, the troubles that began in 2008 underlined just how inadequate this was for a country that requires the creation of a million new jobs a year just to keep up with new demand. Mexico's so-called 'demographic bonus' – by which a wave of young people gave the population pyramid a large bulge in the middle – is being transformed from an asset into a liability.

❋ ❋ ❋

The combination of laudable stability and inadequate growth is not just the defining characteristic of the Mexican economy in the new political era on a conceptual level. It is also played out in the lives of many Mexicans as a grinding struggle to keep aspirations alive.

Diana León lives on the low-income outskirts of the capital with her two younger siblings, her mother and her father. She was fourteen in May 2011, and I have known her since she was three years old. Together with her family, she hovers on the cusp of poverty, clinging to the hope of one day reaching the middle class. Diana is exactly the kind of person that Luis de la Calle and Luis Rubio consider the font of optimism for the nation.

The family lives in a cinder-block house up a steep, deforested hillside. It was built by her grandmother, Mercedes, with what she saved during a lifetime of domestic service and selling at local markets. Whenever it has been in a position to do so, the family has made small improvements to the house. Over the years, the local authorities have brought drainage and electricity to the *barrio*, but the road up the hill was only paved around 2009.

Mercedes was born in Oaxaca, but moved to the capital as a young, single mother in one of the waves of urban migration that accompanied periodic crises in the rural economy. Around 2003 she was diagnosed with uterine cancer and was given a hysterectomy at the Hospital General, a health institution that caters for poor people with no access to other parts of the state system. The hospital kicked her out on the day of the operation, although she was bleeding and could hardly walk. After that a very aggressive course of radiation left her cancer free; but it may have damaged her gut permanently, for she continued to get weaker and thinner. In between endless waits for appointments with state sector doctors, Mercedes would somehow get together the cash to visit cheap, private doctors who cater to people just like her who believe payment automatically brings better treatment. It did not. Mercedes also went to see a succession of quacks and witches who did little more. The family was devastated when she died in 2010.

Mercedes had helped instil in Diana the idea that she has the potential to go far. She is a bright kid, a good student, and the family's hope for the future. Her younger brother, Oscar, is able and creative, but has learning difficulties and struggles in school. There is no institutional support for him. Her little sister, Padme, is hampered by childhood rheumatic arthritis. Flare-ups – brought on by throat infections – leave her temporarily hobbling in pain and unable to hold a pencil properly.

Their father, Oscar, ekes out a living with a variety of self-employed activities. In the autumn of 2011 he was focusing on assembling small painting kits for children and then selling them for a small mark-up, earning about 4,500 pesos ($375) a month; but he was optimistic things would soon improve. Before that he made belts out of biscuit wrappers. The whole family helps with whatever his current project is.

A few years ago Oscar bought a battered old car. This helped with the transportation of his wares, which get crushed on the buses and metro trains, but the family sold the car after Oscar got an infection in one eye, put off attending to the problem and eventually lost the eye in 2011. The family economy temporarily collapsed because of the cost of the operation. Since then, they have joined the federal government's expanding Seguro Popular health insurance scheme, which now at least provides them with some kind of safety net.

Diana willingly helps her mother with domestic chores and cares for her younger siblings, but she finds it a strain. Her tasks became more onerous in 2011, when her mother began to suffer from searing headaches and her sight started to fade. Luckily they had recently bought a washing machine, but Diana still often finds herself up until 3 a.m. finishing her homework.

Diana goes to a state school near her home that has a good reputation. She came close to being kicked out one year because she almost failed to get together the 900 pesos ($75) that the director demanded from all pupils at the start of term. Diana knows this is illegal, but says there is nothing she can do.

Despite getting some of the best marks in the class, she was left out of a scholarship programme, which, she says, benefited others who got worse grades and had fewer financial difficulties. She misses her best friend, who struggled in similar ways, and who died when she tripped and fell off the balcony of her home because the family had no money for a railing.

Diana's role model – her father's cousin, Carmen – urges her to stay strong. Carmen came from a similarly disadvantaged background, but became an accountant. She is not completely secure, but she does have basic amenities and a relatively comfortable life. Her eldest child graduated as a lawyer, and her youngest works in web page design. Carmen's family is a model of the middle-class future that some dream of for Mexico; but it also shows how the extended family in Mexico steps in to fill holes left by the state. She helps Diana's family out when she can.

The absence of the rampant inflation and devaluations of previous decades, combined with some improvements in basic public services, has helped the León family keep their heads above water and feeds their hope of a better future. But working hard and staying out of trouble is no guarantee of advancement. They also need to hold off the stream of structurally rooted bad luck that haunts them – and they need one clever teenage girl to keep believing that all her efforts will be worth it in the end.

As she approached her fifteenth birthday, Diana was filled with trepidation. She dreamt of going into advertising and fantasized about the time when she would show everybody how far she could climb. She was under no illusions about the size of the gradient ahead. 'I don't want to grow up yet', she told me. I'm not so sure she was ever really a child.

Such stories of struggle, resilience and creativity are found all over Mexico. They represent both the belief that it is possible to move up through the existing system, and at the same time they illustrate why so many give up and either fatalistically accept that things will never really change or drift into criminality. For all her disadvantages, Diana's intelligence, the emotional support she receives from her family, and her access to education provide her with more reasons to be hopeful than many of her contemporaries. One of the biggest challenges facing Mexico today is to create a context in which the role that good and bad luck play in determining the outcome of stories like hers begins to diminish. Aside from improving public services and safety nets, the central task for the government has to be finding ways to increase the number of opportunities available.

All Mexico's major political parties agree that the way to do this is to promote faster economic growth without jeopardizing stability. Their ideological differences are reduced to contrasts in emphasis. The PAN stresses the need to keep the books balanced, but also recognizes that more state action is required to reduce poverty and inequality and to fuel domestic consumption. The PRD promises more public investment to kick-start growth, but also pledges that macroeconomic indicators would be safe in its hands. The PRI tends to be rather shiftier about where its priorities lie, claiming instead to embody effectiveness rather than principle.

Most mainstream political leaders also broadly agree on what the main obstacles are to achieving the longed-for combination of dynamism and stability, even if they posit different solutions. Tax revenue is generally recognized as insufficient, public spending condemned as often wasteful, and continued corruption singled out as unacceptable. There is also broad consensus that the oil industry is in a mess, that big business is overly protected from competition, and that the informal sector serves as both blessing and curse at the same time.

Measured as a percentage of GDP, Mexico's tax revenue is consistently the lowest of all the OECD countries. Mexican revenues totalled 17.5 per cent in 2009, compared to 48 per cent in Denmark, 34.3 per cent in the UK and 26 per cent in the USA. The country's closest developmental peers fared better, as did most of the rest of Latin America. Furthermore, around a third of Mexican tax revenues come from oil production. This reduces the ability of the state-owned oil company Pemex to reinvest in exploration and new technology, and highlights the fact that non-oil revenues are scandalously paltry. The context of falling production makes this particularly worrying.

Mexico's revenue problem is not so much that tax rates are low, but rather that so few people and companies actually pay the amount of tax they theoretically should. The informal sector is the most obvious culprit when it comes to tax avoidance, but the fact that so many within it earn amounts below the minimum taxable bracket means the issue is difficult to separate out from the problem of poverty. There are no such concerns when it comes to the elaborate collection of loopholes that have long allowed Mexicans at the top of the income scale to pay very little tax. In 2001, the US giant Citigroup bought the Mexican bank Banamex for $12.5 billion. The sale was said to show international confidence in the

Mexican economy, but the fact that the authorities authorized it free of capital gains tax shocked many Mexicans, particularly since the Mexican owners of Banamex had been bailed out by the government just a few years before.

A similar situation affected the mining sector at the end of the decade. Gold mining has become particularly attractive in a context of record-breaking prices. The mining companies, many of them Canadian, pay income tax but are not required to pay any royalties on the non-renewable resources they remove from the ground at considerable environmental cost.

Such jaw-dropping cheek encourages the general public to assume that the rich are either left to get richer tax free or else systematically fiddle their books and get away with it. President Felipe Calderón reinforced this popular wisdom when, at the end of 2009, he accused big business of getting away with paying around 1.5 per cent tax, instead of the 28 per cent required by law. 'Philanthropy, sponsorship of sporting and cultural events, and gifts of medical equipment are all very well,' he said, 'but they should also pay at least a part of the taxes that Mexicans need.' The harsh words triggered a backlash from business leaders, who insisted they had not only paid everything they owed, but created most of the jobs in the country as well. It also prompted a barrage of criticism from other commentators, who thought it grotesque merely to appeal to the patriotism of the wealthy rather than force them to pay up.

Middle-class Mexicans are the most vocally resentful, convinced that they are paying for the tax vacuum left by the informal sector, the rich, and the inefficiency and lack of ethics in government spending. It is common to find pillars of respectability fiddling around the edges. Self-employed private doctors regularly offer patients the option of not paying VAT, in exchange for not requiring a receipt. I know of one established left-wing intellectual who calls for increased public spending, but also puts his tax code on other people's restaurant receipts to increase his deductible expenses. Aside from salaried employees, taxed at source, who always make their purchases in formal establishments that hand out receipts, and the odd eccentric who sees paying taxes as a civic duty, few Mexicans make the contributions that they should.

Strategies to deal with this can be divided into those proposed by people on the right, who prioritize broadening the tax base downwards, and those from people on the left, who prefer the idea of improving the enforcement of existing rules and closing loopholes for the biggest earners.

President Fox belonged to the first group, and twice tried (and failed) to push through a reform eliminating the long-sacred VAT exemption on food and medicines. Following an orthodox neoliberal argument, his government insisted that this was the only practical way of increasing revenue, because it was the easiest to collect and police. Fox's efforts were felled by the political furore this produced in a country where so many spend so much of their meagre incomes precisely on food and medication.

President Calderón's approach was rather more sophisticated, but only slightly more successful. His 2007 reform established a minimum corporate tax to reduce evasion. This helped increase revenues somewhat, but nowhere near enough. In 2009 he also tried to partially eliminate the food and medicine sales tax exemption with a 2 per cent tax, promising that the revenue would be channelled into anti-poverty projects. The reform ended up as a 1 per cent rise on general VAT, without touching the exemptions.

Politicians are also reluctant to engage in a full-scale debate over the need to reform local taxes, which barely exist in Mexico, since local government is funded almost entirely by federal transfers. Local property taxes amounted to only 0.2 per cent of GDP in Mexico in 2010. This was about a fifth of the proportion in Brazil, a twelfth of what was collected in Chile and a fifteenth of revenues in the US, while the amount raised this way in the UK is twenty-two times greater.

Distrust of the way the state spends the money it does have provides another disincentive to take the political risk of forcing the population to pay more tax. It is hard to convince ordinary Mexicans that they should tighten their belts to fill state coffers when the media exposes case after case of wanton waste. The need for more income consequently dovetails with calls on the state apparatus to cut its excessive costs.

Mexican politicians and high-level bureaucrats get salaries and benefits that are often much better than their counterparts in the developed world. They live in a bubble of privilege that includes everything from chauffeurs (often used for domestic errands) to subsidized haircuts. The Mexican adage 'To live outside the budget is to live in error' was coined during the glory days of one-party rule. It has held true in democratic times, with the institutions created to ensure the transition being among the most spendthrift of all.

A CIDE research centre study released in 2010 concluded that the Mexican Supreme Court costs three times as much to run as the US Supreme Court. It is nearly eight times as expensive as the Constitutional

Tribunal in Spain. The Mexican court also employs far more staff and resolves significantly fewer cases, while its magistrates receive incomes that are around 45 per cent higher than their US counterparts and nearly double those of their Spanish peers.

Mexican elections are also among the most expensive in the world. The International Foundation for Electoral Systems compared the costs of elections per voter in fourteen countries across Latin America in 2009. While the figure stood at over $17 in Mexico, the average across the remaining countries was under $1.

Ambitious Mexican politicians have also responded to the coming of genuinely competitive elections by spending ever more tax pesos on promoting their image. Those already in public office, particularly governors or legislative leaders, tend to dress this up as public information. It is hard to pin down the figures, but slickly produced prime-time infomercials, in which governors show off the roads they have built, do not come cheap.

While frittering away public money on self-promotion generates anger in informed circles, the greatest popular censure centres on graft. Corruption is often named by ordinary Mexicans as the root cause of everything that is wrong in the country. The promise to stamp it out has been an obligatory component of election campaigns for years. The failure to take more steps to do so after the PRI lost the presidency is one of the great disappointments of the transition, as well as a brake on economic progress.

Marta Sahagún de Fox sank into the comfortable sofa in her large airy office in her husband's presidential library and delicately wiped away a tear. 'I'm only human and of course I feel sadness, indignation and anger', said the former first lady, her voice breaking with emotion. 'I also feel dignity, courage and strength.'

It was a typical Sahagún response to a question about the allegations of corruption that hung over her time in Los Pinos, which had ended a couple of years before. A series of books had accused her of everything from excessive expenditure on her wardrobe to securing lucrative government contracts for companies associated with her sons from a previous marriage. They were also said to have used government property to throw wild parties at taxpayers' expense. The best known were written by famed Latin American muckraker Olga Wornat, who had published similar works on President Carlos Menem in Argentina. Mexican investigative journalist Anabel Hernández also wrote two, before turning her attention to drug-related corruption.

Sahagún was also dogged by stories from businessmen who claimed she had demanded gifts in exchange for audiences with the president. One said she had made him give Fox a red jeep as a birthday present. The couple could later be seen driving it around the small town in the central state of Guanajuato where the Fox family hacienda and the new presidential library were located.

Congressional investigations into the allegations of corruption and nepotism would fade without reaching any clear conclusion. 'Oh, the doubts!', sighed Sahagún, looking over towards her desk, behind which was a photograph of Mother Teresa of Calcutta. 'I have an internal peace and tranquillity that nobody can take away from me, and every day I go to bed knowing that I have done my duty.'

The allegations against President Fox and his family were less extreme than those that have stuck to several previous Mexican presidents in the popular imagination, but they were still serious. What was probably most damaging, however, was the way in which they underlined the superficiality of Fox's early promises to eradicate the culture of corruption from the Mexican political system. Instead of explaining why there were no 'big fish' in jail as he had pledged there would be, he reduced the corruption issue to exaggerated claims of near saintly purity for himself and his wife.

The much less flamboyant Calderón and his more discreet family were not generally accused of getting rich on the back of political office. Even so, the second PAN president was equally hesitant to launch a genuine crusade against corruption during his administration, even though 'Clean Hands' was one of the most frequently used slogans of his presidential campaign. He was also damaged by accusations that the drug cartels had infiltrated the upper levels of his security apparatus.

One case of classic-style alleged graft eloquently illustrates how little was done. First of all, it was only revealed because of a US investigation launched in 2007 into allegations that US companies were paying tens of millions of dollars to officials in the Mexican state-owned electricity company CFE. Despite public US statements describing the practices, though not naming the officials, the Mexican authorities did nothing until the *Houston Chronicle* named CFE's head of operations, Néstor Moreno Díaz, in August 2010. Soon after that, court documents detailed transactions that included the gift of a $1.8 million yacht, a $297,000 Ferrari Spider sports car and $170,000 to pay off credit card bills.

Shortly after the Houston stories Moreno Díaz resigned, as stories began to emerge of his obviously suspect lifestyle and flamboyant imperiousness – he was said to get his subordinates to line up to say goodbye when he left the office. The following month, his yacht – *Dream Seeker* – was seized and an arrest warrant was finally issued in August 2011. Police did arrest him a few weeks later, but he was released within hours on a judge's order. A little more legal toing and froing and the former top official was a fugitive again. He was still missing at the beginning of 2012, as was the Ferrari.

For all the passivity of the PAN presidents, there are some indications of a moderate reduction in federal corruption levels, primarily because political pluralism means that federal budgets are under more scrutiny from opposition political parties and the media. This is not true in the regions where the feudal-style governors operate with almost no oversight. Decentralization of power has also added new fuel to the state-level corruption markets in a way that appears independent of what political party is in power.

Transparencia Mexicana (the Mexican branch of the anti-corruption organization Transparency International) is less concerned with major scandals and more with the day-to-day graft that conditions access to services for ordinary people, and which the organization surveys every two or three years. These studies suggest that overall corruption levels in Mexico have changed little following the transition to democracy. In 2001, 10.6 per cent of procedures surveyed involved bribes that averaged 110 pesos (about $11 at the time). Transparencia concluded that Mexicans spent 23.4 billion pesos ($2.3 billion) on bribes that year. In 2010 the survey found a corruption rate of 10.3 per cent, with bribes averaging 165 pesos ($14) and total expenditure estimated at 32 billion pesos ($2.6 billion).

The frequency of bribes required to access federal social programmes fell dramatically over the decade, but the money paid to get a job in government increased greatly. Bribery of the police – ranging from avoiding detention to getting an investigation started – remained scandalously common. Corruption in some states got worse, while it got better in others; but the trend sometimes switched back again.

The huge quantities of money wasted are perhaps less important than the way persistent corruption encourages Mexicans to maintain a fluid view of rules and regulations. This feeds into the reluctance to pay taxes, and also into a sense that it is normal to have to pay extra for such basic public services as attendance in an emergency room or to secure a child a place at a state school.

This ethos also affects the private sector, where consumers are extraordinarily tolerant of paying over the odds. A poll carried out by the research company Demotecnia in October 2010 concluded that only 10 per cent of mobile phone users were dissatisfied with a service that is not only often patchy, but also significantly more expensive than in many countries where incomes are much higher.

Eduardo Bohórquez López, the head of Transparencia Mexicana, insists that the picture is not all negative. He believes that the implementation of a constitutional reform in 2008 that mandated all levels of government to standardize accounting procedures will revolutionize transparency. Bohórquez is similarly enthusiastic about a new generation of activists, particularly young people using new technologies, who are starting to monitor how public money is used and how private companies take advantage of consumer passivity, though he also admits that their efforts still have limited resonance with both the general public and the powers that be.

The attempt to get legislation allowing for class action law suits proved a particularly salutary experience in this respect. Most Latin American countries already provide routes by which relatively small groups can represent the rights of an entire collectivity in court. A determined group of consumer activists spent four years lobbying the federal legislature to get something similar in Mexico and had received a positive response from some key legislators. They envisaged a time when a class action suit could help force improvements in the standards of care in all public hospitals, or force down mobile phone charges for all consumers. But the law that was eventually passed in 2011 to allow collective legal action in Mexico restricted it to those directly involved in the case, which rendered it all but pointless.

Daniel Gershenson, head of the group Al Consumidor, was almost more upset about the way he felt the politicians had strung the activists along. He later learned that, just as a stronger version of the law seemed on the point of being approved, the private sector lobby had swung into action behind the scenes to ensure that only the watered-down version got on the statute books: 'I have to admit that we were a little naïve to think it would be any different.'

※ ※ ※

Rarely have so many paid so much to so few. The Mexican economy is bursting with sectors that are controlled by a handful of companies, and often by just one or two. A 2010 study by the OECD and Mexico's Federal Commission for Competition estimated that the average Mexican household spends a third of its budget on goods produced in markets where competition is severely limited and prices consequently inflated. The proportion is even higher in low-income households.

More competition (so the free-market mantra goes) would encourage innovation, investment and better services at lower prices, which would mean more consumption. More consumption would mean more growth, which would create demand for more jobs and so lead to greater prosperity. This reasoning is accepted by politicians across the political spectrum. Sworn political enemies Felipe Calderón and Andrés Manuel López Obrador can sound interchangeable on the issue. In 2010, the president said: 'Monopolistic and oligopolistic practices prevent the kind of growth in employment required to improve the well-being and quality of life of Mexican families.' His old leftist rival's Alternative Project for the Nation proclaimed: 'Competition should be a priority of the state and the government should be committed to guaranteeing it formally and structurally.'

Agreement is one thing, action quite another. The monopolies and oligopolies of Mexico today are the business world's contribution to the broader phenomenon of the 'de facto political powers', and are often directly associated with the shrinking of direct state involvement in the economy that ran parallel to the demise of one-party hegemony in politics. Most of Mexico's successful business figures laid the foundations of their market dominance in the new political era by earlier interpenetration with the PRI regime. For some, the symbiotic relationship began many decades ago, in the era of import substitution industrialization; for others, it was associated with the mass privatization of state-owned companies in the 1990s.

The problem today is not just that the companies are taking advantage of market dominance established in years gone by, but that the regulatory bodies cannot or will not do their job. Even when they do act, the brigades of lawyers employed by the corporations can stall their rulings for years in the courts, and sometimes get them overturned. Part of the problem is that many regulatory laws were designed to be vague, so that they could be interpreted in a way that reflected the priorities of the PRI president in office at any given time. Now that presidents no longer have the power to set the agenda in that way, there is almost always ample opportunity to challenge a regulatory decision and protect the status quo.

Take corn tortillas. Mexicans may be eating fewer than they used to, but they still eat an awful lot – an average of four to five a day. Queues form every lunchtime outside little shops where screeching machines churn out the tortillas, which are then piled up, wrapped in a piece of brown paper and sold by the kilo. Walmart superstores have similar outlets that make them little money, but are deemed a necessity to keep the customers coming in.

Not that it really matters where tortillas are sold, since they largely go to swell the profits of a single company, Gruma, which controls 70 per cent of the market. Gruma is a classic case of a long-established company that has done very well out of the new economic and political conditions. The leap to dominance came with the post-NAFTA removal of state control of the market, and also from government measures that encouraged a move away from tortillas made from fresh dough (produced by many different companies and then distributed to outlets), to tortillas made from dehydrated flour, produced by Gruma. In the meantime, the company began expanding abroad to supply the growing international market.

There was a brief crisis in Mexico in early 2007, after tortilla prices soared. Gruma and the other few companies that control the distribution of corn blamed rising international corn prices, but were accused of hoarding and of speculation. After a tortilla protest march in Mexico City, the government negotiated a deal with the companies to cap prices, at the same time as it approved new corn imports from the US and elsewhere. For many critics, the solution epitomized the problem. Instead of investigating the big companies for alleged monopolistic practices, the government sat down and hammered out what it called 'a gentlemen's agreement'.

The details vary from case to case, but similar stories of soft-pedalling on monopolies and oligopolies pervade the Mexican economy. Mexico has the highest per capita consumption of soft drinks in the world, with Coca-Cola accounting for some 70 per cent; the beer market is dominated by two companies; the distribution of liquid petroleum gas, the cooking fuel used in the vast majority of Mexican homes, is controlled by a handful of families. Intercity road transport, air travel, banking and medication distribution are all also limited by the fact that a small number of companies provide the vast majority of services, and attempts to break such strangleholds rarely succeed.

In 2004, a group of Mexican businessmen imported a boatload of concrete from Russia, claiming that, even after paying the transport costs, they would still save 10 per cent on Mexican prices in a market dominated by the company Cemex. However the ship was kept in dock for almost a year, unable to unload. Its crew finally gave up and sailed for home. The businessmen claimed that Cemex had used its influence behind the scenes. Seven years later, the investigation launched by the regulator was still stuck in court.

Sometimes the economy develops in a way that suddenly pits the giants against each other, as in the struggle over control of technological convergence in digital communications. This has put the telecommunication companies owned by Carlos Slim (Telmex and Telcel) that dominate fixed and mobile phone services up against the two networks that hold sway in commercial TV (Televisa and TV Azteca).

The ins and outs of 'the battle of the titans' are complex, but essentially boil down to Slim trying to get into the TV market, while the existing networks gear up for an assault on his dominance of mobile phones. Ironically both sides accuse each other of monopolistic practices. For years, Telcel kept competitors in the mobile sector at bay by charging high fees to connect to its network. By engaging in endless court cases, it had succeeded in neutralizing the rulings of the sector regulator that interconnection fees should be lowered. Then, in early 2011, a Supreme Court ruling gave the regulator more teeth and it immediately slapped a $1 billion fine on Telcel for 'monopolistic practices'. Shortly afterwards, the communications ministry formally ratified the prohibition on Slim entering paid TV contained in the 1994 concession, when he bought Telmex from the state.

Some celebrated the new regulatory assault on Slim as the government getting serious about combating the biggest monopoly of all. Others saw the decisions as helping the expansionist plans of the TV networks. Slim might be the wealthiest man in the world, they argued, but Televisa and TV Azteca were the nation's most important opinion formers. In the run-up to the 2012 elections, that kind of influence was priceless. In the meantime, there was a noticeable shift towards a more pro-government tone in TV news coverage, particularly in relation to the drug wars. A coincidence? Most media watchers assumed not, although I knew of no one who had conclusive proof that an actual deal had been made. Slim, meanwhile, was generally perceived to have a good chance of redressing the balance after the elections, when politicians are less worried about what the networks say.

It appeared that the unavoidable shake-up in communications triggered by technological change was getting sucked into a logic dominated by the interests of established oligarchs and how these fitted with the political context of the time, rather than meeting the needs of the Mexican economy to keep pace with what is happening in the sector internationally. In the meantime, telephone connections remained expensive and erratic; internet connections pricy, patchy and slow; and two networks continued to dominate 96 per cent of open-channel programming.

If sectors as diverse as tortillas, cement and telecommunications demonstrate how vested business interests help to mould policies in ways that do not necessarily favour the wider economy, things are not necessarily any easier in sectors where the state theoretically runs the show. The most important of these is the oil sector, where the brakes to dynamism have less to do with personal fortunes than political capital.

A middle-aged housewife called Pati stood in front of a row of riot police in the Mexican capital and berated them for betraying the nation: 'You should be ashamed of yourselves. You should join the people and stop them selling off what belongs to Mexicans. The oil is ours.'

It was spring 2008, and Pati was taking part in a series of marches and rallies organized by Andrés Manuel López Obrador and aimed at torpedoing a government energy reform proposal in the legislature at the time. The reform in question was actually a rather timid attempt to make the state-owned oil company Pemex a little more efficient. It contained no plans to sell off Mexican oil into private hands, foreign or otherwise.

The impassioned movement against the reform only made sense when placed in the context of Pemex's role as a nationalist symbol, rooted in its formation in 1938 from the expropriation by the state of the foreign companies operating in Mexico at that time. The protests were symbolically led by women who called themselves the *Adelitas*, in reference to the nickname given to female participants in the Revolution, originally drawn from a folk song.

Most Mexicans recognize that Pemex urgently requires reform if the oil sector is to become a motor for growth; but the political battle over the Calderón reform underlined how the Mexican economy is held back not only by the problems of the present, but also by the ghosts of the past.

The 1970s oil boom accelerated the company's degeneration into a morass of mismanagement, inefficiency and corruption. The oil workers' union, the STPRM, became so powerful that it could twist the corporatist relationship to its own advantage and accumulate substantial benefits as its leaders became impressively rich. A layer of fat-cat bureaucrats at the top of the company also did everything possible to protect their substantial privileges and opportunities for graft. Government dependence on oil revenues meant that dolefully small amounts were spent on exploration and the acquisition of new technology.

In the late 1980s and early 1990s, the liberalizing ethos within the Mexican government led many in the global energy sector to assume that Pemex would be privatized along with most other state-owned companies. They underestimated just how much Mexican presidents fear resistance to change within the company itself, as well as a backlash among the general population. Governments have also been deterred from taking the plunge by the knowledge of the extent to which their budgets would shrink without the option to use the company to top up their paltry tax revenues – a crude reality that not even the purist neoliberal technocrats in the finance ministry can easily overlook.

President Carlos Salinas, who privatized almost everything in sight during his term, went after a legendarily corrupt Pemex union boss with whom he had a personal feud, but he did not dare do much more. President Ernesto Zedillo reorganized things a little, but stopped short of a full liberalization drive. The more timid President Fox shied away from the issue almost completely, despite his private sector roots and ideals.

In the meantime, Fox created yet more problems for the company by cranking up production, which rose by 50 per cent at the key Cantarell oil fields between 2000 and 2004. Production eventually reached 2.1 million barrels per day, but then quickly fell off: by 2010, the field could squeeze out less than a fifth of that. In the time-honoured fashion of Mexican presidents before him, Fox administered the abundance with little obvious benefit to most Mexicans, at the same time as he pushed the wonder field into terminal decline much faster than sensible management would have done.

President Felipe Calderón, who had been Fox's energy minister for eight months, made energy reform the economic priority of the first half of his administration. True to tradition, he did not fully embrace the private sector ethic that every serious observer assumed he subscribed to. Instead, the proposal he sent to the legislature in 2008 boiled down to giving Pemex a little more autonomy from government interference. There were also some rather complicated ways of introducing limited private investment into refining and deep sea operations, all wrapped in rhetoric that claimed the project was fundamentally statist. The obvious ambiguities provided the space for López Obrador to plausibly argue that the president was trying to privatize by the back door. At the time, the former presidential candidate required a cause around which to mobilize his supporters, in order to prove that he was still a political force to be reckoned with after failing to get the 2006 election annulled.

The lack of ideological honesty and programmatic clarity on both sides condemned the ensuing debate to sterility. The right-leaning, pro-business government lost a golden opportunity to openly argue in favour of private sector participation, at a time when polls were beginning to show that the traditional nationalist rejection of this was losing some of its passion among the general population. It might not have succeeded in getting such a reform approved, but it could have helped move the discussion forward. It also let go a chance to address the bad experiences of past privatizations – negotiated in the back rooms of political power under the PRI – that had helped create a new oligarchy, which had done so much to stunt competition in the new political context.

The left, meanwhile, failed to focus on developing alternative proposals for reform within the state-owned framework. The Brazilian oil company Petrobras and Norway's Statoil had both transformed themselves into world leaders while remaining under control of the state. There was no reason why Pemex could not do likewise, but this required an openness to new ideas that did not exist within the context of López Obrador's claim to be mounting an emergency rear-guard defence of the nation's assets in the face of a conspiracy to privatize. With Pemex sinking fast, the central debate around the presidential initiative became whether or not the reform was an attack on national ownership. The question of whether it was a good framework for managing the country's energy resources in the twenty-first century was relegated to near irrelevance; and those experts who argued that ownership was less important than the strength of the agencies regulating the sector were sidelined altogether.

Seven months of tortuous party political negotiations eventually produced a reform that had cross-party support, but no more lucidity or coherence than the original proposal. All parties nevertheless lauded it as a great achievement. The legislators boasted about the way they had overcome the climate of political polarization to hammer out a deal that provided everybody with something to celebrate. López Obrador claimed that his protest movement had blocked imminent privatization. President Calderón called the reform 'historic' and, in a televised message to the nation, seemed to claim that it would make poverty a thing of the past.

Within a year, government and opposition parties alike accepted that a new energy reform was needed. Booming oil prices made this somewhat less urgent than it might have been, in fiscal terms, as did the discovery of some small and easily accessible deposits, but the underlying problems remained as acute as ever.

Towards the end of 2011, the PRI's presidential candidate, Enrique Peña Nieto, surprised many by announcing that he would make changing the rules to open Pemex up to more private investment his 'signature issue'. It was time, he said, to go beyond the ideological discourse that had held the industry back. The PRI, he added, was the party to do this because the PRI could rely on the historical credibility of having nationalized the industry in the first place.

Peña Nieto, at least initially, made much more of his oil plans abroad than at home, suggesting a certain nervousness about kicking off a full-scale political battle. Even so, it was a remarkably bold move from a candidate who usually skirted around controversial issues. It was also surprising how little reaction it caused within Mexico, particularly from López Obrador as he geared up for his second presidential campaign. Could it be that a more mature debate on the oil sector was on the horizon? If this turned out to be the case, the time wasted over the reform in 2008 would seem even more unnecessary.

With the Mexican economy unable to provide the million new jobs required every year to soak up new entries onto the job market, the informal economy is the only way for many people to survive. Notoriously difficult to define, estimates of its size vary enormously – from 30 per cent of the workforce up to 60 per cent. No company, for example, could be more apparently formal than mobile giant Telcel, yet much of the business of selling both pre-paid and contract services is outsourced to tiny street-corner firms that often employ people informally. Whatever measure is used, the sector has not diminished since 2000. If the ever-diversifying organized criminal economy is included, then it has grown significantly.

I also find the term 'informal economy' rather problematic because, while it stems from the lack of rules and regulations defining how and where it operates, it suggests an intrinsic lack of seriousness that belies the discipline of many of those who populate even its purest forms. Take José Luis. For fifteen years he earned his keep from tips received for waving cars into parking spaces on a pleasant leafy couple of blocks in the central Colonia Roma in Mexico City. Sometimes the owners gave him their keys so he could move the vehicles around, and sometimes he earned extra cash washing them as well. José Luis usually worked six or seven days a week, turning up promptly around 8 a.m., after making the journey from his home on the eastern edge of the metropolis. With every passing year, the journey got longer, until by 2009 it reached an average of an hour and a half each way. By then he also faced the additional problem of newcomers muscling in on his patch, as the area became increasingly trendy. These included the son of the doorman of a nearby apartment building and burly security guards from a newly opened local private clinic. Somehow they worked out an arrangement in which they all shared the territory until about 8 p.m., unless the wakes held at the funeral parlour on the corner or concerts at the new folk music club kept them busy until much later.

One day in 2010, José Luis accidentally bumped a car he was moving and made a small dent. When the owner threatened him with the police, he decided it was time to move on. With José Luis effectively sacking himself, the doorman's son took up the open position of senior car parker within the network of informality that turns a primarily residential street into a source of survival for dozens of Mexicans who work hard for little gain – and with almost no security.

The most successful of these might well be Magos, who runs a taco stall on one corner, storing equipment in the branches of a tree overnight and employing helpers when business is brisk. Javier, one of several rubbish collectors who supplement the inadequate municipal service in return for a tip, is one of her most regular customers. He went 'informal' after losing his job as an accountant's assistant in the 1995 crisis. The block also attracts a number of vendors who wander through selling everything from brooms to potted palm trees. The number of casual construction workers waxes and wanes as empty plots, once occupied by buildings that collapsed in the 1985 earthquake, are filled by new apartment buildings aimed at yuppies. A small, largely hidden, army of cleaners and nannies is periodically joined by electricians, plumbers and other self-employed tradesmen. Together they epitomize the results of a 2011 OECD study, which concluded that, of twenty-eight nations surveyed, Mexicans work the longest hours for the least pay.

The informal sector is frequently blamed for holding back Mexican productivity levels, making it a contributory factor, as well as a symptom, of the formal economy's inability to provide sufficient jobs. One possible way out of this chicken-and-egg situation is to reform the existing labour legislation in a way that replaces its closed-shop corporatist paradigms of decades gone by with a new, more flexible ethos that encourages job creation within the formal sector. The first major obstacle to this has been political, and has ensured that two PAN administrations have come, and almost gone, without a labour reform. Even though the unions are now much weaker than they were, the proposals to make it easier to hire people on short-term contracts, as well as easier and cheaper to fire staff, are still politically very delicate.

There is also the question of how much this would really help to detonate job creation in the formal sector, given that it is debatable that Mexicans prefer badly paid formal-sector jobs with reduced benefits or the chance to earn a little more in the informal sector with no benefits at all. This is particularly true, given that many social security provisions that currently come with formal employment are designed with people somewhat higher up the ladder in mind. The Fox and Calderón governments' expansion of health coverage through the Seguro Popular has also further reduced incentives to seek out low-paid formal-sector jobs.

The bottom line is that the informal sector has been a valuable buffer for the failings of Mexico's economic model. Without its extraordinary flexibility and sponge-like ability to absorb workers cast adrift by formality, the unemployment rate would be completely unsustainable. Even the informal sector, however, is not infinitely expandable.

The approaching evening was just beginning to take the edge off the heat when the line of migrants began snaking up the scrub-covered hill towards me on a fairly remote part of the 1,969-mile (3,169km) border with the US. They walked slowly but steadily in single file, carrying little backpacks that presumably contained a bare minimum of water, something to eat and perhaps a sweater for the night chills. There were about twenty-five of them, mostly young and youngish men, but also a few women. One had a twelve-year-old girl in tow.

They said they were expecting to be in the desert for around forty-eight hours, hiding by day and walking by night. The terrain was rugged and rattlesnakes were common, but torches were forbidden for fear of the Border Patrol. Some had already tried the same route days or weeks before, but had been unceremoniously repatriated at the nearest major crossing point, where three lines of high fencing, cameras and constant patrols make it well-nigh impossible to cross undetected. Now they were trying again. They would perhaps try again and again, until either they got through or their resolve finally cracked. As they set off into the sunset, towards the border line itself, the girl flashed me a look of steely determination. She was soon indistinguishable from the rest. Not long after that they all disappeared from view.

It was 2008, and the latest huge wave of Mexican migration north was beginning to tail off. Over the previous decade or so, the annual net increase in new migrants to the US had been around 500,000 and the total number of Mexico-born people living over the border had risen to about 10 million, or around 10 per cent of Mexico's population. There had been a long history of migration by young rural males from a handful of states, but now this traditional demographic group had been swelled by more women, more city dwellers and more people from other regions of the country. The money they sent home kept (and keeps) millions of families afloat.

PRI presidents had tended to gloss over the migration issue (which was perceived as an embarrassment), but Vicente Fox changed all that. The first president of the post-PRI era called migrants 'heroes' and sought to harness their energy in the service of the new era of hope that he claimed to have brought.

Fox genuinely cared about migration. His vision stemmed from his home state of Guanajuato, which is one of the core central and northern Mexican states where migration has such a long history that it has developed into a kind of cross-border symbiosis.

The best-case scenario was represented by small towns like Chavinda, in the state of Michoacán, from where migrants had been heading north for decades because the local agricultural economy could not sustain the population. Many Chavinda migrants had obtained US residency or citizenship, and every Christmas they returned en masse to drink in the culture of the old country and to parade the material benefits of the new.

When I visited Chavinda in 2006, the normally sleepy little town square, with its neatly cut ornamental trees, buzzed with activity. Every few hours a newly wed couple emerged on the steps of the church under a shower of rice. The priest said he performed four marriages a day, compared to one a month during the rest of the year. Mingling with the *mariachi* musicians and knocking back the tequila, the tougher variety of bi-national youth in baggy trousers (and sunglasses turned the wrong way round on their heads) cruised the narrow streets in big cars, stereos blasting, while their preppy college equivalents flitted around in spotless outfits. Without Chavinda, the migrants felt rootless. Without the migrants, Chavinda would have gone under.

Fox sought to replicate such experiences all over the country by intensifying existing programmes designed to encourage relations between enclaves of migrants in the US and their communities at home. The idea was to channel more funds into projects that went beyond individual family survival and spurred wider development. Favoured initiatives included paving small access roads to isolated communities, constructing new school buildings, buying ambulances and putting a good number of new roofs on old churches.

Remittances did rise quickly, as did the number of expat associations and the projects they paid for (jointly with government funds). But while this helped to alleviate poverty temporarily, it could not trigger sufficient growth to act as a brake on migrant flows. The problem was not just the number of projects, but also the fact that so few were directed towards the creation of viable businesses that could grow and multiply the effect. The few that were aimed at this were undertaken without the kind of improvements in education, training and support that could help them become self-sustaining in the future.

The biggest disappointment of the Fox years, however, was the failure of the president's energetic attempts to secure a more liberal attitude to mass Mexican migration in the US. Instead, Mexican migrants found themselves facing ever tighter border controls, which (though they had begun around 1994) intensified after 9/11 and again with the drug wars.

Fox's successor, Felipe Calderón, largely dropped migrant issues from his political and media agenda. Migration from Mexico was once again treated as an embarrassment that highlighted the country's inability to provide enough jobs of sufficient quality to stop people voting with their feet. Meanwhile, it kept getting more difficult to cross.

Between 2000 and 2010, up to five hundred people perished each year in the treacherous currents of the Río Bravo or in ever more dangerous desert crossings undertaken to avoid detection by the ever more vigilant US authorities. They were also pushed further into the hands of ever more unscrupulous people traffickers. The *coyotes* or *polleros* had for decades included many honourable locals who sold their knowledge of the best routes by which to cross the border. They got tougher as the border got tighter, but as late as 2001 it was still easy to find smugglers hanging out in the market square of Agua Prieta, just over the frontier from Douglas,

Arizona, negotiating their fees in full view and happy to openly discuss how business was going with passing reporters. A few years later that idea would seem laughable.

The initial change came with half-hearted Mexican efforts under Fox to respond to US pressure to pursue people-smugglers as a condition for future immigration reform. It developed into a more chilling dynamic, as a new generation of smugglers emerged. Prices increased from a few hundred to thousands of dollars, at the same time as evidence piled up of a rise in the number of assaults, rapes and murders of migrants en route. By the time the border area exploded in drug-related violence towards the end of the decade, organized crime had taken over much of the people-smuggling business. Some cartels started kidnapping migrants for ransom as a lucrative side business.

Ever since the first stage of the border crackdown in the mid-1990s, migration experts in both Mexico and the US had insisted that flows were largely unaffected by the increased dangers of the journey. Desperation, they argued, would mean migrants were always willing to take the risk. By 2010 many were not so sure. A new government house-to-house employment survey suggested that the number of migrants leaving Mexico had fallen fairly steadily, with seasonal variations, from over a million in 2006 to around 400,000 in 2010. Much of this was obviously related to the economic troubles in the US, but there was also anecdotal evidence on the border that many repatriated migrants were deciding to give up and return home, rather than try again.

While questions remain as to whether this trend will continue once the US economy has fully recovered, it seems clear that tighter border controls and the colonization of people-smuggling networks by organized crime are encouraging those who have made it to the other side to stay longer than they might otherwise have done. The same government survey estimated that the number of annual returnees actually fell from over 500,000 in 2006 to around 300,000 in 2010, confounding predictions that the recession in the US would trigger a mass return. Mexicans who lose their jobs in the US apparently prefer to be unemployed and in hiding from the threat of deportation at a time of intense anti-immigrant feeling, than to return to an even more uncertain future in Mexico, with a subsequent hazardous journey back again once the US economy picks up. For those who are more established, the increasing difficulties of making periodic visits has fuelled efforts to bring their families north, on the grounds that this requires just one successful crossing rather than many. Each year between 2000 and 2008, the proportion of minors among those Mexicans repatriated from the US was about double what it had been in the previous decade, according to National Migration Institute figures. This suggests that more children are making the journey, rather than waiting for their parents to come and visit.

I met Diana García and her son outside a special 'module' for deported child migrants in Tijuana in 2008. These were set up by the government to provide some security to minors who would otherwise be simply shunted back over the frontier by the US authorities along with the adults. García had been living illegally in California for several years with her husband, while her mother looked after her four children in Mexico City. The plan had been to bring the family over in stages, beginning with her ten-year-old boy. 'I pack onions for $8 an hour in California, while in Mexico I can earn 40 pesos a day. Four dollars a day!', she said. 'What would you do?' But the plan was not working out. Mother and son had endured seven failed attempts to sneak through the mountains, and García was wondering whether she should finally give up.

The changing dynamics of migration associated with the need to keep border crossings to a minimum can be expected to have important economic impacts in Mexico in the future. These may well include a slow waning of remittances, as migrants focus their efforts on staying put and reuniting families on the northern side. Arguably even more importantly – if the greater difficulties in crossing the border are indeed deterring potential migrants from even setting out – this will increase pressure on employment in Mexico even further. The efficacy of migration as a pressure valve for social tension seems set to fade.

Mexico's economic promise is real, and the country is full of hard-working and creative people who appreciate the consolidation of macroeconomic stability following the political transition. But with every year that passes, this has been exposed as not enough. Even if much of the blame for the mediocre growth in the new millennium can be ascribed to international factors, that still leaves the issue of the domestic brakes on development. While it was always unrealistic to expect the coming of electoral democracy to suddenly unleash the country's economic potential, it was surely reasonable to hope that it would bring a new ethos that might at least set the ball rolling. If the approaches chosen by the political elite to this issue – which is of enormous and direct concern to all Mexicans and their livelihoods – have lacked imagination and determination, what hope was there for a display of administrative flair in areas that have traditionally been relegated to the background, such as the environment?

CHAPTER 7

Environmental Time Bombs

Just as the rainy season was getting going in the early summer of 2007, President Felipe Calderón knelt down to plant a pine in one of central Mexico's most important forests. 'To plant a tree is to plant a better country', he said. The president had brought along his youngest son for the photo opportunity, in order to underline the point about the future. He had put on a poncho to emphasize his solidarity with the locals.

Calderón's main objective was to back up his claim to be the greenest president the country had ever seen. Mexico, he said in a speech during the event, was taking a vanguard role in a global reforestation effort promoted by the United Nations Environment Programme, which had set a target of a billion new trees in a season. While Spain was committed to planting 20 million saplings over four years, the president emphasized, Mexico was going to put 250 million in the ground before the year was out.

By the beginning of 2008, Calderón began boasting that his target had not only been met, but that it would be increased to 280 million for the season to come. 'There were those who laughed', he gloated, 'those who didn't believe it possible.' Not long after that, the UN formally recognized his 'global leadership' in reforestation.

But there was a problem. Before the second season had even got under way, exposés in the media were contrasting pictures of the previous year's freshly planted saplings, full of promise, with the dried-up sticks they had become. The original presidential pine, apparently tended with reverential care, was doing pretty well; but this was not the norm. A widely reported Greenpeace study of a selection of reforested areas concluded that only 10 per cent had survived.

For months the government denied the claims. After the release of a report by the official federal auditor in March 2009 it went quiet. Overseen by independent forestry experts, the report shied away from estimating survival rates, but it did identify serious deficiencies in the programme that had rendered the reforestation all but pointless.

It was a particularly embarrassing situation, given that Mexico's relatively long history of federal reforestation programmes had long ago provided the country with proof that mass tree planting is not a simple business. The first projects, in the 1980s, were designed primarily to create jobs rather than thicken tree cover. The government bought the trees from locally run nurseries and gave them to communities, which often never even bothered to plant them. Many were, at the time, focused on clearing their land to cultivate saleable crops, so why would they? In the 1990s the programmes began to include incentives to reforest, but they remained a resounding failure from the point of view of how many of the plants survived.

Fox extended and expanded things still further – and got similarly grim results. Then Calderón plucked a new, enormous, target out of the air and launched his mass reforestation effort with unprecedented fanfare, but without changing anything fundamental about the way things were done. According to the official auditor's analysis of what went wrong, the infrastructure was obviously overstretched, and the nurseries were unable to produce enough trees, which were distributed far too widely across the country. Moreover, many of those that were produced were undersized and yellowing before they were even put in the ground, and about 15 per cent died during transportation. The auditor's report also emphasized such basic mistakes as planting the wrong species in the wrong kind of soil. The biggest problem of all was probably that, once planted, the trees were largely left to wither in neglect. Either the president did not know the history, or he never expected the scrutiny that exposed a high-impact story filled with optimism as a bit of a farce.

From the exuberant jungles that cover huge swathes of the south, to the temperate pine forests of the centre and the vast deserts in the north, and from the long, rugged sierras, high plateaus to the lowland plains, all sandwiched between 9,330 kilometres of coastline, Mexico is, by any measure, an extraordinary country in environmental terms. Classified as 'megadiverse', it provides a home to around 10 per cent of all known flora and fauna on the planet, hundreds of which are endemic to Mexico. It takes first place for reptiles, second for mammals and fourth for amphibians and vascular plants. A tenth of the globe's bird species fly over its territory. Mexico boasts large oil and gas reserves, as well as abundant deposits of metals yet to be mined. An enormous array of agricultural products grows on a large variety of different types of soil.

Such richness, however, carries with it a particular vulnerability to unsustainable exploitation, as well as to newer challenges, such as climate change, and ill-conceived (or ill-executed) plans to deal with the problems. The dangers are heightened by the fact that, as in most developing countries, environmental concerns have traditionally been viewed as luxuries for the rich. Environmental issues have become a staple of political rhetoric and a focal point for citizen action only in the last few years, and both governments and the general population still tend to relegate them to the background if other priorities are also in play.

Some of the major problems have, indeed, been around for much longer than anybody can remember, encouraging the sense that they can be dealt with at a later date. Nowhere is this clearer than in attitudes to deforestation and erosion. Many of the areas now at risk of tipping from semi-aridity into desert were cool, luxuriant forests before the conquistadors arrived in the early sixteenth century. As Joel Simon elegantly charts in his 1997 book *Endangered Mexico*, the first phase of the devastation began in the early colonial period, with the thirst for timber around mining centres and then sugar plantations. Marauding herds of newly introduced farm animals came next. European weeds came after them.

The assault continued in the centuries that followed, with the arrival of the haciendas and mass cultivation for export. The twentieth-century drive to industrialize put new pressure on the land, born of the need to feed the rising populations of urban centres. The land redistribution that began in the 1930s hardly touched the big estates in the fertile valleys, and instead provided small farmers with plots in marginal areas – plots that they were then encouraged to over-farm.

The so-called 'Green Revolution' – which focused on intensifying agricultural production – started in Mexico in the 1940s, before being exported across the developing world, along with the acute dependence on chemical fertilizers and pesticides that was at its core. These increased yields spectacularly, until the backlash of ecological imbalance set in. Many small farmers ended up with exhausted plots, on which hardly anything grew at all. If they had control of forested land, they cut down the trees; if they did not, they migrated and swelled the cities. At the time almost nobody in government paid attention to the destruction of the rural environment that accompanied the phenomenon of urban migration.

During the decades of the PRI's economic miracle and the oil boom that followed, concerns about industrial pollution were easily dismissed as unpatriotic diversions from the business of promoting national development.

Juan Antonio Dzul was a teenager when the Ixtoc 1 oil rig exploded and sank in June 1979 in the Gulf of Mexico. An estimated 480 million litres of oil poured into the sea over the next ten months. Champotón, the fishing village where he grew up, was about 120 kilometres from the rig. 'The oil covered the reefs and washed up on the shore. Fish died and the octopuses were buried under the oil, which filled the gaps between the rocks where they live. We threw our nets at sunset and then couldn't pull them back the next day because they were so heavy', he told me. That spill was the worst on record before BP's Deepwater Horizon exploded in 2010 and revived old memories.

The government's scramble to plug the well included putting a funnel on top and injecting mud, saltwater, cement and golf balls (in the hope that they would expand once inside). They used booms and skimmers, and dumped large amounts of chemical dispersants on the surface slicks. This sent the globules of oil down to the sea bed, where they devastated shrimp larvae. With the oil washing up on the beaches, most international concern focused on the threat to those that doubled up as nesting grounds for the endangered Kemp's Ridley sea turtles. Usually newly hatched sea turtles follow their instincts and immediately head down the sand into the sea, but this would have meant swimming right into the approaching slick. An emergency operation airlifted them into cleaner waters beyond.

The Ixtoc spill was quickly forgotten – not just in the world, but in Mexico, too. The domestic media of the time remained wary of displeasing the regime, and those directly affected were not in the habit of complaining too loudly about their lot. 'Nobody protested back then. We just stopped fishing for a while until things got back to normal', recalled Dzul. A slow, largely natural regeneration did take place; but according to the fisherman, even today he comes across black coatings on the rocks that are several centimetres deep and release the unmistakable smell of oil when broken.

The Ixtoc spill came just before a wave of protests did take place over oil pollution, particularly in the southern state of Tabasco. They grew to be such a nuisance that Pemex paid out large amounts of compensation for lost crops, damaged land and contaminated water. The movement died down after a few years, and in most sectors concern about pollution was once again relegated to the status of unaffordable luxury in the context of a series of severe economic crises.

The government finally created the country's first institutions explicitly charged with protecting the environment in the late 1990s. This was partly a spin-off from the negotiations of the NAFTA trade agreement with the US and Canada, and US fears that American companies would take their jobs south, attracted by the opportunity to pollute with impunity. Local elite-based environmentalist groups had also emerged and consolidated into organizations with the capacity to influence government policy.

President Ernesto Zedillo appointed Julia Carabias Lillo as the country's first environment minister in 1994. An earnest biologist with a solid academic track record focused on finding solutions to environmental problems, she was receptive to dialogue with activists outside the government. The sincerity of her commitment was rarely questioned. But her political effectiveness at overcoming entrenched interests and bureaucratic blindness was.

With the fall of the PRI in 2000, many assumed that the continuing opening-up of the political system would move environmental issues closer to the centre of the national agenda. It seemed like a natural development of the dynamic already established in the previous decade, as well as in tune with international trends and the democratizing ethos that accompanied the end of one-party rule.

'A lot of people, including myself, thought there would be some big changes', says respected academic and veteran environmentalist Exequiel Ezcurra. 'This didn't happen.' Ezcurra was one of a group of similarly established professionals invited to join the Fox government. He became the head of the semi-independent National Institute of Ecology. Like most of his peers, he left around the middle of the presidential term, frustrated at the lack of substance behind the president's rhetorical commitment to the issues.

President Calderón employed fewer notable environmentalists than his predecessor, but his personal concern for the environment appeared more genuine. Nevertheless, although he had considerable success in raising Mexico's environmentalist profile abroad over climate change, there was little evidence that there was any shake-up in day-to-day policy making at home – at least not until a disaster struck, and sometimes not even then.

The federal government's relationship with sceptical NGOs with access to the media did not improve, and it became increasingly common to hear activists talking as if the country were on the edge of environmental catastrophe. This was still not a particularly pressing issue for most of the population, which continued to put the environment far down its list of priorities (well below the economy and security). Even so, it added to the widespread feeling of impending doom that took hold in much of Mexico during Calderón's administration, as the drug wars escalated and the economy struggled.

But are things really that bad? In some ways they certainly are. The political transition has made little difference to most of the major environmental problems facing the country: the old ones have continued to advance, and new ones have emerged. From peasants struggling to eke out a living on deteriorated land to city slum dwellers inundated with sewage, and from receding beaches to rivers running blue with contaminants – the sheer number and variety of environmental emergencies is staggering.

Even so, in other areas things are inching forward in a positive way. A dramatic expansion in better-managed protected natural areas, new and accessible databases on such long-taboo issues as pollution, and bicycle lanes in the capital all illustrate the fact that environmental concerns are now firmly established on the political agenda, albeit still far from the centre of it. Public consciousness and activism are rising slowly but surely.

Ezcurra pins much of the blame for the lack of the sea change he had hoped for on the more general failure of Mexico's democratic transition to dismantle the old top-down administrative habits of old and to replace them with something more responsive to citizens. The consequences of this lack of innovation have been particularly acute with respect to environmental concerns, because the old system had so few established channels through which they could be fed up to political decision makers. The public's input is largely restricted to the opinion polls that politicians survey, and which usually show that the majority of the public do not pay that much attention to environmental issues. Measures mandating consultation exist in some instances – new roads, for example – but these are rarely more than a formality, unless the protests of those affected grow into enough of a nuisance to force a modification of that particular project.

A determined community of Huichol Indians stopped the construction of a road through their land in the central state of Jalisco in 2008, with the help of national support. The road did not have the necessary permits and violated international treaties on indigenous rights, signed by Mexico. But while the victory was significant locally, there is little to indicate that it has encouraged the authorities to take more care about how they develop their infrastructure projects.

The limited communication also means squandering the energy of a new strain of grass-roots activism that goes beyond protest to claim a more propositional role. The most famous of this new crop of activists come from small rural communities, and focus their efforts on trying to halt the degradation of the land they farm and, in some cases, spearhead longer-term projects of regeneration. They have become known as 'peasant ecologists', and their potential contribution could be much greater if they received more support. For most of these new activists, the best hope of attracting attention still comes when their causes are taken up by the big national environmentalist groups that have now established themselves as a clearly defined lobby.

The NGOs play a key role in drawing attention to problems and possible solutions, as well as in supporting grass-roots organizations. At the same time, however, their tendency to automatically dismiss all government initiatives as empty rhetoric gives the authorities little incentive either to try new approaches to complex problems or to improve programmes shown to be flawed.

The limited number of specialist environmental reporters exacerbates the polarization and lack of communication. In stark contrast to the subtlety of political and economic reporting, most environmental stories (with a few notable exceptions) are based either on exaggerated official claims or on apocalyptic NGO reports. There is little room for a more nuanced vision of the challenges and the attempts to address them.

The aftermath of President Calderón's rush to plant 250 million trees in 2007, the majority of which subsequently died, illustrates how this situation can block progress even when everybody agrees on the basics of what should be done. The government never openly accepted that the project had been a failure, but it did stop promoting it as a great success. If pushed, it cited a study of the 2008 season by the Autonomous University of Nuevo León, which put overall survival rates at 40 per cent. This was hardly much to shout about, particularly since, while two of the states surveyed registered rates of over 60 per cent, four had below 10 per cent.

The quiet appointment of a new head of the National Forestry Commission in 2009 did, however, suggest a tacit official recognition of

the problems. Juan Manuel Torres Rojo began discreetly refocusing reforestation efforts on a few strategic areas, at the same time as he increased
post-planting monitoring and government support for maintenance. 'I
don't want to say that the project got out of control. Let's just say that it got
complicated and there was a lack of strategy', he told me in 2011. 'We have
evolved since then.'

Nobody seemed to want to draw attention to these positive developments.
The government was disinclined to remind the public of its earlier mistakes.
The big NGOs that had done so much to point out the original absurdities
seemed reluctant to applaud the subsequent improvements. Both sides
consequently lost a perfect opportunity to welcome the rectification of a bad
programme, the very fact of which could have served as a springboard to
something much more genuinely ambitious – the reversal of deforestation.

The rate of deforestation in Mexico actually improved significantly during
Calderón's term in office. The estimates vary wildly, according to how a
forest is defined, but those published by the Food and Agriculture
Organization (typically the lowest but the most consistently produced)
conclude that the area lost per year declined from around 235,000 hectares
between 2000 and 2005 to 155,000 hectares between 2005 and 2010.
Experts have credited everything from more programmes to improve agricultural productivity, to migration from rural areas (which relieves the
pressure on marginal land). Mass reforestation was obviously not an
important factor, but more support for the rectified programme would
have boosted its ability to promote a broader range of community forest-
management programmes that offer one of the most promising routes
towards reversing the trend altogether.

Environmentalists around the world began pushing the community
focus several years ago. They argue that it is both more effective than
grand-scale reforestation and better than purist conservation efforts, such
as national parks – especially in a country where the resources to police
such reserves are severely limited. Many activists also claim that it is far
more sensible to help people find a way of making a living out of their own
trees than to set up big carbon credit programmes that are vulnerable to
being monopolized by oil, mining, car and gas corporations. They also say
that Mexico leads the way.

The land reform of the 1930s left a legacy of communally held forests,
and over 70 per cent of woodland was still collectively held in 2010. For

decades this meant little more than a piece of paper, as the government granted private companies concessions to exploit the timber, regardless of who formally owned the land. These concessions were phased out from the 1970s and communities took back control of their forests. Some of the projects born of this change have become remarkably successful, particularly in the southern state of Oaxaca, where rural community organization is traditionally strong. In some areas, deforestation and erosion have not only slowed but have been reversed. Even the odd dried-up old stream now gurgles again.

My favourite example of innovation within the community paradigm comes from the tappers of the chicozapote trees that grow in the jungles of the Yucatán Peninsula, on the border with Belize and Guatemala. In the rainy season, the chicozapote produces a sap called 'chicle' that was the raw material for most chewing gum from around 1870 until petrochemical substitutes came along in the 1950s. During the boom years, when chewing gum symbolized the American Dream, an estimated 20,000 *chicleros* set up camp deep inside the Mexican side of the jungle for the season. By the end of the twentieth century the business was only kept limping along by Japanese gum manufacturers, whose consumers still retain a taste for a bit of the natural product in their mix. Then, just as the end seemed nigh, a group of former state bureaucrats came up with the idea of a certified organic biodegradable product and brought the tappers' cooperative on board. By the time I visited in 2009, they had several contracts to supply high-end chain stores in Europe.

'We live off the jungle, so we look after it', a *chiclero* called Ricardo Baños told me from half way up a tall, straight chicozapote trunk. Supported only by a rope wound around his hips and the tree, he cut a zig-zag wound in the brown bark to reveal bright red wood. Blindingly white chicle trickled down the channel into a bag at the bottom of the tree. Spider monkeys played in the foliage above.

Community forestry projects work best where community organization is already strong, as in many indigenous communities, and are particularly helpful as a way of discouraging farmers from clearing their land of trees to plant crops. They also help deter poor peasants from sneakily cutting down trees on communal land to sell the trunk for a small sum. They are not, however, a panacea for all Mexico's deforestation problems. They can help somewhat with forest fire control, indirectly, but have little impact on urbanization – the other major cause of deforestation in Mexico. They are all but powerless when the pressures come from organized crime.

Logging by armed gangs is a minor cause of deforestation on a national level, but its impact in specific areas can be devastating. In spring 2011, the P'urhépecha community of Cherán in the central state of Michoacán decided it had had enough of the loggers, who had left parts of their communally held forested land all but bare. When they tried to resist, they suffered retaliation, to which they responded with a self-defence strategy. This amounted to a mini-uprising and included barricades at the entrances to the town. Cherán ground to a halt. Children were kept away from school and the economy began to dry up. Masked community spokesmen patrolling the barricades told reporters that they believed the Michoacán authorities were colluding with the loggers, and demanded that the army be deployed in the area.

After that, things got even more complicated. The government sent troops and claimed they had controlled the situation. Community leaders said the federal forces were doing little more than milling around the mountains. 'We look after the forests and you protect the loggers', Salvador Campanur told President Calderón and assembled ministers during a meeting between victims of drug war-related violence and the government in June 2011. 'The devastating ecological impacts are your responsibility.' Later that year, the community took its claim to autonomy further by refusing to allow the Michoacán electoral authorities to organize the state's local elections in the municipality.

The escalation of the deforestation problem in Cherán into an explicit challenge to political authority stemmed from frustration with the state's inability to protect natural resources from the de facto power of organized crime. But powerful groups with an interest in overexploiting the environment do not necessarily have to wield guns or operate outside the law to get away with it. Sometimes they even find ways of doing it with government funds and support. The vulnerability of the authorities to pressure from vested interests that profit from activities that damage the environment – a vulnerability that has arguably increased in the context of the political transition – represents another major reason for the continued bleak vision of the country's environmental future.

When Hurricane Wilma barrelled into the mega-resort city of Cancún on the north-eastern tip of the Yucatán Peninsula in the early hours of 21 October 2005, it bent palm trees to the ground and felled electricity poles like twigs. Then it parked on top of the city for two days and dumped phenomenal quantities of rain. By the time the weakened storm meandered off towards Florida, the streets were filled with floating debris, some of the poorer and flimsier *barrios* of the city had been destroyed, and even the sturdiest of the battalion of big and brash seafront hotels were looking distinctly the worse for wear. But what fell down or cracked because of Wilma would prove far less significant than what floated away. Cancún's famed white sand beaches had all but disappeared.

The first stage of what would become the Cancún mega-resort was built in the early 1970s on a long, thin, mosquito-infested island that had previously been inhabited by three fishermen. It was a short hop from the mainland, near a village with a population of five hundred. The initial zoning regulations and a limit of three floors – about as high as the palm trees – gave way to chaotic development in the late 1980s, and the construction accelerated from 2000. The expansion of the resort obliterated the mangroves that once filled the area and kicked off the slow but sure death of significant parts of the second-biggest coral reef in the world, a short boat ride away. Where it was not trampled to death, the reef was poisoned by sun screen or smashed by pleasure boats going off course.

By the time Wilma struck, Cancún boasted 28,000 rooms and received some 3 million visitors a year. The whole area, which includes the fast-developing stretch of coast to the south known in the brochures as the Riviera Maya, accounted for about a third of national tourism income.

Cancún's struggle to resurrect its beaches after the hurricane opened a whole new chapter in the resort's destructive history. In panic mode, the government funded the implantation of 800,000 cubic metres of sand, sucked up from the sea bed, only to see it drifting off again within months. By 2009, the situation had become so serious that the beach in front of the Gran Caribe Real Hotel was cordoned off with yellow crime-scene tape and patrolled by soldiers, while the authorities investigated its owner for poaching sand from his neighbours.

It had become as clear as the normally cloudless skies that Wilma was only partly to blame for the erosion. The real culprit was the construction of too many high-rise complexes, crammed together along a dune that could not cope any more. The holiday paradise that looks out over a calm and impossibly beautiful turquoise sea had not only destroyed much of the surrounding environment, but it had also begun to destroy itself.

After the first post-Wilma beach reconstruction ended in disaster, the authorities and the tourist industry devised a much bigger plan. This involved 6 million cubic metres of heavier sand, dredged from a bank just off the island of Cozumel, forty-five nautical miles away. The federal, state and municipal authorities promised to foot the $80 million required to carry it through. Local activists warned that moving the sand would leave Cozumel more vulnerable to hurricanes, and would alter currents in a way that threatened marine life. They pointed out that it was likely that the new beaches would be gone again in a few years' time anyway.

Their campaign failed. The environment ministry approved the requisite impact studies in double-quick time, and dredgers brought in from Dubai began work at the end of 2009. 'We sell ourselves as a place of sun, sea and sand', local business leader Rodrigo de la Peña summed up the situation for me at the time. 'That's rather difficult to do if we don't have the sand.'

Cancún, it seems, is too big to fail, and its beaches were wide and gleaming again in time for the 2010 Easter high-season influx. When President Calderón opened them, accompanied by his environment minister, he stressed that the government's support for the project, 'despite considerable resistance', was 'incontrovertible proof' of its commitment to the tourism industry. The crisis deemed solved, local authorities authorized a new 180-room eleven-storey hotel, and enthusiasm surged again for the imminent construction of a second international airport, eighty kilometres down the coast. By 2011, a new state governor was beginning a campaign to get Formula One motor-racing to come to the resort.

Cancún epitomizes a national tourism policy born in the middle of the twentieth century that has always measured its success primarily in terms of the numbers attracted to large coastal resorts. In many cases, the developments also brought juicy profits for political patrons, who bought up land relatively cheaply in the area before construction began, and then ploughed federal funds into the infrastructure as the value of their property soared.

The model originally took off in Acapulco in the immediate post-Second World War era, vigorously promoted by President Miguel Alemán. The resort milked its glamour days when Elizabeth Taylor regularly moved her court there, along with the likes of Lana Turner, John Wayne and Frank Sinatra. But the times when it seemed obvious that John and Jacqueline Kennedy would honeymoon in Acapulco slid away as slums crept up the steep hills cradling the legendary bay and untreated sewage flowed into the water. By the 1990s, Acapulco had transformed itself into the standard holiday destination for the working classes, whose numbers boomed after a new high-speed road to the capital was opened in 1993.

The resort could also rely on US 'spring breakers' (looking for sex, sun, sea and sand). There were a few exclusive resorts on its fringes, as well as the odd drug-lord mansion. In the meantime, the federal government sought to repeat the original formula in a whole array of other mass resorts that were mostly further up the Pacific coast.

For a while, in the 1990s, it seemed that people in power might also begin throwing their weight behind other kinds of less damaging tourism. They started putting more energy into promoting Mexico's colonial cities, as well as its archaeological sites. There were even some attempts to galvanize eco- and conservation tourism. Sector pioneer Ron Mader believes this was motivated, at least in part, by Mexican pique over Costa Rica's success at establishing itself as a Mecca for ecotourism, despite having less biodiversity to boast about.

Whatever the causes, many assumed that the new political era that came with Vicente Fox's election in 2000 would provide a major new boost to more environmentally friendly forms of tourism. They were proved wrong. More than a decade later, Mader says, official support remains uncoordinated and patchy, down to the near total absence of the most basic statistics on independent travellers in the country.

Mexico-focused travel writer Barbara Kastelein puts the failure to change the model down to 'an addict's mentality' – a mindset that cannot let go of the idea that big resorts are the best way to attract large numbers of high-spending tourists and provide the greatest quantity of tourism-related jobs. In 2010, Mexico's tourism industry accounted for about 9 per cent of GDP and, according to official figures, around 2 million direct jobs. While this is certainly impressive, it is debatable whether big resorts, the profits from which are vacuumed up by large national and international hotel chains and tour operators, are more beneficial to the economy as a whole than small-scale developments that distribute less income from less-affluent tourists more equitably.

The lobbying power of big tourism companies, particularly hotel chains, reinforces the lack of imagination and audacity in tourism policy. Fox's first environment minister, a well-respected environmentalist called Victor Lichtinger Waisman, felt the full force of their ire when he began releasing embarrassing beach pollution data and suggested that red flags be put up on particularly dirty beaches to warn swimmers of the risks. His resignation in 2003 was at least partly associated with this issue. Lichtinger's replacement, a career politician called Alberto Cárdenas Jiménez, who had no previous commitment to environmental issues, made sure that his first official engagements included a breakfast with tourism sector leaders in Los Pinos.

This is not to say that the needs of green tourism have been completely ignored; just that efforts in this direction tend to fall by the wayside in the face of pressure from powerful business interests. A reform banning all development projects that destroy mangroves stands as a notable exception. Mangroves serve as a first line of defence against coastal erosion. They are a breeding ground for many commercially exploited fish and are a fiesta of other biodiversity. The ban became law without debate – and apparently without the implications registering until it was too late – when a federal deputy slipped in a surprise last-minute addition to broader reform approved unanimously by the legislature a few days before Christmas 2006. Activists have since accused the authorities of wiggling around the restrictions in several projects, but it is also significant that the 'hotel lobby' has tried and failed to push through a full-scale counter-reform.

Not being able to hack apart mangroves is also, perhaps, a minor irritant for the lobby in a context in which the old formula has, if anything, been reinvigorated. In 2009, the government announced plans for a brand new development, twice the size of Cancún, on an undeveloped stretch of the Pacific coast state of Sinaloa that is currently occupied by coconut palm plantations and the odd fishing village. The plans include several golf courses and marinas. The development borders an important wetland area that the authorities promise to protect, but environmentalists are inevitably sceptical.

Major new tourism investments – and there are at least two other big projects in the pipeline in Baja California – have not been deterred by the rising violence of the drug wars. If anything, the killing has further bolstered the model. Aside from Acapulco, damaged by a full-on turf war, the other resorts have been largely violence free. Hotel occupation numbers have not been greatly impacted by the wider problem – something that further underlines the fact that international tourism and domestic life are worlds apart.

Anecdotal evidence also suggests that the kind of people who previously took road-based holidays to explore Mexico's hidden treasures are now more inclined to fly to the big resorts for fear of stumbling into a convoy of narcos on some rural road. The security situation also encourages the development of the all-inclusive variety of hotels run by the big chains, with security guards on the door. The drug wars are not the impetus for these kinds of projects – which cater to tourists unlikely to consider alternative holidays – but the violence bolsters the priority given to them within tourism policy.

While government policy has played an active part in strengthening a tourism model that does an enormous amount of environmental damage, the authorities tend to play a rather more passive role in the continued problems of industrial pollution. On the positive side, the growth of the environmental agenda, with greater media scrutiny in the context of the transition, has made it harder for companies to pollute with quite the alacrity that they did in the past.

The Met-Mex Peñoles metallurgical complex in the northern city of Torreón began operations in the early twentieth century, processing lead and zinc ores. The first complaints about itching eyes and throats and bad smells were documented in 1937. Workers filed a formal complaint with the health authorities in 1961. This led to studies that found arsenic in the air. Soon after that, production of arsenic at the plant was discontinued, though it was not stated why. Otherwise Met-Mex Peñoles continued to operate as normal.

Over the decades that followed, an eighty-metre high mountain of slag emerged out of nowhere, wafting black dust across the city. Residents began noticing that a large number of their children had obvious neurological damage. Several studies indicated that children attending nearby schools had high levels of lead in their blood, but still the authorities did nothing. It was not until 1999, with the protests getting more attention in the media, that they began moving people out and cleaning up the site. A further study that year found that only 6 per cent of nearly 2,400 children tested had 'acceptable' levels of lead in their bloodstream.

It is hard to imagine such serious and blatant disregard for public health concerns over such a long period of time in the current context. Even so, Mexico has a long way to go before the extensive legal framework that now exists, and that theoretically guarantees standards, is routinely respected. Enforcement requires a degree of coordination between the different authorities that is a rare animal in the post-transition, and is one of the main reasons why industrial pollution remains such a major problem in Mexico.

In the summer of 2010, the federal government presented a new hazardous-waste inventory, which concluded that Mexican industry was producing 1.6 million tonnes of hazardous waste every year. The inventory did not include the energy, metal and mining industries, but it is clear that even the waste that was documented had nowhere safe to go. At that time, Mexico had only two working hazardous-waste sites, with a capacity of 684,000 tonnes. The federal authorities had been trying for years to build new facilities, but this required the backing of municipal authorities. And given local scepticism over safety guarantees and the lack of compensatory projects, backing was difficult to secure. The waste had to go somewhere. A 2008 government study of eighteen states identified around two hundred 'highly contaminated areas'. While it is clearly an advance to have more official data on industrial waste and pollution, this does not make the findings any less frightening. Nor does it seem to result in major steps to deal with either the general issue or specific instances.

The contamination of the valley of Tehuacán in the central state of Puebla, is not just dramatic, but ironic, too. Overlooked by volcanoes and laced with underground waterways, the valley provided archaeologists with their earliest evidence yet of corn domestication, and the city of the same name was once famous for its mineral springs and spas. Then, in the 1990s, the municipality filled with factories plugged into the global denim industry. Soon the water discharged from the laundries washing the clothes they produced was running an ever more intense shade of indigo, as the industry focused on the trend for new clothes that look as though they have been worn for years.

As well as monumental amounts of stone washing, distressing denim often includes the use of large amounts of potassium permanganate – a bleaching agent once commonly used (illegally) to trigger abortions. 'As well as being blue, it burns the seedlings and sterilizes the earth', sixty-seven-year-old Mariano Barragán told me as he directed the water from an irrigation canal around his corn field that was already caked in a grey-blue crust. 'What can I do? It's the fashion.'

Tehuacán's factories produced clothing for some of the world's best-known brands, and local campaigns attracted the attention of union-based international solidarity groups in the US. This eventually prompted many of the biggest companies to stop handing out contracts to Tehuacán factories. While that removed the international attention, the factories continued to produce for the domestic market.

When I reported on the story in 2007, representatives from every level of government – all of which bear some degree of responsibility for water in the area – recognized that the pollution was serious. They also all claimed that they were doing all they could, but that the others were not.

Sometimes the different levels of government do close ranks – as in the case of the network of industrial pig farms that briefly attracted the world's spotlight at the start of the flu pandemic of 2009, triggered by a new virus discovered in Mexico that April that mixed swine, avian and human strains. The show of unity, however, served to protect the company.

Within days of the announcement of the new virus on 23 April, the world's media scrambled to a small village called La Gloria, in the middle of a cactus-peppered dusty mountain plain that straddles the states of Puebla and Veracruz. We went there in search of a four-year-old boy called Edgar Hernández, who, in those early stages of the crisis, was the first known sufferer of the flu, identified when a batch of samples of suspicious cases was sent to specialized labs in the US and Canada. Once we had pursued the boy for the obligatory quote, we talked to the villagers. It turned out that Edgar had fallen ill towards the end of an epidemic of acute respiratory illness that had rampaged through the village from early March. Now the villagers assumed that they, like Edgar, had been suffering from the new swine flu. Many also assumed that the virus had originated in the local complex of industrial pig farms, owned by a subsidiary of the Virginia-based pork giant Smithfield Foods, about which they had been complaining for years. Global environmental campaigners fuelled the charges by reminding the world of the company's dubious history: a decade before, two of its US subsidiaries had been fined $12.6 million for discharging pollutants into a river. It had also been found guilty of falsifying documents and destroying records. At the time of the flu outbreak, Granjas Carroll, the subsidiary, had seventy-two farms spread out across the plain and produced about a million pigs for the domestic market every year. The farms consist of metal barns crammed full of pigs, next to large, pestilent ponds filled with their waste. Hogs that die before they are fat enough to be sold end up decomposing in nearby pits.

Local opposition to the company, which arrived in the area in the mid-1990s, took off in the new millennium, when a small group of activists from La Gloria began campaigning against plans to construct a new facility on the outskirts of the village. They said they were already suffering from clouds of big black flies and a putrid stench wafting up the plain from the nearest farm, eight kilometres away. They also charged that the farms were contaminating the groundwater.

The protests in La Gloria developed into a wider movement, which called for improvements in environmental standards in existing facilities, as well as a halt to the expansion plans. Several of its leaders received threatening anonymous phone calls. At least one got death threats. The authorities took five of the activists to court on a potentially serious charge of blocking a road during a protest. The protest leaders believed the company was behind the charges and claimed they had evidence that executives were on chummy terms with the local governors – Fidel Herrera in Veracruz (where La Gloria is located) and Mario Marín in Puebla (where the road was allegedly blocked). Both governors are prime examples of the kind of feudal-style local strongmen whose abuse of judicial independence became famous in the post-2000 political context.

The company responded to the new accusations over swine flu by insisting that its pigs were so healthy that it was impossible for the virus to have emerged from its facilities. It stressed that people living in Xaltepec – the village right next to the nearest farm – had not fallen ill. Michael Hawn, a high-level company executive from Virginia who was in the area at the time, told me that Granjas Carroll was actually a model company that had been misunderstood by the residents of La Gloria. 'I mean, I love Mexico – the culture and everything; but there are things that are quite a bit different here', he said. 'This is a poor village that could really have done with the jobs we offered. They had an emotional response.' I asked how many jobs had been planned. 'At least five', he replied. It hardly seemed like a very good deal, however poor the village was.

What was even more telling was the way the state and federal government closed ranks behind the giant. The federal authorities immediately ruled out the possibility that the farms might be the source of the virus, emphasizing that they had passed all health and environment checks.

Veracruz Governor Fidel Herrera, meanwhile, went on a charm offensive in La Gloria. He flew into the village in a helicopter early on in the crisis to ruffle Edgar's hair, give him a football, and promise him a stipend to pay for school supplies. The state government financed a beach holiday for the family, and gave them a second-hand pickup truck. It also commissioned a statue of Edgar for the village square. The so-called 'kid zero', wearing a crumpled T-shirt, shorts and trainers, was cast in bronze for posterity. He had a rather odd smile on his face and an even odder frog in his hand – meant to symbolize the pestilence he had overcome. There was no explanation of why it was not a pig.

The governor also paved the road into the village, kitted out the tiny local health clinic, and built the church a new bell tower. 'The virus didn't hurt – it helped', Herrera announced in August, after unveiling the statue of Edgar on his fourth visit in as many months. 'Today La Gloria is living in glory.'

The governor did not return after that. Nothing came, either, of the promises of a new sports field and a mobile phone antenna. By then swine flu was no longer a major issue. The impact of the virus had been much less than was at first feared, when it unleashed global panic, prompted the Mexican government to deploy the army to hand out blue surgical masks at street corners and all but shut down the economy for a couple of weeks. The debate turned to whether politicians around the world had overreacted and been suspiciously willing to fill the coffers of the pharmaceutical companies that made a killing out of developing a vaccine.

Studies of the local epidemic in La Gloria by a team of epidemiologists from the National Autonomous University of Mexico also found no direct evidence to suggest that the new virus originated in the pig farms. The team took blood from about half of La Gloria's 3,000 inhabitants during the summer of 2009 and found swine flu antibodies in about a third. This represented a particularly concentrated cluster, but interviews dated the earliest sufferers to early March – a month after a case had appeared about 300 kilometres north-west. 'I think we will probably never know the origin', said Dr Malaquías López-Cervantes, the leader of the study. 'The pig farms would have been a propitious place for the virus to mutate, but there is no evidence that it happened there.'

I went back to La Gloria a year after the swine flu media whirlwind to find that the activists had gone silent. The five who had been taken to court were most concerned about getting the lingering case off their backs. Smithfield's pig farms were still there, glinting in the harsh mountain sun, surrounded by security fencing, and so highly mechanized that it was rare to see a worker anywhere near them – or indeed a pig. The animals' presence was felt in the squeals from the barns and the stench of the slurry pools.

A mechanic called Jorge Bernál stood outside his workshop near one of the farms and talked in hushed tones. He had once been a vocal member of the protest movement, but not anymore – though he still insisted that the farms were continuing to poison the environment. 'We stopped them building any more, and that's good; but we can't make them do much more', he said with a fatalistic shrug. 'The company just has too many friends in high places and we do not.'

For all the criticism directed at him by domestic environmentalists, President Felipe Calderón retained a solid self-image as a 'green' president. In an interview with *El Universal* newspaper in February 2011, he lamented the fact that, in the context of the drug wars, he would not be remembered primarily 'as a president committed to the environment, which is my favourite issue'.

Much of Calderón's claim rested on the way he energetically picked up the climate-change banner as soon as he took office. He began by commissioning detailed studies to identify exactly where Mexico's vulnerabilities lay and peppering his discourse with reference to the phenomenon.

Mexico's coasts are obviously in danger from altering weather patterns. Hurricane Wilma wrought its havoc during the most intense Atlantic storm season on record in Mexico, although some scientists were reluctant to blame climate change directly. There is greater consensus over the accelerated erosion along some parts of the coast that reflects longer-term trends.

Mexico's lowland river deltas are also particularly susceptible to the kind of flooding that put the Gulf state of Tabasco under water for weeks in 2007. Tabasco had flooded to some degree almost every year for as long as anybody could remember, but nobody recalled anything like this. The rivers that criss-cross the state all burst their banks, and when I hitched a ride in an aid helicopter soon after the start of the crisis I could see almost no land at all. Cattle huddled together on the occasional patch of higher ground. Villagers, doing the same, waved energetically at every passing aircraft in the hope of help.

In the state capital of Villahermosa, the floods submerged whole *barrios* that had been built in high-risk areas that should have been kept empty. Thousands of people in these areas refused to heed calls to evacuate. Worried about looting, they preferred to wait for the water level to slowly recede over several weeks. They whiled away their days, stuck on their upper floors or camped on their roofs, watching the world go by in canoes punted up canals that had once been streets. 'Hey, *muchachos*,' I remember a man calling out from a boat one evening, when the softening light made it all seem almost romantic, 'Venice has got nothing on us, don't you agree?'

Nobody died in the Tabasco floods, but downpours in mountainous areas that send hillsides crashing on top of remote villages tend to be less forgiving. Again such tragedies have been a feature of Mexican life for many years, but are expected to happen more often as storms get more extreme and continued deforestation makes the ground ever less stable. A single out-of-season downpour in February 2010 buried most of the small, picturesque, old mining town of Agangueo, in the central state of Michoacán. The authorities said the river of mud killed thirty-four people and left 80 per cent of homes uninhabitable.

The problem of climate change in Mexico is not just about too much water; it is also about too little. Even if global warming is kept below the catastrophic levels that some predict, the north and the centre of Mexico are threatened by ever more intense droughts, with potentially devastating impacts on local agriculture.

Small maize and bean farmers without access to irrigation are, as ever, the most unprotected. Less rain means yet greater pressure on them to leave their land and head for the cities. Slums in those cities are also particularly vulnerable, as pressure increases on local water supplies – supplies that are sometimes also required to keep golf courses in tourist resorts green.

Climate change also represents a major threat to Mexico's extraordinary biodiversity. The annual migration of monarch butterflies from eastern Canada to one small patch of a particular central Mexican forest, where they spend the winter, counts among the great wonders of the natural world. It is a particularly delicate one, since even a partial thinning of the fir forest can expose the millions of orange and black insects to potentially fatal night-time frosts, as they hang from the boughs in great, huddled clusters.

The colony's main enemy used to be the illegal logging of organized crime. The government sent the army into the area in 2008 and slashed the amount of forest lost in the season from 259 hectares to 53 hectares. But just as independent environmentalists monitoring the area were beginning to sound uncharacteristically optimistic, a new challenge emerged in the form of a plague of beetles. Though always present, the beetles had become much more rapacious because of unusually warm temperatures. The plague saw the authorities themselves cutting down thousands of affected trees in an effort to save the rest.

As well as cataloguing the dangers of climate change for Mexico, and drawing up some plans to prepare for them, Calderón sought to make an impact on the world stage by spearheading efforts to break down the gulf between the rich polluters and the rest by keeping the debate centred on how to deal most effectively with the problem, rather than on who was to blame for it. He argued that, while the big emitters should bear most of the costs, even countries with very low emissions could not afford to just wait impassively for disaster to strike, and urged them to take a more active role in preparing themselves for what was to come.

I always thought it rather unfair of local environmentalists to dismiss the president's pronouncements on climate change as mere grandstanding, and the praise he received in the international community as little more than naïve. Calderón, at least to me, appeared genuinely concerned. A reliable source insists he was one of the last leaders to give up on desperate last-minute efforts to hammer out some kind of agreement at the climate change summit in Copenhagen in 2009. Mexico did much to ensure that the follow-up summit, in Cancún a year later, ended somewhat more hopefully.

Good intentions – and even solid personal commitment – are rarely enough in the most propitious scenarios; but they can seem almost irrelevant in the context of Mexico's weakened presidency. They certainly did not hold much initial clout in Calderón's pledge to cut 50 million tonnes (or about 6 per cent) from the projected greenhouse gas emissions for 2012, his last year in office. Mexico accounts for some 1.5 per cent of global emissions, largely because of its heavily polluting oil industry, heavy use of road transport, and 112 million people – not much when compared to China or India, perhaps, but enough to give it a voice.

Calderón anchored his reduction promise in a plan to reduce the flaring of gas in offshore oil fields exploited by Pemex. Flaring had increased dramatically in previous years, largely as a side effect of the oil beginning to run out. Dwindling wells tend to produce more associated natural gas that can, given the right technology, be compressed and piped ashore or re-injected. Pemex simply burns it off – a colossal waste of money, as well as a major source of pollution. The sector regulator ordered Pemex to dramatically cut flaring in early 2010. A year later it was complaining that the company had largely ignored the directive.

With the government unable to ensure that a state-owned enterprise complies with regulations on an issue so close to the president's heart, it is hardly surprising that imposing environmental discipline on local authorities or the private sector is also a major problem. Nor is it difficult to understand why old developmental paradigms that ignore the environment are difficult to shift or, indeed, why voices of community-based activists are usually ignored unless they can stage dramatic protests. The environment is part of the political debate in Mexico today, and there have been important steps forward. But it is also clear that, without structural changes speeding things up, a myriad dangers will continue to edge Mexico closer to some kind of brink.

Few areas of the country face as many diverse and difficult environmental headaches as Mexico City and the urban sprawl surrounding it. The issues of limited citizen input, damaging private sector interests, institutional confusion and diminished state authority are all present – further exacerbated by political competition. The central and southern parts of the metropolis fall under the jurisdiction of the Federal District, while the rest lies within the State of Mexico. Meanwhile the capital is not only the seat of the federal government, but federal bodies also have a say in running key parts of the infrastructure. From 2000 until at least 2012, the Federal District, the State of Mexico and the federal government were all controlled by different political parties.

The Mexican capital is probably best known internationally for its poor air quality. This has actually improved considerably since the 1980s, when the city was considered to be the most polluted in the world. There are still days when your eyes sting, and asthma rates are still relatively high, but air pollution also now seems like a minor issue compared to some of the other environmental challenges facing the metropolis.

The march towards gridlock is proving particularly difficult to reverse. A recent expansion in public transport networks and efforts to encourage cycling in the Federal District have helped slow the slide somewhat, but such initiatives simply cannot keep up with the influx of ever more vehicles. As anybody who regularly moves around the city knows, the jams keep getting worse and travel times just keep getting longer. The roadside outside my (fairly central) home fills up most mornings before dawn with people dozing in their cars, having succeeded in beating the rush hour into town from the suburbs.

Mexico City also faces an enormous rubbish problem that became suddenly obvious at the end of 2011, when the city was inundated with clandestine dumps after the closure of its already overstuffed landfill. The Bordo Poniente had received almost all the 12,000 tonnes of waste produced by the Federal District every day, but the authorities had done almost nothing to prepare for its long-imminent closure. The situation settled down again after a few weeks, thanks to a cobbled-together collection of deals with small private dumps at some considerable distance from the city (and involving some considerable cost). Still the underlying problems of a chaotic and anachronistic refuse-management system, partially controlled by mafia-style bosses, remained.

But it is water – too much of it and too little – that arguably takes the prize as the most intractable problem of all. The Valley of Mexico lies at an altitude of 2,420 metres, almost surrounded by mountains. Millions of years ago, these cut off the natural drainage of the area and produced a system of lakes, fed by forty-five rivers that run down into the basin. A nomadic tribe that called itself the Mexica (and that would later become known as the Aztecs) settled here in 1325 and built its great capital Tenochtitlan on an artificially extended island. The Aztecs organized their watery environment in a supremely pragmatic way, from the canoes that collected human excrement and carried it to fertilize floating gardens elsewhere in the lake, to its use as a huge natural moat to protect the centre of their expanding empire. But while they saw their environment as essentially propitious, they never forgot that it was also delicate and dangerous. A complex cosmology and religious practice emphasized the capriciousness of the elements and ensured that the Aztecs rarely overstretched their efforts to control them.

Conquistadors would write eulogies to the dazzling engineering and organizational talent they found when they arrived in the valley and conquered the Aztecs nearly two hundred years later, but their subsequent construction of their own city on the same site followed a very different ethic. They replaced the Aztec attempt to maintain a balance with the lakes and rivers with a drive to dominate them. This triggered one of the most extraordinary urban environmental transformations ever seen. A river basin inhabited by around a million people would mutate into an urban jungle of 22 million, half of whom live on land that was once covered with water.

The early destruction of the flood breaks the Aztecs had built to protect Tenochtitlan during the seven-month rainy season provided early warnings of what was to come, and the new city found itself under water several times in the first few decades of colonial rule. The Spanish sought to deal with this by constructing a tunnel through the mountains to carry away excess water. Inaugurated in 1608, it was hailed as a triumph. A few years later, the city suffered a flood that lasted for years and killed thousands of people.

City engineers spent the next few centuries funnelling the rivers flowing into the valley into the city drainage system, which channelled them out of the valley again. It still was not enough, and the periodic floods continued. The next monumental attempt to solve the problem came after independence, with the inauguration in 1900 of a new route out of the valley for rainwater run-off and sewage – the Gran Canal. This helped drain larger areas of the valley and the city expanded into them. Another major flood followed, as did more channelling of rivers into the drains.

With the Gran Canal obviously unable to cope with the urban explosion in the middle of the century, the government built sixty-eight kilometres of huge tunnels in the hard rock underneath the lake bed. The Deep Drainage System, inaugurated in 1974, once again took the rain, river water and sewage out of the valley. Once again, this was supposed to be the definitive answer to the problem. Once again this proved not to be so.

By the late 1990s, the system was being used all year round, instead of just during the rainy season, as had originally been intended. This ruled out even basic maintenance during the dry season, as had been envisaged in the original plan. The installation of pumps to boost the capacity of the Gran Canal eventually allowed engineers access to the central tunnel of the Deep Drainage System in the 2008 dry season, so that maintenance could finally resume. They found large sections in such a critical state that they threatened another catastrophic flood if the system was not patched up immediately. It did not help matters that climate change appeared to be increasing the incidence of freak downpours out of season.

A taste of what a modern major flood might look like came in February 2010, when a thirty-six-hour storm took everybody by surprise in a month traditionally known for wind and sun. With maintenance workers down in the main tunnel of the Deep Drainage System when the storm began, the city could not get rid of the unexpected additional water fast enough. Tens of thousands of homes around the city were suddenly flooded with dilute sewage.

The worst-affected areas included a vast working-class suburb called Valle de Chalco, which runs along the main motorway east out of the capital through the State of Mexico. A swampy flood plain thirty years ago, it has grown into a teeming mass of breeze-block homes and pollution-pumping buses carrying residents to and from jobs in other parts of the metropolis. The Río de la Companía, once a small, dirty stream in the middle of it, has mutated into a foul-smelling open canal protected by walls that have already failed on several occasions. This time rain and sewage rushed out of a fifty-metre hole and turned several *barrios* into a pestilent canal system. Water levels reached two metres high in places. Shelters filled up with suddenly homeless families. My own eyes and throat began stinging within an hour of arriving in the area, while the corroded snouts of the stray dogs I saw wandering around hinted at more lasting health risks.

Ramiro Martínez stood hugging his chest, gazing up the canal that was once his street towards the home he had fled when the malodorous water began rushing under his door. 'We only had time to grab the children and get out of there.' He broke his pensive silence and began to cry, gently. 'The level rose very quickly. Now everything we had is lost.' A makeshift raft passed by, carrying other flood victims, cloths pressed against their noses, on their way to inspect their own ruined homes. The vessel punted slowly to the end of the road and then disappeared around the corner.

It took soldiers working round the clock ten days to block up the hole, using 340,000 sandbags and some complicated engineering that allowed the area to be drained. It took days more for the area to be disinfected. When things were just about beginning to get back to normal, angry flood victims who said they had not received the promised government help held a protest that closed the motorway and ended in a pitched battle with riot police. Another unusual downpour fourteen months later found the soldiers back again, filling in another hole.

The fundamental irony about Mexico City's water crisis is that, at the same time as the city struggles to cope with the threat of another great flood, the taps are beginning to run dry. In centuries gone by, the capital relied on springs in the mountains that ring the valley; but as the population expanded and these dried up, it became dependent on pumping water up from the underground aquifer below the valley. Soon the city engineers were pumping faster than the rain could replenish the aquifer, and the spongy formations holding the underground water began to compress. The areas near the pumps started sinking at an alarming rate. They did so unevenly, too. In the 1940s, the historic centre sank forty-five centimetres a year, which is why so many of the old colonial buildings there tip, dip and crack in strange places. There is one church tucked away in a small square that makes me feel nauseous as soon as I enter it. The engineers moved the pumps out of the city to places like Valle de Chalco, but the new pumping areas were soon swallowed up by urban sprawl and the same problem of sinking and cracking was repeated.

The authorities, meanwhile, began bringing in a third of the water used in the metropolis from the other side of the mountains, from what is known as the Lerma-Cutzamala system. Even this was not enough as the city kept growing and, as it grew, occupied the mountain sides at the edge that had once helped channel at least some of the rain that fell in the valley back into the aquifer. By 2009, chronic water shortages affected around 1.5 million people living in disadvantaged areas of the Federal District, and probably as many again in the State of Mexico.

By then the Lerma-Cutzamala system was also beginning to feel the strain, as lack of maintenance combined with irregular rain patterns. The authorities began warning that the water could run out in the not-so-distant future, ramming home the point by periodically cutting supplies to middle-class areas, as well as to the working-class *barrios* long used to the problem. To some extent this was scaremongering, designed to prepare the way for cuts in water subsidies; but it also underlined a reality. Mexico City is slowly but surely using up its own precious aquifer and exacerbating the sinking problem, at the same time as it spends huge amounts of money pumping additional supplies from outside the valley, and depriving others of their local resources in the process.

Meanwhile, the water that does flow in Mexico City's homes is considered unsafe to drink by the majority of the population, which means that many spend a disproportionate amount of their income on bottled water: Mexico has the highest per capita consumption of bottled water in the world. In what amounts to a de facto privatization of drinking water, four major multinationals (Danone, Pepsi, Coca-Cola and Nestlé) dominate the market, making enormous profits by purifying water extracted from the country's aquifers at minimal cost. Much of this additional water eventually finds its way back into the drainage system, only adding to the flooding potential.

Moreover the sinking puts ever greater pressure not only on the buildings, but also on the drainage system. The Gran Canal – once hailed as the permanent solution to the flooding threat – is now an active problem. Its original drainage slope has reversed, which means that, were it not for pumping stations, the sewage it contains would run back into the city. The Río de la Companía sewerage canal through Valle de Chalco is highly prone to fracture, because its wall has had to be built up several metres over the years as the surrounding plain sinks.

Just as in the seventeenth, nineteenth and twentieth centuries, the answer the twenty-first-century engineers have come up with is to build yet another tunnel. Inaugurating work on an extension of the Deep Drainage System that is due to be completed in 2012, President

Calderón pronounced: 'This will solve the flooding problem in the city once and for all.'

A wiry academic with wild, white hair and an encyclopaedic knowledge of all things to do with water in the Mexico Valley, Jorge Legorreta laughs at the very idea: 'They all said that.' Legoretta imagines a network of reservoirs in the surrounding hills to capture the water running down into the valley before it is fed into the drainage system. He claims that this, together with roof-top tanks to store rainwater for use in buildings, would solve the flooding problem, significantly reduce the pressure on the aquifer, and slow the sinking of the city: 'We have to revive some of the knowledge of how to manage the environment that was lost with the fall of Tenochtitlan.' Nobody in power seems to be listening to such offbeat ideas, despite five centuries of evidence that the existing paradigm is fundamentally flawed.

The weight of that history literally loomed before me in 2010, on the day I drove out to Valle de Chalco to report on the floods. The great, extinct Iztaccihuatl volcano was reflected in the glassy lake of sewage and rain that was spreading from the burst canal over the motorway and into the maze of streets beyond. A bright, sunny day had replaced the rare winter storm that had caused all the problems. The storm had also cleaned the air, making the image especially sharp, and had covered the volcano in snow. This would make the flood even more difficult to control, as the meltwater flowed down into the streams that fed into the canal, which ended up in the city's drainage system.

This perverted picture-postcard image spelt out nature's revenge. It also felt like a reminder of how often Mexico's most complex environmental problems can also seem very basic. A river basin fed by forty-five rivers that swell when rain falls remains a river basin fed by forty-five rivers that swell when rain falls – even if it is covered in concrete and even if those rivers are channelled into drains. This natural reality screams for attention in any major water policy.

The fact that policy makers seem to have so much trouble acknowledging this even today stands as testament to the power of the ethos of environmental domination established by the conquistadors. That in turn is just one expression of the intangible legacy of three hundred years of Spanish rule. The persistence of extreme inequality, in all its facets, contains multiple echoes of a time when a tiny minority felt completely justified in monopolizing not only the territory's natural resources, but almost all other expressions of wealth and power as well. Independence, but particularly the Revolution, went some way to addressing this; but then it got rather lost under the imperial PRI presidency. Much of this book amounts to a chronicle of the way the transition to party-political plurality has so far only partially lived up to its promise to recharge the cause of citizenship and democratize the handling of matters as diverse as security and the environment. Citizen empowerment in this new context has tended to emerge almost despite the political elite, rather than in association with a drive from the top to push democratization further. While I have already highlighted the part played in this rather disappointing story by the PAN governments and by the looming continued presence of the PRI, I have so far only skated over the role of another central actor – the left.

CHAPTER 8

Left Behind?

Having done the lion's share of the work of pushing the PRI monolith to the precipice, the Mexican left had to watch Vicente Fox of the right-wing PAN collect the prize for nudging it over the edge in 2000. The PRD swallowed that bitter pill and came within a whisker of taking power in 2006 with the candidacy of Andrés Manuel López Obrador, only to fritter away its new strength in an orgy of self-sabotage.

The momentum that built up behind the PRI and its candidate Enrique Peña Nieto in the run-up to the 2012 election campaign was primarily a response to widespread disappointment with two terms of PAN government. It also reflected the weakness of the left and its main leaders. All the polls showed López Obrador, on his second run for president, trailing around twenty percentage points behind the frontrunner, with less than six months to go before the election. It was just possible that his charisma and strategic talents could turn things around, particularly if Peña Nieto and his party's comeback juggernaut began to stall. Even so, it was clear that one of the great weaknesses of Mexican democracy was the PRD's difficulty in transforming itself into an automatic magnet for the many frustrations over the shortcomings of the transition (if only on the grounds that it was the one major party that had yet to hold power).

The trouble the left has had in convincing the electorate that it offers a route forward in the new era is, at least in part, a function of the trouble it has had in shaking off the old.

❀ ❀ ❀

The left's contribution to the decline of the PRI regime is often dated to 1968 and the Mexican expression of the wave of student activism that flowed over the world that year. A new middle class, with unprecedented access to university education, had done well out of the stability and development of the first half of the regime; but instead of being meekly grateful, it was demanding more say in how things were run. These were the grandchildren of the 1910 Revolution, and President Gustavo Díaz Ordaz was not amused. He accused them of being part of an international conspiracy to undermine that same Revolution.

The students had already got into several clashes with the authorities by the time they called a mass meeting in a square in the Tlatelolco neighbourhood of the capital on 2 October to plan their next moves. With just ten days to go before the opening ceremony of the Mexico City Olympics, designed to showcase the PRI's achievements, the government was under intense pressure to defuse the movement quickly. There were few hints that they planned to do this by way of a massacre.

The rally was winding down when the soldiers arrived and opened fire on the crowd, apparently provoked by snipers from the Presidential Guard placed on the buildings around the square. The government initially said four people had died. Eyewitnesses said they saw hundreds of bodies trucked away. Investigations decades later never clearly established the number killed, but nobody questions that the events at Tlatelolco marked a watershed in Mexican political history.

The 1968 massacre exposed just how absolutist the regime had become, and how far it was willing to go to retain its control. It would come to be seen as the moment that exploded the PRI's claim to represent all sectors of Mexican society, although this reading of the events took some time to grow, as initially news of what had happened was severely restricted.

The crackdown included the imprisonment of many activists. This both decimated the movement and fuelled the belief within the independent left that more radical methods were required, although guerrilla tactics had already proved notably unsuccessful as a means of exerting pressure on the regime. The decades of PRI domination of Mexican politics is peppered with small guerrilla groups that came and went without making much of a mark. The book *México Armado 1943–1981* by Laura Castellanos chronicles the rise and fall of thirty between those dates.

A former member of Emiliano Zapata's revolutionary army called Rubén Jaramillo led the most famous early armed struggle against the regime. He sought to deepen land reform in the *caudillo's* old base in the central state of Morelos. The army killed him and his family in 1962, at a time when he was not in open revolt.

Most of the groups date from the late 1960s and early 1970s. This was a period of guerrilla effervescence across Latin America, although the Mexican guerrilla movement was notably weaker than in many other countries in the region.

The Party of the Poor became the most important rural guerrilla force. It was based in the Atoyac region of the southern sierra, in the state of Guerrero, and was led by a radical teacher called Lucio Cabañas. It withered away after the army killed him in 1974.

A plethora of urban guerrilla groups formed around this time, their ranks swelled after the repression of the peaceful student movement. The Liga Comunista 23 de Septiembre proved to be the most important. It had a presence in several major cities and carried out some high-profile kidnappings (and the odd murder) of prominent business figures, diplomats and their families. The group had fallen into disarray by the early 1980s, though it did not formally disband until 1990.

In his book *Utopia Unarmed*, Jorge Castañeda identifies two main reasons why Mexican armed groups never really took off. Their potential was limited, he writes, because of the lack of contact and cooperation between the peasant-based rural groups and the more middle-class urban ones. The lack of support from Cuba, even at the height of the Cold War, constituted another major problem. Indebted to the PRI for its willingness to act as a buffer to US pressure, Fidel Castro ignored the Mexican guerrillas, at the same time as he provided money, training and arms to their peers further south.

This fragmentation and international isolation also left the Mexican guerrillas particularly vulnerable to the government's dirty war against them. Though rather less extreme than similar conflicts elsewhere in the region, Mexico's dirty war, which reached its height in the 1970s, had all the hallmarks of its more famous counterparts. There were extrajudicial executions, clandestine jails, torture and disappearances, as well as a group of relatives of the victims that emerged to protest against the human rights violations. The numbers, however, were not comparable, and the world did not seem to notice when the armed dissident movement was all but wiped out. While the victims ran into the hundreds in Mexico, in Chile and Argentina they numbered tens of thousands. In Guatemala – a country with less than a tenth of the population of its northern neighbour – the thirty-six-year-long civil war killed around 200,000, most of them during the army's scorched-earth policy of the late 1970s and early 1980s.

The resonance of the Mexican repression both inside the country and out was also limited by President Luis Echeverría's concurrent strategy of promoting himself as a leftist. Populist public spending increased sharply during his term (1970–76). Abroad, he promoted himself as a spokesman for the Third World, and welcomed exiles from the fury unleashed by the generals in Latin America's Southern Cone.

The dirty war continued under President Jose López Portillo, as did populist projects funded by an oil boom. López Portillo also began to tentatively open up the political playing field, pushed by the embarrassing fact that he had won the election with 98 per cent of the vote, by dint of being the only candidate. His government legalized the communist party and made it easier for all opposition political parties to both register and gain minimal representation in the legislature. For years, these parties served as a kind of pressure valve to head off dissident organization, their leaders controlled by a skilful mixture of co-optation and repression that encouraged their own sectarian battles. An amnesty in 1978 also accelerated the decline of the Mexican armed groups. They had faded into near insignificance by the time López Portillo left office in 1982, accompanied by economic crisis.

The powerful earthquake (8.1 on the Richter scale) that hit Mexico City on 19 September 1985 and the following day's strong aftershock sparked yet another strain within the left. The quake killed at least 3,692 people (the number of death certificates), though some say the figure was closer to 20,000. The death toll would presumably have been significantly lower had there not been so many unstable buildings constructed in the context of pervasive corruption. Slow to do anything – and clumsy when it did – the regime's refusal to accept international aid (out of a sense of national pride) added insult to the injury.

Community and citizen groups spontaneously sprang up to fill the vacuum, organizing around issues such as securing housing for the homeless. Armed with a new confidence in their own capacities that (participants would later say) surprised themselves, the new social movements in the *barrios* resisted attempts by the PRI to incorporate them into the party's corporatist structure. Instead of pressing for handouts, these groups demanded rights, and in the process did much to bury the myth of the paternalistic state. Mexican writer Carlos Monsiváis later described it as tantamount to 'discovering the existence of society in the most physical sense of the word'.

While chipping away at the legitimacy of the regime and beginning to shake off the shackles of clientelism were major steps forward, they were little more than pebbles in the system's shoes until the social movements joined forces with leftist exiles from the PRI.

The PRI's longevity was partially built on its ability to contain the latent conflict both by promoting itself as the vanguard of the struggle for social justice and by incorporating most of the other significant political forces into its structure. Leftist President Lázaro Cárdenas did most to establish both traditions. During his *sexenio* (1934–40), Cárdenas consolidated the regime's claims to embody the legacy of the Revolution by distributing land to the peasants and nationalizing the oil industry. He also cemented its political control by incorporating labour and peasant organizations into the state in a way that both harnessed their support for the regime project and helped neutralize their opposition when things did not work out as promised. To round it off, Cárdenas underlined the priority given to stability over ideology by choosing a right-leaning successor.

Over time, the PRI developed an ideological nebulousness that belied attempts to pin it down to any particular part of the spectrum. Even in the final decades of the regime, when orthodox neoliberal technocrats took control of economic policy, it could not be described as an orthodox neoliberal technocratic party. Politics remained largely under the control of old-style operators, the so-called 'dinosaurs'. They were not only experts at ensuring that elections were won, whatever the ballots said, but also past masters at nationalist rhetoric infused with leftist sentiment and symbolism.

By then, however, the contradictions had become much more difficult to manage. Reduced public finances not only diminished the regime's ability to offset popular discontent with populist projects and subsidies, but it had also made the position of the leftists within increasingly untenable.

Cuauhtémoc Cárdenas' failure to secure the PRI presidential candidacy for the 1988 elections produced the first major schism. President Lázaro Cárdenas' son, who had been groomed for power by his family since he was a boy, headed a faction within the party that demanded a return to a left-wing focus in economic policy as well as democratic reform. Once he left the PRI, he provided a perfect figurehead to bring the two main strands of leftist dissent together – the one that had been forged inside the regime, and the other that had cut its teeth outside but was not ready to completely throw off the idealized vision of the Revolution.

Cárdenas ran for president, backed by a loose coalition called the National Democratic Front. As well as former *Priistas*, like himself, and urban *barrio* leaders who had grown out of the response to the earthquake, it also included a good number of former guerrillas and veterans of the student movement of 1968. There were also former communists and other leftists from the cornucopia of tiny political parties already in existence. Small farmers who owed their plots of land to his father's agrarian reform provided Cárdenas with a rural base.

The leftist's popular support ballooned, despite the patently unfair conditions of the campaign, epitomized by a near absence of media coverage of his campaign. The early returns on election night itself showed him ahead in the vote – and then the system crashed. When it came up again, the PRI's Carlos Salinas was ahead. Salinas would be declared the winner, with 51 per cent of the vote; Cárdenas was given 31 per cent, and the PAN's Manuel Clouthier del Rincón 17 per cent.

Cárdenas and his supporters took to the streets to denounce the obvious manipulation, but he was an institutional politician at heart. Fearful of provoking a bloody crackdown, he resisted pressure from within his movement to step up the resistance. The tension subsided, allowing Salinas to consolidate himself in the presidency with the help of negotiations with the PAN.

The 1988 elections might have ended with the re-imposition of the PRI regime, but it is often referred to as the start of Mexico's transition to democracy. The left had proved that defeating the PRI electoral machine in a presidential election was possible, even if there was still some way to go before such a result would be respected. Salinas also went on to try and cleanse his term with a series of reforms that gradually began to level the electoral playing field for elections to come.

The left initially found it hard to capitalize on the opening it had forced. The coalition behind Cárdenas mutated into the Partido de la Revolución Democrática – the Party of the Democratic Revolution, or PRD. Registered as a political party in 1989, the PRD immediately established itself as the biggest of the left-wing parties. Its growth was truncated, however, by the variety of groups with distinct visions and strong leaderships contained within it. These would become known as *las tribus*, or 'the tribes'. Cárdenas' overwhelming presence and the clear aim of bringing down the regime could hold things together when things were going well, but it was not so easy when they were not. Another bout of selective repression targeting PRD activists in the provinces did not help either. An estimated six hundred died in those early years.

Salinas, meanwhile, transformed himself into a very popular president, seducing the nation with his promise of an imminent leap into the First World. This time it was the radical left that burst the balloon, in the form of the emergence of the popular Zapatista indigenous guerrilla movement in the southern state of Chiapas in 1994. Even so, it was the PRI that took advantage of the sense of impending chaos that followed and that included a series of high-level political assassinations.

At a time of uncertainty, Mexican voters reached for the devil they knew, and Ernesto Zedillo easily won the presidential poll for the PRI in the summer of 1994, with 49 per cent of the vote. The PAN's Diego Fernández de Cevallos came second with 26 per cent, and Cárdenas trailed in far behind with 17 per cent. Polling day was deemed largely free of dirty tricks, although the campaign had still been decidedly unfair in terms of media exposure and the use of state resources to favour the candidate of the still, seemingly eternal, party of power.

The PRD had been able to suck up all the major strands on the political left until the emergence of the Zapatistas, who defied similar institutionalization. According to its best-known 'face', Subcomandante Marcos, the Zapatista Army of National Liberation (EZLN) was founded on 17 November 1983 by three survivors of one of the 1970s middle-class guerrilla groups. They set up a base in the Lacandón jungle in Chiapas and persuaded three indigenous locals to join them. Marcos himself got to the jungle nine months later, by which time the group had grown to a grand total of nine people.

Over the decade that followed, the EZLN appropriated the anger engendered by the extreme poverty, discrimination and violence that local indigenous communities suffered from, in a state where large landholders still maintained paramilitary groups to keep uppity labourers in check. The guerrillas also took advantage of the consciousness-raising work done in the area by catechists and deacons sent by Bishop Samuel Ruiz, Mexico's most famous liberation theologist.

Marcos would later explain the decision to launch their uprising on the very eve of 1994 as a combined result of the group members' growing impatience for action and the fact that they knew that the government knew they existed (though probably not the extent of their support). The

North American Free Trade Agreement that Mexico had just signed with the USA and Canada had apparently delayed action against them. The treaty came into effect at midnight on 31 December 1993, providing the guerrillas with a perfect symbolic date on which to come out into the open. President Salinas was pulled out of a triumphant New Year's party in Mexico City to be told that thousands of indigenous guerrillas had taken control of several towns in Chiapas, including the colonial tourist city of San Cristóbal de las Casas.

The uprising was brief, with the badly armed Zapatistas soon withdrawing to their Lacandón strongholds, pursued by the army. After that a wave of national and international sympathy persuaded Salinas to pull back and announce a unilateral ceasefire. In just twelve days of fighting – which left around a hundred and fifty people dead – the Zapatistas had captured the imagination of millions around Mexico and the world.

The Zapatistas had also realized that their original dream of sparking a nationwide uprising was not going to happen, but that this did not necessarily condemn their movement to failure. The David and Goliath image of a rag-tag indigenous army coming out of the jungle in a last-ditch, desperate cry for justice proved to be far more effective than their rudimentary weaponry. Marcos' singular charisma and the lyrical, ironic, humorous and erudite communiqués he wrote challenging Mexico to redeem a historic debt to its indigenous population, engendered far more support than more conventional calls to rise up against oppression.

From the start, the tall, light-eyed and obviously non-indigenous Marcos claimed he was merely the mouthpiece of the group, a mere *subcomandante*. He originally put on his famous mask, he said, so as not to draw attention to himself. When the limelight found him, however, he lapped it up, and his claim to secondary status was never taken all that seriously. It took Che Guevara a successful revolution, smouldering looks, martyrdom and a few decades more to become a habitué of student T-shirts. A living, faceless Marcos joined him in a matter of months.

After the first attempt at a negotiated solution in 1994 foundered, the conflict entered a kind of limbo. Fascination with Marcos and the Zapatistas dissipated in a chaotic electoral year, only to surge again when Ernesto Zedillo launched a short-lived offensive against the guerrillas soon after he took office. The government had sought to demystify their leader by unveiling him as Rafael Sebastián Guillén Vicente, the son of a furniture salesman from the Gulf city of Tampico and a former philosophy lecturer in Mexico City. But the *subcomandante* was still Marcos in the collective imagination, and the offensive catapulted him and his movement back into the spotlight, sparking a new wave of sympathy.

A fresh round of negotiations led to the San Andrés accords, signed in February 1996, which mandated constitutional reforms guaranteeing autonomy for indigenous communities throughout the country. Then the talks broke down, the existing accords were never turned into law, and the Zapatistas returned to their strongholds, while their support base in highland villages weathered low-level military harassment, the expulsion of dozens of their international supporters, and the underhand encouragement of conflict within and between indigenous communities. This reached a peak on 22 December 1997, when paramilitaries allegedly linked to the local PRI massacred forty-five men, women and children who belonged to a group sympathetic to the Zapatista cause as they attended a prayer meeting in the village of Acteal.

The authorities also poured money into non-Zapatista civilian communities in Chiapas. The Zapatistas ordered their civilian base to reject government-funded projects or handouts. Instead they relied on international solidarity donations, which, while significant, were insufficient. The movement inevitably bled members.

The fall in fortunes for the Zapatistas contrasted with a recovery for the electoral left, which, after picking itself up from humiliation in the 1994 presidential elections, began to build momentum again during yet another acute economic crisis. The PRD won a significant number of seats in the mid-term legislative elections in 1997 – the first time the PRI lost its controlling majority in Congress. That year Cárdenas also won the first ever election for mayor of the capital, putting him literally on the doorstep of Los Pinos.

But the veteran candidate, with his hang-dog eyes and down-beat, monotonous way of talking, proved a rather uninspiring mayor. Though he easily secured the PRD's candidacy for the 2000 presidential poll, during the campaign he seemed tired, dour and anachronistic. The ever energetic and optimistic Fox had also picked up a coterie of former leftists who had previously worked on Cárdenas' team but had abandoned him for the loud-mouthed rancher who had a chance of winning. They made it acceptable for Mexicans with left-wing sympathies to vote for Fox in order to push out the PRI. Cárdenas came in a poor third again. 'The struggle is long', he said, as he acknowledged defeat on the night. 'We will continue going in the direction of history.'

The PRD entered the new political era with its historic leader on the wane and its guiding narrative in tatters. The PRI had indeed fallen, but it had not been the PRD that had made it happen. But rather than reinvent itself for the new context, the party immediately turned to a new charismatic leader who, like his predecessor, refused to acknowledge that any real change in Mexico was possible unless the left was in power.

Born in 1953, Andrés Manuel López Obrador began his political career within the PRI, in his home southern state of Tabasco. In those early years he acquired a reputation as a committed organizer and a bit of a political ascetic (based primarily on his work with the indigenous community and the fact that he and his family lived within it and enjoyed few of the luxuries that party leaders are accustomed to). His nascent radicalism was also obvious, although it did not develop into an openly confrontational style until he left the party to join the PRD. After losing a deeply suspicious governorship election in Tabasco in 1994 to PRI dinosaur Roberto Madrazo, he marched on the capital in protest. As president of the PRD between 1996 and 1999, he mounted an aggressive campaign against a bailout in which the government took over bad loans from failed banks.

Radicalism, however, has never been a constant feature of López Obrador's political style, and it played no part in the early years of his term as mayor of Mexico City, which began four days after President Fox's inauguration in December 2000. He had beaten the PAN's Santiago Creel by a single percentage point. This bucked the trend that had left the PRD in poor third place in the presidential and congressional elections at the same time, but was hardly a resounding victory in the left's most important bastion.

The new mayor initially focused on getting himself known around the country. He held daily dawn press conferences which earned him regular exposure on the national morning news, at an hour when few other major political figures had even finished their breakfast. When he did not have anything newsworthy to announce, he got coverage anyway by taking verbal potshots at the president. His irony was often sharp, but the cheeky tone remained light enough to earn him chuckles up and down the social strata.

López Obrador easily shored up support among the working classes in the capital when he introduced small monthly stipends for the elderly and other particularly vulnerable groups. The programme provided a modicum of respite for many families looking after ageing relatives, and underlined the point that the mayor cared. Still, administered through cards that could only be used in registered supermarkets, it hardly amounted to a system-threatening redistribution of wealth. Veteran independent leftist Marco Rascón – who became famous in the effervescence of civil society action after the 1985 earthquake through a politicized masked character he created called 'Super Barrio' – condemned it as 'a subsidy for Walmart'.

The mayor expended more effort and resources courting the middle classes by building a second tier above the capital's main ring road, prioritizing private cars over public transport. He was also at pains to develop good relations with telecoms magnate Carlos Slim, already well on the way to becoming the richest man in the world. They worked closely together on the regeneration of part of the capital's dilapidated colonial centre. As López Obrador's popularity rose, it was common to hear big businessmen say they had no problem with the idea of a leftist like him donning the presidential sash.

The US government under President George W. Bush also seemed happy with the idea of a López Obrador victory, confident that he was a long way from being a rabble-rousing, anti-gringo, anti-imperialist along the lines of Venezuela's Hugo Chávez. As late as January 2006, US Ambassador Tony Garza titled a confidential cable he wrote after a meeting with López Obrador 'Apocalypse Not'. Garza, a personal friend of Bush who had recently married the woman who controlled Mexico's biggest brewery, described the leftist as 'humble and friendly'. The ambassador concluded that he was an 'experienced politician' who 'geared his discussion to his audience, showing his willingness to discuss difficult issues, and apparently open to our suggestions'.

As the 2006 elections approached, the sense that the presidency was the PRD's almost by birthright still reverberated around the party. A wider regional ideological shift further augmented the sense of inevitability. President Chávez in Venezuela and Evo Morales in Bolivia represented the more radical continental wing, and were on the point of being joined by Rafael Correa in Ecuador. Luiz Inácio Lula da Silva in Brazil and Michelle Bachelet in Chile provided more moderate models.

Mexico had been politically rather out of tune with the rest of the region in the twentieth century. The PRI had transformed the only Latin American country with a revolution in the early decades into an outpost of relative stability in a region buffeted by ideological civil wars and military coups. As the new millennium got going, Mexico finally seemed ready to join regional trends with López Obrador at the helm.

Heading a coalition of the PRD and two minor left-wing parties (united under the slogan 'The poor come first'), López Obrador enjoyed a solid lead of over ten points in most opinion polls when campaigning began. He was, however, already leaking some of the support he had worked so hard to win, as his meticulous moderation gave way to a discourse centred on the idea that there was an establishment plot to keep 'the people' out of power.

This started in response to President Fox's ultimately doomed attempt to get him banned from the race by seeking to prosecute him over a minor planning dispute. López Obrador had adroitly turned this into a political victory, but then seemed to get bogged down in the radicalized discourse he had used to achieve it. This intensified as the campaign really got going. López Obrador's face hardened, the volleys of insults he fired at his political opponents got shriller, and his disdain for all those who thought differently from him, even on the left, became more manifest. His decision not to attend the first presidential debate in April opened him to charges of contempt for the voters as a whole.

At the same time, López Obrador's hard core of supporters from the urban poor tightened around him and radicalized as well. They lapped up the way he transmitted a genuine commitment to end inequality, and they admitted no failings in his character, actions or judgement – even when people around him were exposed as corrupt. López Obrador lived in a comfortable but modest middle-class apartment and drove around in the kind of car the working class could hope to afford one day. This was rare for a successful Mexican politician, and his supporters held this up as proof that he was not only untainted, but untaintable. His slogan 'Honestidad Valiente' ('Courageous Honesty') drove home the idea.

López Obrador's increasingly abrasive style played directly into the deeply negative campaign strategy chosen by the PAN's Felipe Calderón, which sought to cast the leftist as an unhinged extremist. The electoral propaganda proclaimed that he was 'a danger to Mexico', destined to plunge the country into another economic crisis with irresponsible populism if he was not stopped. By the time election day came around, López Obrador and Calderón were running neck and neck in most pre-election polling.

On election night, the electoral authorities refused to release their quick count of a sample of polling stations. They said the result was too close to provide certainty. Rather than wait, the two frontrunners claimed victory anyway. The PRI's Roberto Madrazo, obviously not in contention, accepted defeat. The preliminary official count, finally completed a few days later, gave Calderón a wafer-thin advantage of 0.58 per cent. López Obrador cried 'fraud' and the post-electoral crisis began.

At first, the *Lópezobradoristas* focused their efforts on pressing for a full recount. When this apparently reasonable demand failed, they turned their attention to persuading the electoral tribunal to annul the poll. When that failed – despite the tribunal suggesting that the campaign had been rather less than fair – they sought to disrupt Calderón's inauguration on 1 December.

The five months of constant mobilizations included a six-week occupation of Reforma Avenue, which cut the capital in two, as well as regular mass marches and rallies that filled the capital's huge Zócalo plaza every time. López Obrador summed up the ethos of the protest at one such show of strength, on 1 September. 'They are worried that we are no longer willing to accept the rules of the game', he told the crowd of around 100,000 that stretched out below him. 'Let them go to hell with their institutions.'

It was never clear why López Obrador threw his famed tactical skills to the wind – and with them the election that had once seemed to be his for the taking. Nor was it obvious why he should turn complaints about its fairness into a full-scale assault on the country's electoral institutional framework. The election had clearly been flawed – even the electoral tribunal said so – but the evidence of dirty tricks paled in comparison to the habits of the past. Even some of those who genuinely believed Calderón had won unfairly thought it irresponsible and counterproductive of López Obrador not to live with the result. They pointed to the unprecedented level of representation that the left had won in the legislature in the congressional poll held at the same time. This, they argued, could have provided a perfect platform from which to build a more solid project to take to the electorate in 2012.

The Mexican *comentocracia* tended to surmise that López Obrador had let arrogance and overconfidence cloud his political judgement during the campaign, and then let frustration and immaturity lead him into a political tantrum. More sympathetic analysts emphasized the way Fox's crusade against him, combined with Calderón's negative campaigning, had fomented an atmosphere of extreme polarization that wedged him into a radicalized corner. They argued that the decision to actively contest the result allowed his fired-up supporters, who could not conceive that their time had not come, to release their anger in a controlled way, and so averted the risk of violence.

López Obrador's will to win may also have been somewhat sapped by the raised expectations among his core supporters. A documentary called *0.56 per cent* – referring to the final margin by which he officially lost the election – includes a scene shot from inside his car as he leaves a rally and is mobbed by men and women whose desperation and adulation verge on aggression. '*No nos falles*', they literally scream, one after the other, through his open window – 'Don't let us down'. At another point in the film, López Obrador muses on the limits he would face if he did actually become president. 'It's much easier in the streets', he says, with an only half-ironic smile.

The motor behind the electoral left had somehow got stuck. Theoretically, this opened the way for more radical organizations to pick up support, although they faced other challenges that they also had trouble overcoming.

A bead of sweat was visible through the eyehole of his famous black balaclava. Latin America's most celebrated living rebel was feeling the heat, but a glass of water would have meant taking off the mask – and that was out of the question. Subcomandante Marcos made do with a puff on his pipe and a subject that was close to his heart. 'My new book's coming out in June', the Zapatista leader announced. 'There's no politics in the text this time. Just sex. Pure pornography.' Decadence? Not quite, he added: any profits from the book would go to the revolutionary cause.

It was the spring of 2007, a full thirteen years since the Zapatistas' uprising shook Mexico and turned them into an international *cause célèbre*, and nearly seven years since the end of one-party rule that they had helped to bring about. I had covered the Zapatistas fairly consistently since then, but this was the first time I had ever sat down face to mask with Marcos. The interview had not been easy to set up, but most journalists no longer even tried. The era when big-name foreign correspondents waited patiently in jungle huts, night after night, for a chance to talk to the man dubbed a post-modern revolutionary icon was a distant memory. So were the queues of enthralled young women outside his tent.

But if the romance and mystery had long faded, at the same time as his middle-aged paunch had grown, the *subcomandante* was still a fascinating character. He remained the man who had not only spearheaded the construction of the biggest group of rebel fighters since the Revolution, but had also been astute enough to lead its transformation from a doomed, anachronistic, traditional Marxist guerrilla organization into arguably the most unconventional and innovative modern armed group the continent had ever seen.

I had not been easily persuaded by Marcos, and the Zapatistas, when I first arrived in Mexico in 2000, steeped in the experience of covering Central America's civil wars. The Zapatistas did not fit my image of a real guerrilla group, given that there was so little fighting involved; and Marcos' celebrity rather trivialized it all for me. I also found it difficult to take the mask seriously, given that by then everybody knew his name.

Over time I have come to appreciate how much the Zapatistas in their prime revealed about Mexico, and how many of the country's real struggles are played out intensely at a symbolic level, like a kind of passion play. Their response to the new political era also exposed just how unique, and frankly rather strange, the radical Mexican left remained, and how hard it was to identify where its strengths stopped and its weaknesses began (and vice versa). Where else, I wonder, could you find yourself interviewing an unarmed outlaw, officially at war with the state, in the sweltering back room of a solidarity internet cafe in the heart of the capital, with a policeman dozing in a car parked at the end of the street? The rebel's response to my question of when the mask would finally come off only underlined the point. 'When Subcomandante Marcos is no longer necessary', he replied earnestly. 'I hope it's soon, so that I can finally become a fireman as I've always wanted. Firemen always get the prettiest girls.'

The end of PRI hegemony in 2000 had provided the Zapatista guerrilla with a fresh opportunity to regain attention and relevance, and Marcos initially handled it with spectacular aplomb. President Fox sent the long-dormant constitutional reform proposal based on the 1996 San Andrés peace accords to Congress as soon as he was inaugurated in December 2000. He also met Zapatista demands to withdraw military checkpoints on a number of roads in their areas of influence, and released dozens of Zapatista prisoners. Marcos responded with an inspired piece of political theatre, which he called the 'March of the People the Colour of Earth'. The press called it the 'Zapatour'.

It began mid-morning on 25 February 2001, in the Zapatista bastion community of La Realidad in the Lacandón jungle, with Marcos taking the bullets one by one out of the bandoliers across his chest and handing them to an indigenous comrade. Then he took the ammunition out of his revolver, which, together with his assault rifle, he raised above his head as the clicking from the bank of photographers reached a crescendo. Fully disarmed, the *subcomandante* waved and walked slowly up a dirt track to be driven away in a large SUV, leaving the rest of us struggling to get out of a jungle traffic jam in order to follow.

For the next two weeks, Marcos and the twenty-three-person indigenous *comandancia* (which theoretically told him what to do) travelled across the nation, accompanied by a discreet police escort that had been negotiated even more discreetly with President Fox's representatives beforehand. A substantial contingent of the Zapatista international fan club went too, including a group of officious Italians (in camp, white jumpsuits) who were responsible for maintaining an inner security cordon. Mexican nationalist sensibilities, and a touch of machismo, ensured that they were soon replaced with locals. Still, the international festival feel was always present, the strains of Manu Chao's cult album *Clandestino* wafting out of almost every bus.

Crowds of extraordinary diversity greeted Marcos everywhere he went. They ranged from true enthusiasts to those who just wanted to see the famous guerrilla in a mask. Rock tour-style T-shirts went on sale with a picture of the *subcomandante* on the front and the major performance dates on the back.

At each stop, Marcos gave speeches filled with elliptical tales and hard-hitting rhetoric focused on the evils of capitalism, as well as offensive personal jibes aimed at President Fox. The rebel leader also made it clear that lasting peace in Chiapas was now possible. Marcos and the *comandantes* finally rolled into the Zócalo in Mexico City on the back of an open lorry on 11 March, to a rapturous welcome from a full plaza.

The real climax to the Zapatour came a few weeks later, when several tiny men and women in balaclavas addressed a joint session of Congress. Marcos, in another masterly propaganda coup, countered the charges that the movement was all about his ego by waiting outside. 'The *subcomandante* is just that, a *sub*, and we gave him the mission to bring us here. Now it is our moment', said Comandante Esther, her head scarcely visible above the lectern. 'My name is Esther, but that's not important. I'm a Zapatista, but that's not important, either. What is important is that I am indigenous and I am a woman and I am speaking in this symbolic place.'

The sense that something new was beginning ended abruptly a few weeks later when the legislature approved a watered-down version of the reform that augmented indigenous rights but fell far short of the recognition of autonomy that had seemed in the bag. The Zapatistas dismissed it as a betrayal and, back in their jungle strongholds, went almost completely silent for several years.

I have never seen a really convincing analysis of why the Zapatistas decided so abruptly to disengage from the new political era in Mexico, particularly at a time when their popularity was riding so high. The decision bore some similarities to the way in which López Obrador torpedoed his own electoral chances six years later.

Some observers, particularly those based in Mexico City, speculated that Marcos could not cope with events moving out of his personal control and with the corresponding dynamic that was pushing him towards becoming a conventional politician. Others, especially those based in Chiapas, said that the indigenous *comandantes* and Zapatista communities in Chiapas were uncomfortable with the national agenda taking over from their local concerns and had pulled the movement back to its bastions to attend to those. The movement's most committed supporters argued that the guerrillas were right to surmise that the failure of the initial constitutional reform effort had proved that – political pluralism or no political pluralism – the system could not be changed from within.

Whatever the reason, the Zapatistas deflated the bubble they had blown and turned inward. They said nothing to the outside world until 2003, when they announced their intention to construct de facto autonomy in the communities they still controlled. By that time, however, the broader context had changed again, and while the residual sympathy they commanded ensured that they still enjoyed a certain protection, interest had faded dramatically.

Domestically, left-wing attention had turned to the momentum growing behind López Obrador's presidential bid. The rest of the world, meanwhile, was too caught up with Al Qaeda and the wars in the Middle East to see much relevance in a largely peaceful bunch of rebels, far from the global centres of conflict. Moreover Marcos himself was still nowhere to be seen. Aside from a crime novel featuring a Zapatista private eye, his communiqués were sporadic and often impenetrable.

Marcos did not appear in public again until August 2005, when he began a series of mass gatherings of supporters in Zapatista strongholds to prepare for what became known as the 'Other Campaign' – an effort to build a network of leftist radicals who felt disenfranchised by electoral politics. Timed to coincide with the real presidential campaign for the 2006 elections, Marcos's new foray into the public arena did not go down very well with many of the Zapatistas' erstwhile supporters on the electoral left, because he took every opportunity to pour scorn on López Obrador. He described the PRD candidate as 'a serpent's egg' and 'a traitor', who, behind his egalitarian rhetoric, was propping up a system of exclusion and exploitation. He told participants in the Other Campaign that the only rule defining membership of the new movement was that they could not support the Zapatistas and López Obrador at the same time. Several leftist intellectuals who had once gushed over Marcos would later blame him for helping to lose López Obrador the crucial 250,000 votes that could have assured him the presidency. Around the time of the Zapatour, the PRD tried hard to persuade Marcos to take off his mask and accept a seat in the Senate. Now they abhorred him.

Nearly five years after the Zapatour, Marcos left the jungle again in January 2006, this time making the first stage of the journey on a motorbike, presumably in homage to Che Guevara. (The film *Motorcycle Diaries*, about the Argentine's rite of revolutionary passage, starring Mexican actor Gael García Bernal, was popular at the time.) After that, the *subcomandante* and a handful of collaborators travelled the length and breadth of Mexico, to sit in endless meetings with a bewildering array of organizations, whose only common ground was that they all identified themselves as being on the fringes. These ranged from dispossessed indigenous communities, powerless to stop dams and prevent agribusiness from destroying their lands, to street vendors evicted from the capital's kerbs to make way for the retail magnates, and transvestite prostitutes facing extortion by the police.

The Other Campaign was never supposed to replicate the mass appeal of the Zapatour, but it was intended to infuse alternative politics with a new energy. The indigenous issue that had been so central in 1994 and 2000 was now, Marcos insisted, part of a bigger attempt to create a new kind of revolutionary movement based on the principle of respect for difference. He claimed that Mexico's politicians, media, and its earnest left-wing academics were oblivious to the nationwide social uprising about to explode.

'Nightmares don't announce themselves', he said when I interviewed him in 2007, towards the end of his intermittent eighteen-month tour. 'Or more accurately, they announce themselves with a huge supper. And in our country, the rich and the governing class have been stuffing themselves for too long now and their nightmare is coming.' Marcos added that he believed the 200th anniversary of independence and the 100th anniversary of the Revolution – both dates falling three years later – would light the fuse. Soon after that, he returned to Chiapas and went silent again, but there was a buzz of expectation in the air as 2010 approached.

In the event, the year came and went without any revolutionary sparks, and even earnest members of the Other Campaign admitted that it had ended up as a bit of a damp squib. It seemed to most outside observers that Marcos had played his final hand in search of a way of maintaining his status as a rebel icon in the new political era – and that he had lost. Spring 2011 brought reports that he was seriously ill. This prompted a denial and a flurry of dispatches written by him analysing the drug wars. I know few journalists who even bothered to read them.

✻ ✻ ✻

The Zapatista movement was always a two-pronged animal that mixed its struggle against the national institutions with a community-based movement focused on local issues. Though its national platform waned, that still left the local agenda – but it, too, faced new challenges. The threat once posed by the army and paramilitaries had been replaced by infrastructure projects, tourism developers and government-funded anti-poverty programmes. The international solidarity that had once helped keep things afloat had also dwindled away, and an increasing number of young Zapatistas were heading north to the US in search of the material progress their communities could not provide. The local movement also faced the problem of encouraging loyalty among a new generation who barely remembered the uprising in 1994, if at all. Somehow, however, the movement soldiered on.

In November 2009, I made a short visit to the Zapatista community of La Garrucha, located in the heart of one of the jungle canyons that had always been strongholds of the rebels. In 2003 it became one of the five civilian Juntas de Buen Gobierno – Councils of Good Government – that knitted together the self-government project. These councils were supposed to sort out problems ranging from stolen chickens to full-scale land conflicts within communities under their de facto jurisdiction, and between them and non-Zapatistas in the same area. The armed wing of the movement was supposed to watch from a respectful distance, protecting them from the state they rejected, but not interfering either.

I got to La Garrucha after dark and, after registering my arrival with a woman at a little office at the gate, was courteously given my own room, with a couple of planks to sleep on (luxuries not afforded the woman and her children, who slept on a plastic sheet on the floor of the office). I was up at dawn, watching a thick mist take a full hour to rise enough to reveal the shadows of the settlement's buildings, and even longer to divulge the murals painted all over them. One featured a moon with a bandana covering its face, looking over an idyllic pastoral scene of corn cultivation, while another had a huge image of Emiliano Zapata with few additional adornments. The murals' slogans took still longer to become legible: 'Masked in Order to Unmask Power' read one; 'We sow our seeds with the wind of life and dignity' proclaimed another.

Little by little, La Garrucha filled with gentle-paced activity. Women made breakfast in a communal kitchen, men chopped wood and buzzed around a little building site, and a group of small children wandered off to the community school. A couple of young international-solidarity types tried to look inconspicuous and failed. It hardly looked like a hotbed of revolutionary dynamism, but nor did it seem like a community on its last legs.

Eventually I was taken before four Junta members, seated behind a long desk, who told me they would not respond to a single one of the questions I had earlier written down, at their request. There was no explanation, and I knew from past experience that there was no point in pushing for one. When Zapatistas are in mute mode, you have to be far more skilled a conversationalist than I to get them to say anything at all, let alone anything of interest. Hanging around the settlement for the rest of the morning was equally futile, and I eventually gave up, frustrated but grudgingly impressed. Their silence suggested that they felt their backs were up against the wall, but it also seemed to be rooted in genuine disdain for outsiders. If the world had long forgotten them (they seemed to be saying), then that was the world's loss, not theirs. It made me question how accurate it really was to think of the Zapatistas as a spent force, as most observers did by then. Marcos' grandiose plans might have failed, but the Zapatistas' local low-level rebellion still retains a gentle intensity that does not seem about to disappear anytime soon.

The small redoubt of Zapatistas is also part of a broader phenomenon of community-based alternative organizing, which they originally helped to inspire but which is now far beyond their control. This is particularly evident in an indigenous community police force, which patrols in the mountains of the southern state of Guerrero and is credited with keeping things there much calmer than in similar areas.

❄ ❄ ❄

The Zapatistas are not the only guerrillas still hanging on in the new era of political pluralism. There are several more very small groups, also rooted in the legacy of the 1970s, that have never made the transition out of strategic and ideological convention.

The best known and the biggest of these is the Popular Revolutionary Army (EPR), which announced its existence in 1996 and is based in Guerrero and parts of Oaxaca. The EPR surprised many with its capacity to mount simultaneous attacks on six natural gas, propane and crude oil pipelines in September 2007, later explained as an action to demand the restoration of two of its leaders who had disappeared. But the group did almost nothing of note in the rest of the decade, and some guerrilla watchers suggested that they have been significantly weakened by drug traffickers encroaching on their territory.

Most of the handful of other recognizable names stem from splits within the EPR. They include the Insurgent People's Revolutionary Army (ERPI), whose most prominent leader, Comandante Ramiro, was found dead in 2009. Another EPR breakaway, calling itself the Revolutionary Democratic Tendency (TDR), has a more urban bent, but no more clout – unless, that is, it was behind the kidnapping of PAN godfather Diego Fernández de Cevallos, as some have speculated.

Fernández de Cevallos was abducted from one of his many properties in the central state of Querétaro in May 2010. A wealthy lawyer and former presidential candidate with a reputation for being an extremely adroit back-room wheeler dealer, he was held for seven months and eventually released, complete with godlike beard, after the payment of a ransom that reportedly topped $20 million. A group calling itself the Mysterious Disappearers initially claimed responsibility for the kidnapping. Then it changed its name to the Network for Global Transformation. Some guerrilla watchers surmised that it was actually the TDR by another name, since the latter group is known for occasional kidnappings.

Jorge Lofredo, who uploads every single communiqué that is put out by armed groups throughout the region onto the website of his Argentina-based organization Cemeda, has raised the possibility that they might be a criminal gang using revolutionary rhetoric as a façade. Others have speculated that it might be the first real sign that Mexico's guerrillas are teaming up with organized crime, although this seems unlikely, given that they are so weak and fractured that it is hard to imagine what advantage drug traffickers could find in such an alliance.

The persistence of Mexico's traditional guerrilla groups, for all their insignificance and apparently delusional hope that the historic conditions for an insurgency might coalesce in their lifetimes, still serves as an ever-present symbolic token of potential political revolt – a potential that refuses to fade away despite the democratic transition and that sometimes bubbles to the surface, though not in an armed form. The largely peaceful uprising by the Popular Assembly of the Peoples of Oaxaca (APPO) that took hold in the eponymous city and state in 2006, did not just bubble – it boiled.

The uprising in Oaxaca was triggered by the autocratic style of the state's PRI governor, Ulises Ruiz Ortiz, who was elected in 2004 in a poll mired by dirty tricks. The governor then made this much worse through his clumsy handling of the restlessness that is always latent in one of the country's poorest states, with one of the highest indigenous populations and a strong tradition of organized discontent.

Governor Ruiz had apparently forgotten one of the axioms of PRI rule, which held that repression is usually much more effective when mixed with co-optation. The tension began to rise with the killing of several community leaders in mysterious circumstances, but the governor made little attempt to defuse the anger this generated. It exploded when he applied the same logic to the annual protest of teachers who occupied the Zócalo in the city in May 2006.

The long-dissident Section 22 of the National Union of Teachers, representing the 70,000-odd teachers in the state, had organized similar protests every spring since at least the early 1990s. The negotiations usually took two or three weeks, after which the teachers would go home with a slightly higher pay deal than the national average, and enough other concessions to keep them passive until the following year.

In 2006 this ritual cycle broke down. The Oaxaca teachers seemed more determined than usual to get themselves permanently reclassified into a higher pay band, and Ruiz refused to negotiate at all. Instead he ordered the strikers to return to work or lose their pay and risk their jobs. When they responded by blocking roads around the state, Ruiz launched a pre-dawn raid to evict them from their camp in the city. Initially sent scrambling, the teachers regrouped and pushed back into the Zócalo, at the same time as helicopters began shooting tear gas down at them from above. By mid-morning, the protestors were back in control, incensed, emboldened and determined to broaden the movement into what became known as the APPO.

The Popular Assembly of the Peoples of Oaxaca was preposterously diverse. It included more than three hundred different organizations, ranging from unions, residents' and students' associations, human rights organizations, indigenous groups, intellectuals, feminists and bicycle taxi associations. There was even room for the odd successful businessman who had been alienated by the governor's penchant for giving contracts for major infrastructure and energy projects to companies from outside the state. Word had it that the EPR was also involved, undercover.

The media paid particular attention to Flavio Sosa, an articulate, heavy-set man with a big beard and a lolloping, rhythmic gait, who always seemed to be just where you needed him to be when you needed a quote in the name of the movement. The APPO, however, was essentially leader-less. The huge and disciplined Section 22 inevitably had the loudest voice, but the teachers did not control the APPO as a whole. The rest of its members also demanded to be heard, and all decisions were taken by consensus. The cacophony meant that the only demand they could all agree on was that Ruiz should go.

Ruiz disappeared from public view, aside from very occasional appearances in staunchly PRI towns around the state. It was obviously folly to be seen in the city centre, but he did not even dare turn up at the government offices, which he had already moved to a kind of bunker on the outskirts of the city. He held just one press conference during the entire conflict – in a heavily guarded hotel on the fringes of town. The local congress still partially functioned, but the reality was that the state government had been paralysed by the uprising.

There were many in Oaxaca who complained about the APPO's ugly invasion of the elegant historic centre, the graffiti daubed on the faintly green stone of the colonial buildings, and the sense that anything could happen. They worried as they watched the tourist economy fade away, and there was anger over the 1.3 million children left without classes. The emergence of vigilante justice also demolished the APPO's attempt to portray itself as a paragon of pacifist virtue. They brought alleged thieves to the Zócalo and tied them to lampposts with signs around their necks saying 'This is what happens if you steal.'

But the often-heard charge that the APPO represented a tiny minority of violent extremists who had 'kidnapped' the city was inaccurate. Given the radicalism in the air, the movement was actually remarkably peaceful, and it had genuine and widespread support in the city and beyond. Tens of thousands joined its marches, and the decision to set up barricades around town prompted spontaneous participation. APPO supporters would while away the nights manning these, deep in conversation and consuming provisions delivered by sympathizers.

The barricades were originally set up over the summer to hinder the approach and escape of the thugs who began attacking APPO sympathizers. The attacks started as hit-and-run assaults on the protestors and on the radio and TV stations they had commandeered. They developed into death squads. By the time the conflict ended, different sources put the death toll at anywhere between twelve and twenty-five.

Governor Ruiz always denied any connection to the violence; but even if that were true, there is no evidence that he did anything to stop it. A non-binding Supreme Court investigation three years after the events ruled that Ruiz's failure to act made him responsible for serious human rights violations during the conflict.

At its height, the APPO attracted a steady stream of idealistic young foreigners, a good number of whom posted internet reports of what they viewed as a modern version of the Paris Commune. Most Mexican analysts were rather less ready with the labels, instead emphasizing the movement's diversity, lack of leadership and absence of goals (beyond the resignation of the governor). They tended to see the fact that the APPO did not, in the absence of the formal authority, attempt to assume administrative functions as final proof that it should not be described as revolutionary. As I watched a middle-aged, conservatively dressed woman shed tears of anger as 'robo-cops' removed a barricade under a shower of Molotov cocktails hurled by young men in masks, it felt pretty revolutionary to me.

The APPO was always too radical for the comfort of many, but it was also obviously rooted in legitimate grievances against a local despot. Governor Ruiz was not only continuing the old authoritarian traditions of the worst of the PRI, he was doing so with additional leeway, as the most extreme expression of the phenomenon of the new feudal governors. Caught between his fear of being branded authoritarian if he repressed the uprising and his reluctance to try and force the governor out, President Vicente Fox let the problem fester and grow for months. The 2006 presidential election and the initial stages of the post-electoral crisis also encouraged passivity, as the president sought to keep additional problems at bay.

The change came when the post-election crisis began to settle down and it became clear that the PAN needed the PRI's help to ride out the final stages of the challenge to Calderón's electoral victory. Sorting out the mess in Oaxaca became the obvious way of securing it. When the federal Senate finally discussed whether to declare Oaxaca's government 'non-functioning' – a legal way of forcing Governor Ruiz to go – the PAN ended up voting with the PRI against the resolution.

The outgoing Fox government then turned its efforts to preparing to retake the city. This began by negotiating a pay deal with the teachers. In return they stepped down from the mobilization. The rest of the APPO responded angrily, with a state-wide day of action on 27 October that ended with three sympathizers dead. They included a New York Indymedia video reporter called Brad Will, who was shot as he filmed from behind an APPO line under attack from men with guns.

Fox sent the *federales* to occupy the city two days later, arguing that he had no choice, given the impending anarchy. The rows of federal riot police that inched into town along the main road from Mexico City faced only symbolic resistance. A couple held up a painting of the Virgin of Guadalupe, an older man waved a large Mexican flag around his head, and several people pushed against the riot shields. A chant of '*asesinos*' – 'murderers' – gathered steam at the sight of the automatic weapons carried by some of the officers, but it was drowned out by the noise of a helicopter overhead. As the crowd was inevitably pushed back, there was a rousing chorus of the Latin American left's historic mantra: 'The people united will never be defeated.' Whether this was conviction or bitter self-mockery was not clear.

The *federales* made slow progress on their way to the city centre because of the number of barricades in their way. They removed these one by one with the aid of a small army of bulldozers. Other police contingents got there quicker on back roads, but they faced more militant opposition. In one battle, police buses had most of their windows shattered by protesters hurling chunks of concrete. Piles of burning tyres filled the air with black smoke, which mingled with the tear gas.

The first *federales* entered the city's Zócalo at dusk, after the radicals had already slipped away. That night the officers pulled down the tarpaulins and posters glorifying the revolt that had adorned the ornate bandstand in the middle of the square, the colonnades along the sides and the great laurel trees in between. They built bonfires, defecated on street corners and wandered around rather aimlessly, as if they did not really know what to do next. By the time they bedded down in the recaptured territory on pictures of Che Guevara, the rest of the centre of Oaxaca was empty and eerily silent.

The following day Ulises Ruiz sat once again in the governor's chair and Fox proclaimed that social order and peace had been restored. In fact, the battles went on for another month. The days were permeated with tension and peppered with minor incidents, while the nights were aglow with burning buses, as youths with bandanas pulled up over their noses wheeled around shopping trolleys full of homemade firebombs.

The final crackdown came on 25 November, when an APPO march aimed at establishing a siege of the federal forces in the Zócalo escalated into a full-scale clash. The federal police rounded up hundreds of protestors (and anybody else in their way), using systematic and serious violence that left some detainees permanently crippled. The message was clear: no more rebellion would be tolerated. It was an ironic end to Fox's term. Six years after being hailed as the architect of Mexican democracy, Fox had restored a political dinosaur to power, in order to persuade the PRI to help the PAN hold onto presidential power in the face of accusations of voting fraud.

I went back to Oaxaca in May 2009, three years after the uprising, to find out where all that radicalism had gone. All was apparently calm. By then those arrested in the crackdown had been released, and most had hardly shown their faces since. The Zócalo was once again occupied by striking teachers, but this time the protest was following the old traditions and negotiations would eventually lead to quiet demobilization. Ulises Ruiz, firmly back in power and on the point of leading the local PRI to smash all opposition in the mid-term federal legislative elections, had learned that it was not worth risking another major flare-up.

Explicit anger about what had happened three years earlier was confined to large posters demanding justice for the human rights violations strung up around the Zócalo. A few diehard APPO remnants sat next to them. 'We just didn't manage to maintain the unity that was needed'. Fifty-year-old teacher Alfonso Arellano looked close to tears as he alleged that many of the leaders had been bought off. 'It was a terrible blow and we are scraping the barrel to keep things alive. In the *barrios* there are people ready and waiting to form something new, but we just haven't got the ability to get it together. And how are the enemy doing? Very well, thank you.'

A woman I interviewed in her tiny dressmaking shop close to one of the definitive battles of 2006 summed up for me just how deep radicalism could run in Mexico beneath apparent docility. A picture of respectability in a well-pressed blouse, a tape measure around her neck and kitschy little ornaments displayed on her wall, she initially evaded questions about the aftermath of the uprising. Then she launched into an impassioned description of how she had taken food to those on the barricades and watched an activist have his throat cut by government thugs during the final police assault on the state university campus, where the rebels still controlled a radio station:

> Things exploded back then because of the accumulation of anger over lack of services and bad treatment you receive when you are not wealthy and because there was a movement we could all join, and because we thought, we really thought, it was possible to bring down the governor . . . The rage remains. You mark my words, this is a time bomb.

The following year, the political context in Oaxaca took a surprise turn with the election of an urbane, left-leaning politician called Gabino Cué Monteagudo as the state's new governor. Cué was supported by the PRD, the PAN and anti-Ruiz elements within the PRI. Even López Obrador made an exception to his general disdain for such coalitions and provided tacit support, as did some former APPO leaders like Flavio Sosa. Such a seemingly contradictory alliance, which ended eighty-one years of PRI domination of the state, would have been much more difficult to construct had the 2006 uprising not underlined how fed up people really were.

❄ ❄ ❄

In the meantime Andrés Manuel López Obrador was revving up for a second shot at the presidency in July 2012, something few had thought he would be in a position to do after his failed efforts to get the previous elections annulled.

López Obrador had all but disappeared from the mainstream media as soon as Calderón was sworn in as president. The leftist alleged a boycott by the big news organizations, and that may be true. It was also true that, with no official position and very little money, the former candidate was not generating much news anymore – certainly nothing to compare with the cascade of events that accompanied Calderón's bid to put his mark on the presidency and the start of the drug wars.

López Obrador, however, was never going to retire, gracefully or otherwise. The old strategic planner returned to the fore and he went back to basics. The documentary film *0.56 per cent* ends with the man who, during the post-election crisis, had had himself proclaimed 'legitimate president of Mexico' in front of a full Zócalo, giving a low-key speech to a couple of dozen locals in a sleepy, broiling southern backwater.

Over the next few years, López Obrador visited every single one of Mexico's 2,438 municipalities, a good number of them several times over. His support base had always been in the capital, but his tireless town-hopping allowed him to spread it around the country and build an informal nationwide organization focused on carrying him into the presidency next time around. While it overlapped with the constituency of the PRD and the other, smaller left-wing parties, it owed its loyalty and its mission to him alone. 'There has never been anybody like him', Mirna Rodríguez told me at one López Obrador rally in 2010. 'He is superior to them all. Honest, courageous, austere. He works very hard, and we only believe in him.'

López Obrador formally launched the network in early 2011, calling it the Movement for National Regeneration – or Morena – and calling its members 'Protagonists of Real Change'. Each of these (he predicted there would be four million by the time the campaign formally began) was committed to mobilizing at least five more voters.

Morena seemed like an attempt to re-create the movement that had almost taken Cuauhtémoc Cárdenas to power in 1988, only in a more organized way. It also had missionary undertones and picked up on the salvation motif long present in López Obrador's political style. Mexican historian Enrique Krauze wrote a deeply negative profile of him during the 2006 election campaign entitled 'The Tropical Messiah'. US political scientist George Grayson wrote a similarly critical biography called *Mexican Messiah*. Most importantly, however, it was something that even his enemies within the PRD could not ignore. López Obrador's comeback after the 2006 election had by no means been a given. For several years many observers wrote him off as a political has-been. When it became clear that he was not going to give up, he was frequently accused of pushing the PRD into a crisis from which it might not recover.

The division of the PRD roughly along pro- and anti-López Obrador lines started almost as soon as Calderón took office. It began when a number of the party's newly elected deputies and senators quietly withdrew support for his short-lived attempt to set up a parallel 'legitimate' government. Not long after that, some of these began openly criticizing the former candidate's confrontational tactics and 'authoritarian' style.

The discord deepened into open hostility when one anti-López Obrador faction got control of the leadership in 2008. Relations became so antagonistic that the man himself campaigned for a tiny left-wing party called the Partido de Trabajo, or Workers' Party, rather than his own in the mid-term legislative elections of 2009. It proved disastrous. The number of PRD deputies dropped from a hundred and twenty-seven to sixty-nine, while the number of Partido de Trabajo deputies rose from eleven to thirteen.

The following year the internal conflict focused on the party leadership's commitment to a strategy of electoral alliances with the PAN to fight several governorship elections, with the aim of stripping the PRI of some of its key bastions. López Obrador fervently opposed all the alliances (aside from the one in Oaxaca) on the grounds that it was both ideologically and ethically unacceptable to join forces with a party that (he still claimed) had cheated the left out of victory in 2006. The strategy also struck at the heart of his insistence that the PRI and the PAN were essentially different expressions of what he frequently called the 'Mafia of Power'.

Both López Obrador's supporters and opponents within the PRD resisted pushing the party to actual breaking point. Although they seemed close to doing so on several occasions, they always pulled back. As much as they hated each other, they needed each other as well. The party with López Obrador and Morena against them was an electoral damp rag. López Obrador without the PRD did not have access to the kind of state electoral funding required to mount a realistic presidential campaign.

The left's run-up to the 2012 elections was complicated further by the existence of another potentially strong candidate – Mexico City mayor Marcelo Ebrard Casaubón. Ebrard had served as his predecessor's public security and social development secretaries. López Obrador had then helped him to a resounding 19 percentage point victory in the 2006 mayoral election. The new mayor made his presidential ambitions clear almost from the start of his term.

Ebrard's rather elitist demeanour meant he could never hope to compete with López Obrador for the emotional loyalties of the poor. His wonkish style, which includes launching into detailed policy explanations at breakneck speed, has similarly limited popular appeal. He did, however, find the space to cement his left-wing credentials by investing more in public transport, promoting cycling around the city, and organizing showy popular events in public spaces – such as a huge ice rink in the Zócalo at Christmas, and artificial beaches in the holidays for those who cannot afford to leave town. Ebrard has also turned the capital into an island of social progressiveness. Legislation allowing abortion on demand was followed by the introduction of gay marriage – both issues that López Obrador had always studiously ignored.

Ebrard's liberal reputation has many holes. These include insufficient attention to human rights violations committed by the municipal police, excessive control of information of obvious public interest, and the manifest failure to prepare an environmentally progressive solution to the country's imminent rubbish crisis. Even so, he can still lay credible claim to the most modern leftist image in Mexico, having transformed himself into the kind of politician who could be imagined running a European capital.

Ebrard began his political career within the PRI under the tutelage of Manuel Camacho Solís, who remains his close (largely behind-the-scenes) collaborator today. Their exit from the PRI in 1995 was rooted in Camacho's frustration at not securing the presidential candidacy for the previous year's election. This background, along with the fact that Ebrard did not actually join the PRD until 2004, meant his attempt to secure the party candidacy for 2012 was viewed with suspicion by many within the structure. At the same time, however, he could count on the support of some of López Obrador's enemies inside the party.

López Obrador and Ebrard danced around each other's ambitions for years, careful not to let their rivalry become too open. In the meantime the PRD itself was riven with ever more open, intense and complex power struggles as the different *tribus* set about seeking to secure spheres of influence for the future. This had as much to do with preparations for the legislative elections and the race to be the next mayor as with the presidential poll held at the same time. It also put the least palatable sides of the party on open display.

The rehabilitation of a disgraced but seasoned political operator called René Bejarano Martínez was particularly symbolic. Bejarano cut his political teeth in the post-earthquake social movements, and went on to build a clientelistic power base among neighbourhood groups in the capital. This he put at the service of the PRD, in exchange for quotas of power. After taking office as mayor of Mexico City in 2000, López Obrador appointed Bejarano to be his first private secretary.

Bejarano fell dramatically from grace four years later, following the release of a video showing him in the office of a businessman associated with the party, stuffing bundles of cash into a laptop case. After filling up the case, he shoves the remaining wads into his pockets, before gathering up a handful of elastic bands still on the table. He became known as 'El Señor de las Ligas', or the 'Lord of the Elastic Bands'. The scandal earned Bejarano a short spell in jail and several years in the political hinterland, but in 2011 he was voted back onto the PRD's national leadership committee. 'I never left the party', he told reporters with a knowing smile. 'I was just being discreet.'

The PRD's continued dependence on the likes of Bejarano underlined how far the political left was from genuinely embracing the need to push Mexican democratization beyond competitive elections. Having lost the freshness of 1988, and squandered its 'perfect storm' moment of 2006, it was beginning to look so tired, dysfunctional and stuck in the past that it became common to hear and read predictions of imminent implosion. The left, the argument went, had no choice but to 're-found' itself. And then, all of a sudden, some coherence returned, thanks to a single simple act of political congruity.

López Obrador and Ebrard had agreed in May 2011 that they would decide which of them got the candidacy on the basis of an opinion poll that November. They chose this method because it was clear that they could not trust the PRD to organize an internal contest. The party's internal elections in October proved them right. These ended up so riddled with obvious dirty tricks and marred by so many mutual accusations of foul play that they had to be annulled in many districts.

In the polls to decide the candidate the following month, Ebrard came out slightly worse than his rival and graciously accepted defeat: 'A divided left will go straight to the precipice, and I will never be the person who condemns the effort to change the course of Mexico to failure.' The bucket-loads of praise that Ebrard received in the media for accepting the result of the polls underlined how far Mexican democracy is from consolidation, but it was enough to suddenly provide the left with a semblance of order and dignity. After that all major leaders from all the major factions fell into line behind López Obrador, as if the past six years of constant backbiting had never happened.

López Obrador stepped into the limelight provided by the candidacy decision, having shed the radicalism with which he had defined himself since at least 2005. He still insisted on the need for more fairness and equality, but all the ire directed at the 'mafia of power' had been replaced by talk of reconciliation. He also began explicitly courting private sector support. The former mayor's efforts to bury his confrontational image of old were not, however, devoid of a certain edginess. His new slogan – 'La República Amorosa' or 'The Loving Republic' – appealed to widespread weariness with the conflicts of the past few years, but it was also so extreme (and faintly ridiculous) that it was inevitably enveloped in a certain amount of irony. López Obrador may have softened (the message seemed to be), but he is not naïve.

Victory still seemed very unlikely, but the complete electoral debacle many had predicted for the PRD now seemed somewhat less inevitable. To salvage the situation, López Obrador needed to see off the PAN's candidate (Josefina Vázquez Mota) and then, with second place secured, turn himself into a magnet for the votes of all those who did not necessarily sympathize with him, but could not bear the idea of the old party of power returning to Los Pinos. If he managed to get even close to Peña Nieto, López Obrador would cement his status as a remarkable political leader whose curious charisma and dogged determination is mixed with strategic instinct that few can rival. Not even pulling off the near miraculous feat of winning, however, could transform him, or the PRD, into the coherent political expression of the need for further democratization that the country still so clearly needs. The best hope for pushing parties on any part of the political spectrum towards that role still comes from civil society.

Although organized groups demanding accountability represent the most obvious and direct sources of pressure to get Mexico's democratic transition moving again, there are also vaguer social developments that should be taken into account. One of these is a torturously slow, but still unprecedented, growth in awareness and discomfort with the obvious correlation between skin tone, class, wealth and power that impacts the lives of almost all Mexicans.

Racial difference in Mexico is not conceived of as a matter of distinct communities, as it is in the United States and most of Europe, but as a colour continuum with cultural and class associations grafted on. The myth of a unitary national identity developed under the PRI regime brushed over the differences with the claim that all Mexicans were variations of the basic mix of indigenous and European ancestry. It was nevertheless obvious then, and is arguably even more obvious today, that the vast majority of aspirational figures, outside of sport and the odd folk-loric exception, are notably lighter than the vast majority of Mexicans. This is as true of the country's news anchors and top entertainers as it is of the majority of intellectual opinion formers, business leaders and the models used in almost all advertising. Whether the product is washing powder or cars, nappies or cellular phones, newspaper subscriptions, microwave dinners, indigestion medication or low-income housing credits, if there is a person in the picture he or she will almost certainly not be very brown.

According to Anastasia Guerra, who heads the Mexico City-based advertising agency Imaginaria, the industry easily adapted its stereotypes to changing times, to give women more forceful roles and to take on such previously taboo issues as sexual health or sexual orientation. But the skin-colour issue, she told me in 2009, has remained 'untouchable'. The most successful models for adults, she said, are lighter than average, but not so white as to seem like fantasy. The same desire for upward mobility has been reflected in product form by the booming market in skin-light-ening creams that took off around 2008.

Products aimed at children (or at the adults who buy products for their children) tend to be whiter still, reflecting the freer rein parents give to their subconscious hopes for their offspring. In 2010 I went on a mission around the capital to find a non-white doll. I failed. For years, one of the biggest milk brands in the country has run advertisements featuring blond, curly haired kids alongside the slogan 'All of Mexico grows up with LaLa'.

This kind of oblique racism is common in many parts of the world; but in Mexico it is particularly striking because of the nation's official self-identification as universally brown and the traditional lack of any political recognition that there is even a problem.

The Zapatista uprising put discrimination against indigenous people on the Mexican political map in 1994, but this is generally perceived primarily as an issue of culture. The truth is, however, that even when an indigenous woman (or man) speaks Spanish, does not wear traditional dress and does not live in a poor rural community, she is still likely to suffer discrimination because she is probably darker than average. That fact is almost never mentioned even by activists. The vehement Mexican defence of the condescendingly drawn black cartoon character Memín

Pinguín in the face of US complaints about a commemorative stamp in 2005, showed how strong the myth remains.

Since then, however, tentative signs have emerged that this is changing. The first National Study into Discrimination (ENADIS), carried out in 2005, did not even include any direct questions on skin colour. The second (carried out in 2010) had several. The survey made the link between colour and social aspiration particularly clear in a question that asked people to locate themselves on a nine-shade scale. Over 53 per cent of women defined themselves within the whitest three categories, and only 15 per cent in the darkest three. At the same time, however, the survey revealed that 40 per cent of the sample said people were treated differently in Mexico because of their skin tone, and 18 per cent said they had had personal experience of not having their rights respected because of their colour. Given the complete absence of public debate on the issue, the figure seems fairly high.

Fourteen-year-old Diana León, whose struggle to overcome economic disadvantage I have already described in a previous chapter, needs no prompting to talk about the racism that she feels directly affects her life in a low-income urban *barrio*. Like all patriotic schoolchildren, she would like to be in the marching guard that accompanies the flag around her school patio on Monday mornings. The honour is supposed to be reserved for good students (like her), but her teacher has already made it clear that the criteria also include being *güera*, a term used interchangeably in Mexico to mean 'light skinned' and 'pretty'. 'There is a lot of racism everywhere', Diana told me in 2011. 'I know that if, in future, I apply for a job as a secretary, my chances of getting it will be very small if there is someone else applying with lighter skin.'

Growing awareness also ensured that a video of Mexican children in front of two baby dolls – one white and one brown – became a YouTube hit at the end of 2011. Asked which baby was nasty and ugly, they all point straight at the brown one and explicitly explain their reasoning in colour-based terms. Asked to identify which baby is like them, most also point to the brown one, though less enthusiastically.

Derogatory references to assumptions that whiteness is an intrinsic component of beauty and talent are also creeping into popular culture. A typically Mexican-looking singer called Amandititita had a recent fringe success with a song taking potshots at the tall, slim and light-skinned singers promoted on the TV. The chorus went 'I can never be a *güera* Televisa'.

The relationship between skin tone and politics is rather more complex. Drawn from all social classes, politicians range across the spectrum, although there tend to be more darker people in the PRI and the PRD, whose party structures have firmer roots in the popular sectors and provide party activists from poor households with opportunities for advancement. Political advertising also tends to reflect a more realistic vision of the population than commercial propaganda. At least this is true when it is focused on the electorate's problems. When the centrepiece is the politician as a product, it becomes more important to transmit optimism and future victory.

Enrique Peña Nieto's appeal as an early figurehead of the PRI comeback was widely assumed to stem at least partly from his *telenovela*-style good looks. Nobody mentioned his skin tone, but I very much doubt if the governor's appearance would have been considered quite such a significant factor had the same features been etched on a darker background. His aura of being destined for success improved even further when he first dated, and then married, a red-haired *telenovela* celebrity.

López Obrador, meanwhile, chose to call his national movement 'Morena', which means 'dark-skinned' in Spanish. Morena's first promotional video followed a bus travelling through all kinds of Mexican landscapes picking up all kinds of Mexicans (except the white elite), to the strains of a song about rescuing the nation. A darkish-skinned beauty with the aura of a modern Virgin of Guadalupe sang the chorus: 'Morena our daughter, Morena our sister, Morena the mother of the nation, protect the Mexican struggle.'

Morena is an obvious effort to rekindle the old myth of a unified national identity, and to tie it in with unifying Catholic imagery. At the same time, however, it also seemed to contain a jibe at the rising, if also unstated, currency of whiteness that surrounds Peña Nieto.

It seems logical to assume that the slow recognition of colour-based racism as a problem will eventually prompt a political response. It would seem like a natural preserve of the left; but the day any political force finally realizes that there are potential votes to be gained from making the issue explicit will be a victory for the cause of finally burying revolutionary nationalism – the still resilient framework that came with one-party hegemony and that is still helping to hold democratization back.

CHAPTER 9

Unfinished Story

Emerging from an underground chamber and stretching 104 metres into the sky, Mexico's monument celebrating 200 years of independence was supposed to spark reflection on the country's roots and aspirations. But things did not quite work out that way.

The first and most obvious issue was that the anniversary, on 15 September 2010, came and went with nothing to contemplate. There was still nothing for passers-by to see a year later, when the head of construction took a group of reporters into the site to see the foundations. 'It's much more than a hole in the ground', he all but pleaded. 'Really it is!'

The authorities blamed technical problems for both the embarrassing delay and the doubling of the original budget to around $90 million. There was no explanation for why a new thirty-five-storey skyscraper just a block away should have cost only about a third more to build. Obvious mismanagement and serious accusations of corruption aside, there were existential questions, too.

The 1,704 translucent quartz panels that would cover the two rectangular faces of the monument when it finally surfaced came from Brazil. The electricity installation sandwiched between them was German, as was the mechanism used to stabilize the structure in earthquakes and strong winds (which was revealed to be necessary by a Canadian study). Huge Italian steel columns anchored the whole structure to the ground. Was this, some asked, actually a monument to Mexican *dependence*?

The rest of the bicentennial celebrations – which incorporated the 100th anniversary of the Revolution as well – were similarly marred by a fog of organizational mishaps and lack of direction. The planning commission, set up in 2006, went through five different heads before Education Minister Alonso Lujambio Irazábal took over at the start of the anniversary year itself. Even then, the government seemed to have nothing particular that it wanted to say. Aside from the work in progress at the monument, there was a new park built in the grounds of an abandoned refinery, and a long list of infrastructure projects across the country that would probably have been built anyway, but that now included 'bicentenario' in their name.

A televised parade, the biggest event, set out to celebrate the Mexican party spirit and little else, although a twenty-metre-high white statue temporarily assembled in the Zócalo in a haze of dry ice and dramatic lighting was rather spectacular. The only problem was that the Coloso – supposed to represent an anonymous Independence fighter – turned out to have been modelled on a revolutionary general who had ended up before a firing squad as a traitor.

The artist denied any backhanded revisionism of the canon. He said he had merely been attracted to the power of the man's features; but the government still played it safe and cancelled plans to reconstruct the statue permanently in another public space. The different bits were hidden away in a government warehouse – an accidental monument to the mutilated victims of the drug wars, as well as the minefield of Mexican history.

The government did sponsor a series of interesting discussions between academics, broadcast on a public television channel that almost nobody watches. It seemed to believe that encouraging the bulk of Mexicans to get involved in a debate about their past, present and future was courting disaster in the middle of an acute recession, with drug-war violence escalating every month.

In the end, the dedication to neutrality and the government's wariness of encouraging the population to ponder the roots of their nationalism too deeply left the commemorations as underwhelming as they were accident prone.

❋ ❋ ❋

The government was not alone in its confusion over how to understand the historical moment and where it might lead. I, certainly, find it extremely hard to feel confident about almost any prediction. The storm clouds are real and fearful, and can often seem overwhelming; but there are also always reminders that Mexico has come a long way and, if it gets its act together, could get a lot further still.

While parts of the country labour under savage violence and serious governability crises, others would be considered tranquil almost anywhere in the world. The former governor of one state might be suspected of being behind death squads that targeted dissidents, but in the capital same-sex couples can now marry and adopt children. Unregulated toxic waste dumps pepper the country, but small communities win international prizes for innovative sustainable forest management. Around half the population lives in poverty, but home ownership is booming.

To someone who has lived in Mexico since 2000, the present certainly feels like a defining time – although not in an either/or sense. The country as a whole, seen from the capital, does not appear to be in any real danger of collapse, whatever happens in some drug-war conflict areas. But nor is it really possible to imagine it as a place of general prosperity and prejudice-free mutual solidarity anytime soon. A country as large, diverse and important as Mexico – and a place that carries with it the legacy of centuries of injustice – will always be filled with contrasts, some of which will be uncomfortable. But diversity is one thing; disassociation is another. And pieces of a jigsaw do not form a clear image until they are put together.

During the glory days of the PRI regime, a picture of remarkable order was possible thanks to a monopoly on the political power that mattered. Soft authoritarianism ensured that the pieces remained in place, and the gloss of legitimacy was provided by revolutionary nationalism. When this eventually became unsustainable, multi-party democracy was supposed to generate a new kind of order that was better able to respond to the needs and demands of the population, as well as to the times. This hope carried Vicente Fox of the PAN into power in 2000, but then it largely ebbed away. The framework of a weakened and fragmented state that emerged from the transition, and that then seemed to get stuck, appeared to forget about the ordinary voters who might have been able to provide it with genuinely democratic legitimacy that went beyond elections. The diminished state consequently became more vulnerable to the whims of alternative power hubs that have spun out of control and have begun occupying the spaces it has relinquished.

The horror of the drug wars is the most frightening expression of this phenomenon, and it has pushed several parts of the country to the brink. President Felipe Calderón turned a serious problem into a disaster by assuming that the cartels would be cowed by a show of federal force, as if he still had the kind of power his predecessors in the PRI once enjoyed. Instead, his offensive has weakened institutional life still further, and at tragic cost.

The way the drug wars are likely to develop is one of the biggest uncertainties of all, particularly given the imminent change of president in 2012. Even so, as the end of Calderón's term approached there was growing cross-party consensus – even partially echoed by the president himself – that the priority should shift from going after the cartels to reducing the violence. There was also increasing recognition that more attention should be paid to the failures of the judicial system, money laundering, and the social deprivation that makes ordinary young people vulnerable to being transformed into some of the most bloodthirsty killers on the planet.

Politicians still largely glossed over the fact that infiltration of politics by the cartels is a real and present problem in all parties, and the failure to deal with it represents one of the biggest obstacles to reining in the cartels. For as long as this is the case, it is hard to see how there can be a lasting solution to the institutional side of the problem, even if the murder rate falls.

While President Calderón's attempt to show the cartels and the country who was boss backfired, that is not to suggest that there was no need to do anything – it is just that the strategy employed has been counterproductive. The drug wars have already damaged Mexico's democracy, but if the situation continues to worsen, then there is a real possibility that the new president may seek an authoritarian solution. The de facto military occupation of some parts of the north-eastern state of Tamaulipas is not far off this scenario already.

Pushing Mexico beyond its current frenetic limbo (where frantic political activity produces minimal advances) also requires more serious efforts to rein in the other 'de facto powers' that have also accrued enormous influence since 2000 and are chipping away at the legitimacy of the state in the new political era.

The occasional attempt to pursue former feudal governors for the abuses they committed while in office have scuppered a few careers, but have not resulted in the kind of legal cases likely to produce exemplary sentences that might serve as a deterrent to the new generations and lead them to refrain from abusing their power. A new and determined president might be able to impose some limits, but unless this is accompanied by structural changes to make impunity the exception rather than the rule, there will be nothing to stop a reversal in the longer term.

Nobody has taken quite such spectacular advantage of Mexico's new and more fluid political context as teachers' leader Elba Esther Gordillo;

she may well prove irreplaceable when she is finally either pushed out or bows out because of ill health. Yet La Maestra is just the most extreme example of a leader with control of an undemocratic outpost of power who has learned how to play the multi-party system. Albeit on a much smaller scale, this model is replicated all over the country, and it is, if anything, even more difficult to control than governors getting carried away with their new autonomy. They, at least, are limited to six-year terms in office.

Mexico's inability to kick-start the levels of growth required to transform the country from a bastion of poverty and inequality into a burgeoning middle-class nation has many causes, but one of the most crucial is the weakened state. This lies behind the torturously slow efforts to crack down on the country's corporate oligarchs and make them obey regulatory decisions, the inability to raise tax revenue, and the reluctance to directly take on the crisis in the oil industry. It does not matter if a specific plan is inspired by the left or by the right: unless it is backed by institutions that are able to make decisions – and to make those decisions stick – it has little chance of success. The longer this situation continues, the more social tension it is likely to generate – particularly in the difficult international context that seems likely to last for some years yet.

From finding ways of dealing with pressure from the cartels and other 'de facto powers' to removing the brakes on economic growth; from safeguarding individual freedoms under assault from the Catholic hierarchy to minimizing environmental disasters – the elephant in the room is always the need to give the state more coherence and legitimacy.

This is one of the main reasons why the PRI was able to build up such momentum behind its bid to return to power in 2012. Capitalizing on dissatisfaction with the dysfunctional fragmentation of the PAN years, and unified behind the slick telegenic image of candidate Enrique Peña Nieto, the old party of power found a way of combining an image of modernity with a soft nostalgia for the days when at least there was some semblance of order. But the insistence that it is the only party that knows how to govern is belied by the disastrous administrations of many PRI governors. It conveniently forgets that the reason why it lost the presidency after seventy-one years was that the model it had developed in power had become dysfunctional as well.

Peña Nieto formally launched his candidacy after ending his term as governor of the State of Mexico in September 2011, fresh from securing victory for his party in the elections to replace him – by a margin of 40 percentage points. The only way to explain a margin like that, in a state plagued by serious problems that range from high crime rates to rampant urban deprivation, is to conclude that the PRI still manages an astoundingly well-oiled electoral machine that jars (to say the very least) with a healthy multi-party democracy. National politics is a 'whole different ball game', but that election suggested that Peña Nieto still operated on the basis of an ideal in which politics was the PRI and little else, however much he talked of himself as a representative of the 'new generation'.

A return of a scarcely reconstructed PRI to Los Pinos would not automatically bring effective government, any more than the coming of largely free and fair elections did in 2000. It would, however, represent a step backwards for democracy. A defeat for the PRI, meanwhile, would not automatically recharge democratization – though it might help: a new PAN or PRD president, who owed his or her victory to a revival of an anti-PRI vote, would presumably be under considerable pressure to return to the agenda of democratic change.

The discourse of democracy had begun to look tired and empty just a couple of years into the Fox administration, as the new president slipped into apathy. It became too contested to touch after the 2006 elections and the political crisis that followed. After that, it just did not seem to be particularly relevant anymore. Today most commentators have long since stopped referring to the 2000 election as the coming of 'democracy', preferring the neutral term *La Alternancia* – indicating a change of party in the presidency and little more.

This does not mean that Mexicans have actively turned against democracy. In 2010, the Latinobarometro poll found that 67 per cent of Mexicans agreed with the description of democracy as the best system of government available. Even so, this was 10 percentage points less than the Latin American average, and only Guatemalans were more disenchanted. The same survey also found that only 24 per cent considered that Mexico was 'progressing', compared to 68 per cent in Brazil and 55 per cent in Chile. Again, only Central Americans were more pessimistic. The proportion of Mexicans who said they did not know what democracy meant jumped from 3 per cent in 2001 to 25 per cent in 2006. The question was no longer asked in the surveys after that.

With democracy losing a good deal of its mystique, all the political parties began to delve with more regularity into the old language of nationalism, which at least offered the possibility of tapping into the emotion that swells in so many Mexican hearts at the mention of their country and that creates a temporary sense of unity. Several polls around the time of the bicentennial found that over 80 per cent of adults described themselves as being 'very proud' of being Mexican, even if there was little consensus over what the root of that pride was.

President Calderón tended to resort to this most when under pressure, such as when he defended his drug-war strategy against criticism by appealing to patriotic sentiment and branding the cartels the 'enemies of the nation'. Andrés Manuel López Obrador, more steeped in the old canon anyway, makes it a central part of his rhetoric. In the run-up to the 2012 election, he began to talk about kick-starting the nation's fourth great national transformation. There had been Independence, the Liberal reforms of Benito Juárez in the nineteenth century, the Revolution, and now there was López Obrador. Most politicians are also comfortable with a canon within which they had forged their political careers, even from the opposition. In the words of Héctor Aguilar Camín and Jorge Castañeda in their 2009 essay 'A Future for Mexico': 'Slogans and elemental credos of the old narrative remain in the limbic system of the country's political culture. An instinctive repertoire of certainties, proposals and public nostalgias that is present in the majority of professional politicians, not just the Priistas.'

The resurgence of nationalism in political rhetoric does not constitute a full-blown return of revolutionary nationalism, but it has helped perpetuate some important anti-democratic traits in political practice. This includes attitudes and practices such as the ever-present back-room negotiations for quotas of power, as well as seemingly benign factors such as the glorification of consensus that helps flatten debate. These make it more difficult to reconfigure the state from its post-transition fragmented parts into something better able to confront the current whirlwind of challenges and release the country's dormant potential.

Civil society has kept alive the idea by focusing ever more attention on the concept of accountability and the demand that the political elite come out of its bubble and start bridging the gulf between it and the electorate. The movement of victims of the violence – sparked by the poet Javier Sicilia in spring 2011 – is perhaps the most significant of the groups involved, both because of the urgency of the issue and because of the staunchly non-partisan stance of the leadership. Sicilia demanded that President Calderón apologize to the nation for his offensive against organized crime, and also lectured all the other parties about their responsibility in the mess. Even after the movement faded towards the end of the year (as a result of internal divisions and the murder of some of its members), it seemed unlikely to disappear completely, given the commitment and near foolhardy bravery of some of its key members. It was also a potential training ground for political leaders of the future, just as the student movement of 1968, the guerrillas of the 1970s and the community groups that arose in the wake of the 1985 earthquake had been. These helped push the PRI to the brink, even if they frequently got sucked into the bad habits of the political elite once they, too, were invited into the club as political plurality got going.

The newly independent media – even on occasion the commercial TV networks that double up as a 'de facto power' – has also played a crucial role in pushing the accountability agenda. It has consistently publicized scandals involving politicians in abuse of privilege, negligence and even criminality. Most of the moments when it has seemed possible that things can move forward have been prefaced by major media campaigns, either stemming from journalistic investigations or thanks to the way major news anchors now actively support certain civil society groups and their causes. The phenomenal success of the documentary *Presunto Culpable*, owes an enormous amount to the free publicity it received across the mainstream media. Mexicans are now consequently more aware of the ways in which the judicial system systematically creates scapegoats and, presumably, also much more likely to resist something similar happening to them.

The explosion of the social networks has similarly added a whole new dimension to public scrutiny. This can only increase as the number of Mexicans with access to the internet grows from its current paltry levels. A few years ago politicians would feel the pressure of public disdain only when it was sufficiently grave to bring thousands onto the streets to protest. Now it is possible to create as much noise through Twitter and its 'trending topics'. Politicians and the elite have also yet to learn how to effectively control the damage done by an embarrassing YouTube video that goes viral or a misguided post on Twitter – Peña Nieto's teenage daughter caused her father a serious problem when she re-tweeted her boyfriend's description of the candidate's critics as 'envious proles'.

All of this is still a long way from the kind of critical mass required, but it is a step towards re-injecting enthusiasm into the idea that finding a way out of the current tumult requires re-energizing democratization.

In 'A Future for Mexico' Aguilar Camín and Castañeda described democracy as 'a good headline act' that reached a climax with the change of power in 2000 but that was subsequently dwarfed by the new political stage: 'Nine years later democracy seems like a diva that has run out of tricks. The libretto of democracy alone, by its nature discordant, was not enough to give the country the narrative for the future that it needs.'

I prefer to think of democratization in Mexico as a novel that has got rather bogged down by its own sub-plots – interrupted perhaps, lost even, but certainly not exhausted.

Sources

Introduction

Alan Riding's *Distant Neighbors* and *Opening Mexico* by Samuel Dillon and Julia Preston are the most rounded and accessible books on the PRI regime in English that I know. Andres Oppenheimer's *Bordering on Chaos* explores the key moment around 1994. Sam Quiñones' *True Tales from Another Mexico* vividly underlines how the country's diversity was ever more in evidence towards the end of the PRI regime. *Building the Fourth Estate: Democratization and the rise of a free press in Mexico* by Chappell Lawson traces the roots and development of the media's new independence.

Mexican standard works on the PRI, written with the long transition already under way, include: *A la Sombra de la Revolución Mexicana* by Lorenzo Meyer and Héctor Aguilar Camín, Jorge Castañeda's *La Herencia* and Enrique Krauze's *La Presidencia Imperial*. Krauze's TV series *Los Sexenios*, made up of individual episodes devoted to each president, brings it all to life with old news footage.

José Vasconcelos' 1925 essay 'La Raza Cosmica' still makes fascinating reading, and Octavio Paz's *Labyrinth of Solitude* is obligatory. Jorge Castañeda includes most of the classic visions on Mexican identity and posits some updates in his book *Mañana Forever*. Roger Bartra's 1987 book *La Jaula de la Melancolía* (*Cage of Melancholy*) is a complex read, but very rich.

The state-sponsored TV series *Discutamos México* (made to coincide with the bicentenary of the start of the Independence wars in 2010) is somewhat staid, but includes some interesting discussions about revolutionary nationalism in several of its fifteen episodes.

The wave of internationally successful Mexican films made around 2000 (particularly *Amores Perros*, by Alejandro González Iñarritu and *Y Tu Mamá También* by Alfonso Cuarón) also reflect on the country's new cosmopolitanism, openness and confidence of the time. Luis Estrada's 2000 *La Ley de Herodes* or *Herod's Law* is a good film, as well as an assault on the old symbols of revolutionary nationalism. His follow-up *Un Mundo Maravilloso* or a *Wonderful World* was a rather less successful take on the empty optimism of the Fox years. Estrada regained his ability to synthesize the Mexican reality through satire in his 2010 film *El Infierno*, or *Hell*, focusing on the drug wars.

Chapter 1: Narco Trouble

A slew of recent books delve into the drug wars in far greater detail than I do here or in Chapter 5, which also deals with the phenomenon.

Ioan Grillo's *El Narco: Inside Mexico's criminal insurgency* is a very readable, in-depth exploration of the history of Mexican drug trafficking and the development of the drug wars, and has some great on-the-ground reporting. Howard Campbell's *Drug War Zone: Frontline dispatches from the streets of El Paso and Juarez* contains illuminating lengthy interviews with people involved in organized crime on both sides of the border, as well as an interesting analytical framework for understanding them. Ed Vulliamy's *Amexica: War along the Borderline* is a vigorous, anecdote-driven journey along the frontier. Malcolm Beith's *The Last Narco* fills out the myths surrounding the country's most famous drug lord, Joaquín 'El Chapo' Guzmán. Charles Bowden's *Murder City: Ciudad Juarez and the global economy's new killing fields* frames the city's descent into horror in elegant prose. His later book, *El Sicario: The autobiography of a Mexican assassin*, edited with Molly Molloy, provides a window into daily life within organized crime.

Luis Astorga's body of academic work is essential for understanding the history, particularly his 2005 book *El Siglo de Las Drogas: El narcotráfico, del Porfiriato al nuevo milenio*. Anabel Hernández's *Los Señores del Narco* is a carefully documented tome exploring the long relationship between Mexican drug lords (particularly from Sinaloa) and politics, business leaders and US law enforcement agencies. Diego Enrique Osorno's *El Cartel de Sinaloa: Una historia del uso politico del narco* is especially interesting because of his access to the letters written by Miguel Angel Félix Gallardo from jail, and his description of the group's activities in Nuevo León. The rise of the Arellano Felix cartel is meticulously traced in the book *El Cartel* by the revered founder of the Tijuana-based investigative weekly *Zeta*, *Jesús Blancornelas*. Veteran organized-crime investigative reporter Ricardo Ravelo has written several books on Mexican drug trafficking that contain extraordinary amounts of information but can be rather labyrinthine. *Osiel: Vida y tragedia de un capo* contains a wealth of detail on the formation of the Zetas.

El *Mexico Narco*, edited by Rafael Rodríguez Castañeda provides useful vignettes of the drug wars from around the country. *El Narco: La guerra fallida* by Rubén Aguilar and Jorge Castañeda pulls apart the government offensive from a political angle. Marcela Turati's *Fuego Cruzado: Las víctimas atrapadas en la guerra del narco* focuses on the victims of the drug wars and their stories. Juan Carlos Reyna's *Confesión de un Sicario: El Testimonio de Drago* is a particularly chilling and informative testimony of an unnamed hit-man from an unidentified cartel who became a protected witness before leaving the programme to live in hiding.

Julio Scherer García's *La Reina del Pacífico* is based on a series of prison interviews with Sandra Avila Beltrán, who expounds on her life in a world populated by *capos* even as she denies accusations of trafficking herself. The penetration of the narco world into everyday lives is nowhere explored more vividly than in the three books written by *Río Doce* reporter Javier Valdez Cárdenas, *Malayerba*, *Miss Narco* and *Los Morros del Narco*.

The chapter draws on coverage of the drug wars across the Mexican media, particularly radio and TV interviews with relevant actors and victims. The investigative TV news programme *Punto de Partida* is a fertile font of textured reports from around the country. The monthly magazine *Nexos* has some of the best essays on the issue from all points of view. The firmly anti-government weekly news magazine *Proceso* regularly obtains and publishes leaked information and rumours that others avoid. The newer weekly *Emeequis* has some of the best on-the-ground reporting. Some of the national Mexican journalists and chroniclers whom I follow particularly closely on drugs stories are Diego Enrique Osorno, Patricia Davila, Marcela Turati, Héctor de Mauleón, Humberto Padgett and Ricardo Ravelo.

Certain regional media are obligatory reading to find out what is going on in particular drug-war fronts. The investigative weekly *Rio Doce* fills that role in Sinaloa, *Zeta* magazine in Baja California, *El Diario de Juárez* in Ciudad Juárez. In parts of the country, particularly Tamaulipas, the enforced press silence gives certain blogs and Twitter feeds a particularly important role. Among these, blogdelnarco.com contains occasionally essential information amid the general horror. The English-language blog borderlandbeat.com is a good source of information and analysis of what is happening along the frontier. Molly Molloy's 'Frontera List' is an essential compilation of drug war-related stories and discussion of trends.

Some of the most interesting reports in whatever medium rely on information that is almost impossible to confirm or discount. Protected witness testimonies leaked to the media, for example, provide fascinating windows into the inner workings of organized crime and corruption, but should always also be treated with caution. Similarly, the self-promotion and propaganda of the cartels themselves is an essential part of the story, but should never be taken at face value.

Access to government data and analysis of what is going on in the drug wars was very limited and vague in the early years of the offensive. The military and the navy and the federal attorney general's office have always been particularly reluctant to provide information. Although it remained patchy and highly selective, the flow of information freed up enormously during 2010, both in terms of the details the president began to include in his lengthy discourses on the issues, and the occasional reports that the government distributed to the media. Information tightened again in 2011.

The figures I use for drug-related homicides during the first four years of the offensive are drawn from a government database made public in January 2011. This was not updated over the rest of the year. It was partially updated in January 2012. Several national media organizations kept their own unofficial counts, including *Reforma* and *Milenio*. The analyses of the death toll figures and their relationship to the strategy published in *Nexos* by Eduardo Guerrero and Fernando Escalante are particularly illuminating.

Confidential cables between US diplomats in Mexico and the State Department in Washington, released by Wikileaks in December 2010, provide interesting information on the course of the drug wars throughout the country, particularly in Tamaulipas, Monterrey and Tijuana. The most recent cables date from early 2010.

The specific phenomenon of the mass kidnapping of migrants is explored in depth in two reports from the National Human Rights Commission released in 2009 and 2011.

My own direct reporting includes numerous interviews with experts, including Luis Astorga, Jorge Chabat, Raúl Benítez, Samuel González, Edgardo Buscaglia, Alberto Islas, Ernesto López Portillo, Eduardo Guerrero, Alejandro Hope, and Carlos Flores, as well as background briefings with US law enforcement officials and experts employed by security consulting firms who prefer to remain nameless. Particularly relevant interviews and briefings with Mexican government officials include Eduardo Medina Mora, when he was attorney general, José Luis Santiago Vasconcelos, when he was drug tsar, and Alejandro Poiré when he was security spokesman.

Reporting trips to particular areas of the country affected by the drug wars allowed me to gather the experiences of ordinary people, many of whom would not wish to be named for security reasons. I have left out the identities of others in order not to cloud the narrative with a bewildering number of names.

Sources in Tamaulipas tend to be particularly wary of being named. Two female journalists working in the state were especially helpful in providing information and contacts with victims of the violence during a visit to the border city in August 2010. The section on the exodus from Ciudad Mier draws on TV interviews with refugees in the shelter set up in Ciudad Alemán, as well as my own phone conversations with people still in the city, and the descriptions of AP reporter Mark Stevenson, who was there soon afterwards.

The section on La Familia Michoacana and the Caballeros Templarios does not include on-the-ground reporting in the state. My interview with Francisco, the demonstrator drafted in by the La Familia cartel to protest against the arrest of a local mayor, was conducted in Mexico City in 2009. Dalia Martínez and Humberto Padgett provide a rare close-up of the drug business in the Tierra Caliente in their extraordinary piece called 'La República Marihuanera', published in *Emeequis* magazine in August 2011.

The exploration of the horrors faced by Central American and other migrants passing through Mexico on their way to the United States or deported back over the border is based on conversations with migrants in different shelters in Tamaulipas, Oaxaca, Baja California and the State of Mexico, as well as the priests and nuns who run them. It also draws on interviews with relatives of disappeared Mexican migrants from Guanajuato. The reference to the vulnerability of deported migrants is taken from interviews with deportees in Reynosa and Tijuana, as well as with Victor Clark Alfaro, director of the Tijuana-based Binational Center for Human Rights, and government officials.

Chapter 2: Political Wastelands

Mexican books that focus on politics in the wake of 2000 include several that delve into the frivolity of the presidential couple and accusations of corruption. The best known are *Fin de Fiesta en Los Pinos* by Anabel Hernández and *La Jefa: Vida publica y privada de Marta Sahagún de Fox*, a gossipy demolition of Marta Sahagún by Olga Wornat.

La Diferencia: Radiografía de un sexenio by Rubén Aguilar and Jorge Castañeda is a fascinating and unique account of the inside political story of the Fox cabinet, to which both authors belonged. I have also seen a copy of a chapter they wrote on Marta Sahagún and relations with the media that was not included in the published book. Former president Fox's own self-aggrandizing autobiography, *Revolution of Hope* (ghost-written by Rob Allyn), was published first in English in 2007 and includes many implicit insights into his leadership style. Carmen Aristegui's *Transición: Conversaciones y retratos de lo que se hizo y se dejó de hacer por la democracia en México* has extensive interview transcripts with key political actors from before and after 2000. *Los Suspirantes 2012*, edited by Jorge Zepeda Patterson, includes profiles of all the major presidential hopefuls ahead of the 2012 elections. Roger Bartra's *La Fractura Mexicana: Izquierda y derecha en la transición democrática* explores the lack of renewal in the Mexican political elite and includes a heartfelt critique of the failures of the left in particular.

The in-depth coverage of politics, in which much of the domestic media delights, informs the entire book. As with the drug war, the investigative TV news programme *Punto de Partida* has been a particularly fertile source of issues to explore, *Nexos* magazine provides some of the most probing analysis. The account of the ABC crèche demonstrations was taken primarily from videos uploaded to YouTube. Diego Enrique Osorno collected testimonies of parents of the children who died in the ABC fire and others affected by the tragedy, and put them together in a book entitled *Nosotros Somos Los Culpables: La tragedia de la guardería ABC*.

This chapter is infused with the influence of the Mexican analysts and commentators whom I have interviewed over the years, or whose newspaper columns or round-table discussions I pay particular attention to. They include (in no particular order): Daniel Lund, Jorge Zepeda Patterson, Lorenzo Meyer, Raymundo Riva Palacio, Héctor Aguilar Camín, Jesús Reyes Heroles, Denise Dresser, Federico Reyes Heroles, Sergio Aguayo, Roy Campos, Soledad Loaeza, Lydia Cacho, José Antonio Crespo, Jorge

Fernández Menéndez, Jorge Castañeda, Denise Maerker, Juan Pardinas, José Woldenberg, Ricardo Alemán, Lorenzo Córdova and Alfonso Zarate. I also draw on the regular documents produced by Zarate's consultancy company, Grupo Consultor Interdisciplinario, and the rich discussions at the weekly workshops he organizes, particularly from Raúl Fraga and Andrés Ayala Nevárez.

Chapter 3: The Misrule of Law

The rise of the 'de facto powers' is a widely accepted post-transition phenomenon that is a constant theme of many political analysts. Denise Dresser and Jorge Zepeda Patterson touch on it with particular regularity in interviews and in their own writing, such as Dresser's book *El País de Uno* and Zepeda Patterson's two edited collection of profiles of individuals who personalize 'de facto power' – *Los Intocables* and *Los Amos de México*.

My discussion of the feudal governors is informed by an extensive interview with Rogelio Hernández Rodriguez, author of *El Centro Dividido: La nueva autonomía de los governadores*. Patterson's *Los Intocables* includes a chapter on the governors that bursts with extraordinary examples of their baron-like attitudes.

Ricardo Raphael's *Los Socios de Elba Esther* stands out among several biographies of teachers' leader Elba Esther Gordillo. Sabina Berman and Denise Maerker's collection of interviews with influential women in Mexico – *Mujeres y Poder* – includes Elba Esther's own account of her childhood and rising political career. Jorge Castañeda's exploration of Gordillo's political limitations in a 2011 essay in *Enfoque* magazine and, in rather drier terms, in his book *Mañana Forever*, is particularly interesting, given their long-standing personal friendship. Many of Gordillo's interviews, press conferences and secret recordings of her conversations are accessible through YouTube. José Gil Olmos' chapter on Gordillo in his small but fascinating book on supernatural influence in Mexican politics called *Los Brujos del Poder* goes into the detail of the African witchcraft story, also told to me by former collaborator Noé Rivera Domínguez. I have also interviewed several other former collaborators whom I do not name. This section is also informed by interviews with education expert Aldo Muñoz, as well as with other experts and activists associated with the NGOs Mexicanos Primero and the Coalición Ciudadana por la Educación.

Zepeda Patterson's collection *Los Amos de México* includes a profile of Emilio Azcárraga Jean. Andrew Paxman and Claudia Fernández wrote a biography of his father, Emilio Azcárraga Milmo, called *El Tigre. Si Yo Fuera Presidente: El reality show de Peña Nieto*, by Jenaro Villamil, is a highly critical portrait of the former State of Mexico governor, with a particular focus on his relationship with Televisa. Two unnamed sources (with reasons to know) confirmed to me that deals were made, although they did not give me details.

My discussion of the power of the commercial TV networks draws on interviews with Villamil, as well as other media experts Raúl Trejo Delabre and Saúl López Noriega and TV Azteca's president Ricardo Salinas Pliego.

The research centre CIDE is a fertile source of reports and analysis of the problems of the Mexican judicial system and the 2008 procedural reform. CIDE-based Ana Laura Magaloni is particularly clear in interviews and in her own fortnightly column in *Reforma* newspaper, as are Roberto Hernández and Layda Negrete, the makers of the documentaries *El Túnel* and *Presunto Culpable*. I also draw on interviews with activist lawyer and former drug tsar Samuel González and his knowledge of politicized justice.

Over the years, I have interviewed most of the leading anti-crime campaigners, including Eduardo Gallo, Isabel Miranda de Wallace and María Elena Morera. Human rights activists who talked about the early dangers of being portrayed as protecting criminals included former Mexico City human rights ombudsman Emilio Alvarez Icaza. Zepeda Patterson's collection *Los Intocables* includes an in-depth profile of Jorge Hank Rhon. The section based on an interview in jail with Jacinta Francisco Marcial was complemented by a visit to her home town and interviews with her family and lawyers (and many failed efforts to get official comments on the case).

Chapter 4: Lapsed Catholics

The historical account of the Catholic Church in Mexico and its contemporary developments draws on interviews with religious experts Bernardo Barranco and Roberto Blancarte. The latter is author of *La Historia de la Iglesia Catolica en México*. Mexico's most famous expert on the Cristero War is Jean Meyer. Graham Greene's novel *The Power and the Glory* (set during the subsequent years of religious restriction) affords a wonderfully human vision of how it might have been. His travel book *The Lawless Roads* provides a much grumpier take on the reality he found while travelling around Mexico in 1937.

The Marcial Maciel case is covered in detail in Carmen Aristegui's book *Marcial Maciel: Historia de un criminal*. My own reporting of the case included several interviews with the original group of victims, particularly José Barba and Juan José Vaca, as well as visits to Legionario de Cristo schools in Mexico, and interviews with former pupils and a phone conversation with the order's spokesman in Rome.

My coverage of the priest abuse scandal, allegedly involving Mexico City archbishop Cardinal Norberto Rivera in a cover-up, includes interviews with victim-turned-activist Joaquín Aguilar Méndez, who claims he was raped, as well as with his US lawyers from the Chicago-based activist group SNAP. I also visited the parish in the state of Puebla where Aguilar's alleged abuser left behind a trail of accusations before he was moved to California, and I talked to Mexico City archdiocese spokesman Father Hugo Valdemar Romero.

The section on abortion legislation is informed by interviews with pro-choice activists in Mexico City, Guanajuato and Puebla, as well as with women who have had legal and illegal abortions and pro-life campaigners in Guanajuato and Mexico City.

The story of Bishop Onésimo Cepeda and how he obtained a private collection of important art is covered in detail in a piece by Emiliano Ruiz Parra published in *Gatopardo* magazine in March 2011.

As well as Bishop Raúl Vera, I have interviewed numerous priests and nuns who have continued the liberation theology tradition around the country over the years. I have also interviewed many priests from the dominant conservative wing of the Church.

I covered Juan Diego's canonization in 2002 for the Catholic News Service.

Chapter 5: A Bungled War

My own close monitoring of President Felipe Calderón's speeches, interviews and communication style forms the basis of my argument about his development into a full-fledged drug-war warrior. His interventions in the so-called Dialogues with civil society that began in 2010 are particularly revealing.

The 2010 communications overhaul included the appointment of a security spokesman, Alejandro Poiré, whose initial openness had all but faded away by the time he left the post in autumn 2011, to become the director of the national intelligence agency CISEN, just weeks before he was appointed interior minister in November 2011.

The confidential cables sent between US diplomats in Mexico and the State Department in Washington, published by Wikileaks, provide a window on the US priorities of the time. They also indicate that State Department analysis of the political context of the drug wars largely mirrored the dominant trends among Mexican commentators.

The weekly left-leaning news magazine *Proceso* has been among the most consistent platforms for spreading allegations that the Calderón offensive against organized crime is biased in favour of Chapo Guzmán and the Sinaloa cartel.

Presidential adviser, and former Salvadoran guerrilla, Joaquín Villalobos usually kept a low profile, aside from his articles in *Nexos* and one interview with the *Los Angeles Times*. My discussion of his ideas is also informed by an interview with military expert Raúl Benítez, who is also an expert on the civil war in El Salvador. Benítez's knowledge of the military is augmented by the years in which he served in the Fox government as a close collaborator of Adolfo Aguilar Zínser, who was originally appointed as national security adviser.

My discussion of Javier Sicilia and his anti-war movement is informed by my own interviews with him and other members, including Julián Lebarón, Emilio Alvarez Icaza and Father Alejandro Solalinde.

The section on the US role in the drug offensive draws on the Wikileaks cables, as well as on my own background interviews with US law enforcement officials and coverage of US strategy in the US media. Ginger Thompson's reports in the *New York Times* are particularly important. The website narconews.com has covered the investigations into the 'Fast and Furious' gun trafficking operation and the allegations in the Zambada Niebla case in particular detail.

Even after the mainstream media stopped regularly airing cartel propaganda from around 2010, this was still easily accessed through a number of websites, including Blog del Narco, which uploaded unedited photographs, videos and general information sent by contributors without comment. Public Security Secretary Genaro García Luna (and the federal police force under his direction) was particularly given to public relations flourishes, which embellished the truth of security operations to make them seem more dramatic or more successful. Most, but not all, of the videoed confessions by captured *capos* were released by the federal police.

I use the figures on journalists killed or disappeared in Mexico provided by the Committee to Protect Journalists. Other groups give higher figures but do not investigate the possible links between the events and journalistic activity to anything like the same degree.

The Human Rights Watch report *Neither Rights nor Security*, released in November 2011, contains the most damning collection of evidence of the involvement of all branches of the security apparatus in systematic torture, and worrying numbers of extrajudicial executions and enforced disappearances.

Chapter 6: Not Good Enough

Carlos Elizondo's *Por Eso Estamos Como Estamos* provides a close economic analysis of most of the phenomena discussed in this chapter. Luis de la Calle and Luis Rubio wrote an essay in *Nexos* in May 2010 on the middle classes, which lays out the argument in their book released around the same time. Jorge Castañeda is also a loud promoter of the idea that Mexico is already a budding middle-class nation in his book *Mañana Forever* and in his two collaborative extended essays with Héctor Aguilar Camín – '*Un futuro para México*' and '*De vuelta a futuro*'. Zepeda Patterson's *Los Amos de México* includes profiles of some of the richest people in Mexico and analysis of the methods they use to ring-fence their privileges.

The income distribution figures used are taken from the OECD. Poverty figures for Mexico are taken from the government National Council for the Evaluation of Social Development Policy (CONEVAL). The NGO El Poder del Consumidor published an interesting study in 2010 revealing dependency on junk food in poverty-stricken indigenous communities. Remittances figures are taken from the Bank of Mexico. Comparative tax revenue figures as a proportion of GDP come from the OECD. The CIDE is a regular source of reports on wasteful spending.

The *Houston Chronicle* led the way in uncovering the Néstor Moreno Díaz corruption scandal. My own unnamed sources inside the sector provided details about his management style. Transparencia Mexicana's reports provide a detailed picture of which parts of the bureaucracy are particularly bribe-prone and how this changes from state to state and over time. Al Consumidor is one of the highest-profile citizen groups focused on demanding accountability from the private sector.

The OECD report on monopolies followed on from a World Bank book entitled *No Growth without Equity?*, which made many of the same arguments.

Carlos Slim has been the focus of a number of in-depth profiles in the international media. The most illuminating that I know of was written by Lawrence Wright and published in the *New Yorker* in May 2009. My sources on Televisa and TV Azteca are the same as identified in Chapter 3.

Figures on migration come from various US and Mexican government sources. The Pew Hispanic Center puts out periodic reports that draw conclusions based on collations of all these sources, which it clearly identifies. The migration section draws on interviews with experts in the field, including Primitivo Rodríguez and Jesús Bustamante. Victor Clark Alfaro is a fascinating source for the phenomenon in Baja California, both past and present. Juan Carlos Rulfo's documentary *Los Que Se Quedan*, or *Those Who Remain*, is a powerful and profoundly melancholic exploration of the families divided by the phenomenon.

Chapter 7: Environmental Time Bombs

Joel Simon's *Endangered Mexico* gives a very rich overview of the historical environmental challenges facing Mexico.

Much of the information used in this chapter was gathered for stories I wrote for the US-based monthly publication *EcoAmericas*, as well as less specialist media. As well as the sources directly cited in the main text, it draws on numerous interviews over the years with Mexico-based activists in established organizations such as Greenpeace and the Centro Mexicano de Derecho Ambiental and many other smaller campaigning groups. Government officials interviewed include Environment Minister Rafael Elvira Quesada and Environmental Prosecutor Patricio Patrón Laviada, as well as spokespeople at relevant government agencies, such as the National Ecology Institute (INE), and the National Tourism Development Fund (FONATUR).

At the time I interviewed former official Ezequiel Ezcurra he was director of the Biodiversity Research Center of the Californias, based in San Diego. The golf ball reference in the account of the Ixtoc oil spill comes from Abundio Juárez, a former Pemex engineer who was close to the efforts to stop the spill.

The term 'peasant ecologists' was first used to describe Rodolfo Montiel and Teodoro Cabrera, two activists involved in campaigns to stop logging of the forests near their village in the southern state of Guerrero who were arrested by the army in 1999 and later convicted on drugs and weapons charges. They were released two years later through a pardon from

President Fox, but then took their case to the Inter-American Court of Human Rights, which in 2010 ruled that their rights had been violated.

The section on community forestry projects is particularly informed by the work of the Consejo Civil Mexicana para la Silvicultura Sostenible.

Chapter 8: Left Behind?

Elena Poniatowska's *La Noche de Tlatelolco* documents the 1968 massacre through testimonies she collected at the time. *México Armado* by Laura Castellanos traces the rise and fall of the bewildering array of Mexican armed groups between 1943 and 1981. Jorge Castañeda's *Utopia Unarmed: The Latin American left after the cold war* takes the story further and puts it in the regional context. *Opening Mexico* by Julia Preston and Samuel Dillon puts the development of the left in the broader historical context. *Bordering on Chaos* by Andres Oppenheimer has a detailed profile of Zapatista leader Subcomandante Marcos. Alma Guillermoprieto explores the early manifestation of the Zapatistas and Marcos in a chapter of her book *Historia Escrita*. The profile of López Obrador in Jorge Zepeda Patterson's edited collection *Los Suspirantes* is particularly revealing. George Grayson's *Mexican Messiah* and Enrique Krauze's essay 'El Mesias Tropical' provide critical portraits. John Gibler's *Mexico Unconquered: Chronicles of power and revolt* explores the uprising in Oaxaca from his own perspective as a participating observer.

My vision of the history of the left is also coloured by my own interviews with protagonists such as Andrés Ayala, a former member of the Liga 23 de Septiembre, and Marco Rascón, a leading figure in the post-1985 earthquake awakening of civil society who created a masked activist superhero called 'Superbarrio'. My discussion of the left since 2000 is steeped in my own first-hand reporting, mostly sourced in the main text.

Chapter 9: Unfinished Story

The discussion of the legacy of revolutionary nationalism draws particularly on an interview with political anthropologist Roger Bartra, author of *La Jaula de la Melancolía*. Jorge Castañeda and Héctor Aguilar Camín's essay 'Un futuro para México' first published in *Nexos* in 2009, touches on the issue. Castañeda throws himself directly into a culturally determinist explanation of the obstacles in Mexico's route to modernity in his book *Mañana Forever*.

Index